Excel® 2007 VBA
Macro Programming

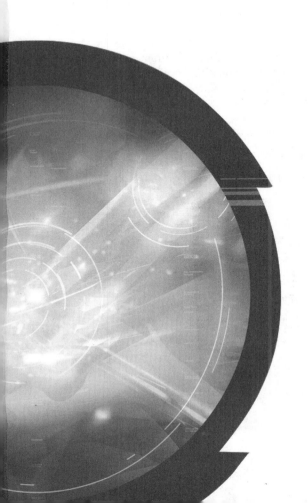

About the Author

Richard Shepherd has worked for many years for major banks and corporations in the United Kingdom writing spreadsheet macros to solve specific problems. He has worked for National Grid plc (electricity distribution), Hertz Car Leasing, NatWest plc (retail banking), Schroders plc (fund management), BNP Paribas (investment banking), Lloyds TSB plc (corporate banking), The Royal Bank of Scotland plc (investment banking), and the British National Health Service.

He has developed advanced spreadsheets and macros for budgeting, business planning, and profit and loss reporting. He originally started working with Lotus 123 spreadsheets but moved some years ago to Microsoft Excel and Microsoft Access. He qualified as an accountant with the Chartered Association of Certified Accountants in 1976 and has been a Fellow since 1981.

He can be contacted at tollside@yahoo.com, but he cannot promise to answer every e-mail!

About the Technical Editor

Todd Meister has been developing using Microsoft technologies for over ten years. He's been a technical editor on over 50 titles ranging from SQL Server to the .NET Framework. Besides technically editing titles, he is an assistant director for Computing Services at Ball State University in Muncie, Indiana. He lives in central Indiana with his wife, Kimberly, and their four remarkable children.

Excel® 2007 VBA Macro Programming

Richard Shepherd

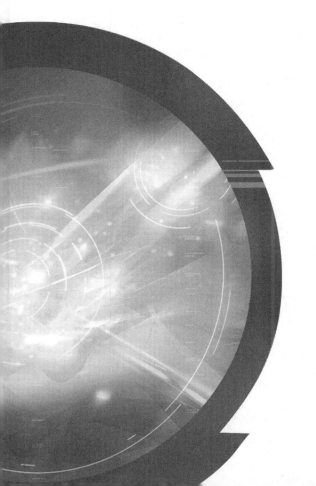

New York   Chicago   San Francisco
Lisbon   London   Madrid   Mexico City   Milan
New Delhi   San Juan   Seoul   Singapore   Sydney   Toronto

Cataloging-in-Publication Data is on file with the Library of Congress

McGraw-Hill books are available at special quantity discounts to use as premiums and sales promotions, or for use in corporate training programs. To contact a representative, please e-mail us at bulksales@mcgraw-hill.com.

Excel® 2007 VBA Macro Programming

1 2 3 4 5 6 7 8 9 0   DOC DOC   0 1 9

ISBN   978-0-07-162700-9
MHID   0-07-162700-6

Sponsoring Editor Wendy Rinaldi	Technical Editor Todd Meister	Production Supervisor Jim Kussow
Editorial Supervisor Patty Mon	Copy Editor Robert Campbell	Composition Glyph International
Project Manager Vipra Fauzdar, Glyph International	Proofreader Bev Weiler	Illustration Glyph International
Acquisitions Coordinator Joya Anthony	Indexer Karin Arrigoni	Art Director, Cover Jeff Weeks

To my wife, Elaine, and my son, Alexander.

Contents at a Glance

Contents

Acknowledgments

With grateful thanks to all the people at McGraw-Hill who have made this book happen. Special thanks to Joya Anthony and Vipra Fauzdar, who have managed this project and dealt with the vast numbers of e-mails this has generated. Others who deserve a special mention for all the help they have given to the project include Wendy Rinaldi (who asked me to write the Excel 2007 version), Todd Meister, and Melinda Lytle.

Finally a big thank you to Elaine and Alexander for all their support on this project.

Introduction

Spreadsheet macro programming has changed enormously within the last 12 years, when we went from text-based macros to VBA. There was also a major change in Office 97, when macros went to VBA worksheet modules in a separate environment accessed via the Visual Basic Editor. It used to be fairly basic: code was entered onto a specially designated worksheet. Although the language was fairly powerful in its own right, it was not a structured language and could certainly not be described as object-oriented. The number of commands was limited, and a fair amount of ingenuity was required to do certain tasks. The main advantage of it was that it was fairly easy to learn and understand; many programmers cut their teeth by initially writing spreadsheet macros.

However, it was also quite difficult to document and for other programmers to understand, since code could be placed anywhere on the macro spreadsheet, and blocks of code were only defined by a range name. This meant that code could be all over the place and following the flow of the program around the macro spreadsheet could become very complicated. Of course, professional developers could comment their code by using a cell to the right and could organize their code and its placement on the worksheet. However, it was still a complicated and unstructured process.

If anyone other than the original author examined the code, it could take days to find out exactly how it worked and what it was doing. Commercial companies frequently found that when the author of a complicated macro left the company, that macro had to be rewritten from scratch because of the time involved in assessing what it was doing.

Since the advent of Excel 5.0, Microsoft has introduced a new programming language called Visual Basic for Applications (VBA). VBA is a more intuitive and robust programming language using an object-oriented design. It has a great deal of similarity with its older and larger cousin, Visual Basic (VB). Once you learn VBA, you will have a fair understanding of how Visual Basic itself operates.

VBA is extremely different from the old macro language, and if the older language is what you are used to, it will involve a total rethinking of how you write and structure your code. The concepts of object-oriented programming (OOP) are as different as chalk and cheese to the old macro language, but there is a huge advantage in terms of what you can achieve on a spreadsheet. With object-oriented programming, you are dealing with the concept of objects. To use an example, the workbook you load is an object. The worksheet where you enter your data is another object, and so are the printer and the screen. All have properties, events, and methods (discussed later in the book). You will start to see object-oriented programming in more detail when you reach Chapter 12 ("The Excel Object Model").

VBA does allow a more structured and object-oriented approach to writing your macros. If this is your first foray into the world of Excel macro programming, you may well find the concepts easier to grasp, since you have no knowledge of the technologies used in the past within Excel. The text-based macros were a completely different language in terms of how and where you entered the code. The concept of VBA is unique and cannot be compared to text-based macros. Unfortunately, knowledge of the old system of writing macros can add to confusion with the new method of VBA and extend the learning curve.

Since VBA is shared by all Office applications, a great deal of the information contained in this book will help with other Office applications such as Word or Access, and also with Visual Basic itself. VBA is more powerful than the previous text macro language and enables you to extend Excel in any way you choose. It allows you to write code to do things not within the Excel menu structure. It even provides the means to access and manipulate other Microsoft Office applications under software control. For example, by using the Outlook object model you could copy address lists onto your spreadsheet, merely by executing VBA code. This would happen even if Outlook were not running, since Outlook only needs to be installed for the object model to work.

By the same token, you can also manipulate the Excel object model from another Microsoft application. For example, you could produce an Excel spreadsheet file from Microsoft Access without Excel ever appearing onscreen or being loaded. Access users will know that it is very easy to write a macro to export a table into Excel, but what if you want information from several tables and you want presentation formatting on the numbers and audit trails on the figures explaining how they were calculated? VBA allows you to do this.

VBA is an object-oriented language that needs a totally different viewpoint from the old text-based macro programming. All objects can have events, methods, and properties, and these can be manipulated to assist your programs. The objects are arranged in a hierarchy (Application Object | Workbook | Worksheet). This concept is explained in more detail in Chapter 12.

Whether you are totally new to macro programming in Excel or simply want to update your skills, this book will show you how to use the Excel object model along with VBA to learn how to program macros effectively.

Objectives of This Book

The first objective of this book is to first show you how VBA works in Excel and the basics of object-oriented programming. The intricacies of the VBA programming language are explained, as are specific keywords and functions. The book then takes you through a number of worked examples showing how to set up subroutines and functions. Full source code is shown for all examples. Finally, it shows you how to hook the subroutines onto the Excel menu system and how to turn a set of interrelated VBA macros into an Excel add-in package. An add-in is a professional application that can be attached into Excel and that works independent of the workbooks that are loaded but provides extra functionality to Excel.

The book shows you not only how to do things that are on the Excel spreadsheet menu but also how to do a number of things outside of Excel's menu structure and make them all look absolutely mind-blowing on a spreadsheet. People seeing them for the first time not knowing that they were done through VBA code will either be amazed and congratulate you on your knowledge, or quietly go away and study the menu structure to see if there is a simple, built-in way of doing this (which, of course, there is not). For example, Chapter 11 will show you how to set up your own menu structures within the Excel menu structure. Chapter 38 will show you how to completely change the appearance of comments in cells.

The book is full of completed examples (you are walked through each step of what the code is doing), which have all been tried and tested. There are also plenty of screenshots so that you can see what your code should be producing. Personally, I have always learned programming by example and experimentation. If I can see the code written down and see what it produces, then I can examine how it works and learn from it. Even if the examples do not do exactly what you want, you'll be able to modify them to suit your own needs.

The book assumes that you already have a good working knowledge of Excel from the spreadsheet perspective but have not dealt with writing macros beyond recording one.

By the time you finish all the examples in this book, you will have a very good knowledge of how to use VBA to solve problems; the only limiting factor will be your imagination. You can contact the author (Richard Shepherd) with any further points at tollside@yahoo.com, but he cannot guarantee to answer all e-mails.

Programming in Excel VBA

In this part, you will learn all about how Visual Basic for Applications (VBA) works for Excel 2007. A number of new VBA features have been incorporated into the 2007 version, and the aim of this book is to show you how to use code to interact with them, as well as the classical features of Excel.

Some areas have changed completely, such as the user interface, the file formats, the command bars, and the charting engine. The infamous Office Assistant (Clippy) has disappeared completely, a change that may well be applauded by some!

You will learn rules for coding, how to write code, how to debug your code—looking for the inevitable errors that occur—and how to build graphical user interfaces (GUIs) so that users can run your code easily. This is really all about the mechanics of code writing and is transferable to other Microsoft applications such as Access or Word.

The final chapters of this book are made up of worked examples to show you how you can harness VBA to deal with problems that you may encounter in Excel. I have always found that one of the best ways to learn a coding language is to go through examples, try them out, understand them, and modify them to suit my own requirements.

I hope that you will be able to use this book to learn all about Excel VBA and the immense power that it can bring to your workplace.

1

The Basics

This chapter is intended to take you through the basic steps of using the Visual Basic Editor window and writing a simple piece of VBA code. It will show you how to use the Visual Basic Editor (VBE) and the Project Explorer and code windows. You will learn how to write a simple macro to display a "Hello World" message box.

Exploring the Visual Basic Editor in Excel

If you use Excel a lot, you are familiar with its spreadsheet layout. When you open Excel, a standard view looks like Figure 1-1. You have a menu bar and toolbars across the top, the spreadsheet itself, and tabs along the bottom that let you access individual worksheets.

The menu bar has changed considerably in Excel 2007 and now uses interactive ribbon controls for the submenu structure instead of the menu structure that previous users were familiar with. To some extent existing users are at a disadvantage with the new menu and will no doubt spend many frustrating minutes trying to find out how they now do something.

Fortunately, the Visual Basic Editor (VBE) window has stayed much the same as in older versions of Excel, so if you have used Excel 2003 to design VBA code, you will not find too many differences.

You can insert data and formulas into the cells, format the cells or the entire worksheet, and insert graphics and graphs. You may even have tried recording a macro by clicking on the Developer item in the menu bar and clicking on the Record Macro icon in the Code control of the ribbon.

Most users are unaware that, in addition to the spreadsheet application of Excel, there is an extremely powerful programming language built into Excel that you can use to design your own applications. You can use VBA code to write macro applications in VBA that do some very powerful things. A *macro* is a procedure written in VBA code that performs

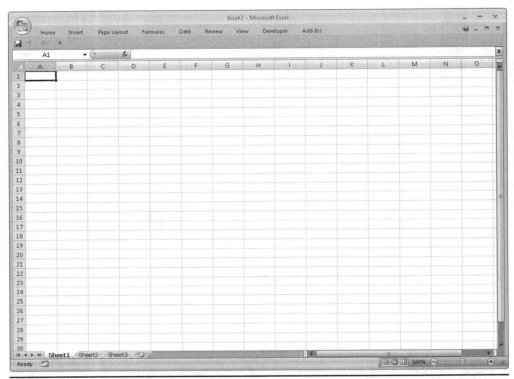

Figure 1-1   *The standard Excel worksheet screen*

certain tasks. This could be something like sorting all worksheets within a workbook into alphabetical order or adding menu structures to the Excel menu. Whatever you decide to do with them, macros automate tasks and make life easier for you and the users of your workbook.

However, before you can start programming in Excel, you need to know where the macros are stored. This is not as obvious as it used to be when text-based macros were entered into a special macro spreadsheet. In the old macro language, you simply inserted a macro sheet and entered your commands anywhere. Now that the macro language has grown and become a full object-oriented language, the method of storing it has also changed. Macros are now kept inside hidden VBA *projects* that are stored and saved within the workbook.

The language works in conjunction with object structures and hierarchies, and you can even create your own objects by using class modules (see Chapter 18). Objects that you create yourself can be reused in other VBA projects if you save them as add-ins (see Chapter 44).

Some people may argue that VBA is not an object-oriented language, but it certainly has all the features for it.

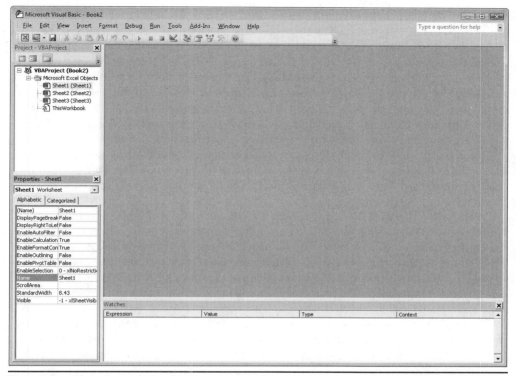

Figure 1-2   *The standard Visual Basic Editor window*

These VBA projects can be accessed through a companion program called the Visual Basic Editor (VBE). Press ALT-F11 to see the window shown in Figure 1-2.

At first glance, this window with its new menu bar, containing menus for File, Edit, View, Insert, Format, Debug, Run, Tools, Add-Ins, Window, and Help, might be confusing. It opens as a separate application window, but it is still very much a part of the Excel application. In fact, this window opens up a whole new ball game in terms of what you can do with Excel. In the next section, I'll explain the windows in more detail.

VBA Project Explorer and Code Windows

The Project Explorer, which shows a Project tree, is in the left-hand side of the screen, just below the menu and toolbar. It shows the VBA project for the active workbook as it stands, displaying the details in tree form so that you can easily navigate between them. If you click a branch of the tree, you'll enter that particular workbook or worksheet from the Visual Basic Editor. The VBA project is the root of the tree, and the workbook and worksheet objects are the branches coming off the tree. As you add and delete worksheets or workbooks, the branches of the tree change to reflect the new worksheets or workbooks being created. You can also add in other objects such as UserForms and modules. Effectively, what you are seeing is a list of currently loaded workbooks and the worksheets within them in an Explorer-like interface.

Remember, VBA is an object-oriented language. The first branch on the tree coming from the root of the VBA project says Microsoft Excel Objects. Coming off this branch are objects for the workbook that contain worksheets. This project tree, as reflected in UserForms in dialogs and in the Excel object model, is discussed in Chapters 9 and 12. Other objects can be inserted into the Project tree, such as UserForms, modules, and class modules.

This is a very important concept to understand because the workbook is an object that can be referred to, and each sheet is also an object that can be referred to. These are not the only objects within Excel, but looking at the Project Explorer simplistically, these are the objects shown there.

Double-click ThisWorkBook, and the code window for the **Workbook** object will open. Initially, it does not show a great deal, and you may wonder what to do with it. If you type something at random such as **What do I do now?** and press ENTER, you will get a compile error. This is because there are disciplines and rules about entering code. Everything that you enter here goes through a Visual Basic compiler that interprets what you have written and converts it into instructions that your computer understands. Unfortunately, it does not understand plain English, which is why you get a compile error.

Click OK in the Compile Error message box and delete your statement. Notice that the statement line turned red when the compile error appeared to draw your attention to the problem. Even if you do nothing about it, it will remain red as a danger signal to show that there is a problem in your code.

The drop-down list in the top-left corner of the window shows (General). Click the drop-down to see another choice, Workbook. Click Workbook to see the code for the workbook event of **Open**. Your screen should now look like Figure 1-3.

What does this all mean? Quite simply, the **Workbook_Open** event happens when you open this particular workbook. This occurs at the point when you choose File | Open and select the file and load it in. The code window automatically shows the statements **Private Sub Workbook_Open()** and **End Sub**:

```
Private Sub Workbook_Open()


End Sub
```

This gives you a code area to write your VBA code against the **Workbook_Open** event. If you check the drop-down list on the right, you will notice there are other events that you can harness code to as well, but for the moment I will concentrate on **Workbook_Open**.

In VBA, if you are not using this event, you do not need this code. Every time you click an event in the drop-down, these two statements are automatically inserted. If you intend to write any code for the event, then you must include these two statements or you will get a compile error. Think of them as start and finish lines in a race—they tell the compiler where the code starts and stops. If you do not want to write any code for that event, you can delete them, but both must be deleted or you will get a compile error. The compiler wants your code neat and tidy, which means it must be structured properly.

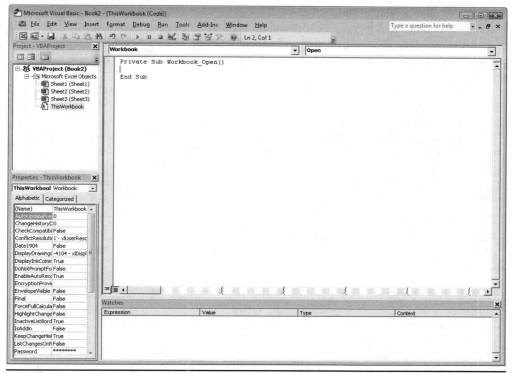

Figure 1-3   *Code window for the Workbook_Open event*

Click the Open drop-down (the box with the down arrow on the right) in the top-right corner and you will see a list of events for the workbook that you can add code to. Each of these events is called at a specific time and corresponds to a specific use of the workbook, and any code found will be run. An example is the **Workbook_Open** event. All the code you enter for this event will be run. If there is an error, the relevant error message will be displayed.

Currently, you have the start and finish of an event. Although there's nothing between the **Sub** and **End Sub** statements, the routine is still live and will fire automatically every time the workbook opens. However, because there is no code in the event, it will not do anything.

Your First Excel VBA Macro

Programming books traditionally help you take your first steps in a program by writing a simple piece of code to display the text "Hello world," and this book is no exception. You will use the **MsgBox** statement to display the statement. This is a simple user interface showing the statement and an OK button that you have probably seen before in Windows.

For this example, you will use another event on the **Workbook** object. You could use the existing **Workbook_Open** object, but this would require you to close the workbook and reopen it because the event is only fired off when the workbook is opened. Instead, you'll use the **NewSheet** event, which gets fired off every time you insert a new worksheet into the workbook.

Select from the drop-down list in the top-right corner the event **NewSheet**. Your window will now have two more statements added for the event **Workbook_NewSheet**. Just as with the **Workbook_Open** event, these are like start and finish lines.

In the blank line under the statement **Private Sub Workbook_NewSheet(ByVal Sh As Object)** but before **End Sub**, type in **msgbox "Hello World"**. Be sure to be lazy and do not use the SHIFT key when typing "msgbox," and see what happens. The word "msgbox" transforms into the upper- and lowercase "MsgBox" because it is a defined statement word in VBA and is already set up to appear in this way. However, you must make sure you spell it correctly—make a mistake, and you will get a compile error.

```
Private Sub Workbook_NewSheet(ByVal Sh As Object)
  MsgBox "Hello World"
End Sub
```

Notice that the **MsgBox** statement is indented with the TAB key. This is a useful way to see where one set of statements begins and ends. When complicated loops are used, without this notation it is easy to get lost and lose track of where a loop starts and finishes. For more on loops, see Chapter 4.

A **MsgBox** statement is a simple way to provide an interface to the user by displaying a message and an OK button. I'm sure you've seen message boxes like this pop up from time to time, and now you know how easy they are to create. They can be quite sophisticated, and Chapter 5 explains in more detail how to use them.

After you type in the word **msgbox**, a box containing all the parameters for this command is displayed. In this instance, you do not have to take any notice of this box, since you are only displaying a text string. However, it can be extremely useful in telling you what parameters are required for a function and in what order they should appear. If, for example, you wanted to give the message box an icon or a title, the parameter box would help you do this correctly. The parameter box is a list box that appears when you reach the parameter for the icon and gives a list of optional constants for the icon of your choice. This type of help is available for all functions when using the VBA editor. Your code window should now look like Figure 1-4.

To make this event macro run and display the message, go back to the Excel window and insert a new worksheet: Switch to the Excel worksheet screen by clicking the Excel icon on the Windows taskbar at the bottom of the screen or clicking the View Microsoft Excel button on the VBE toolbar (the first button). Then right-click the workbook tabs at the bottom right of the worksheet screen (these have names like Sheet1, Sheet2) and click Insert in the pop-up menu.

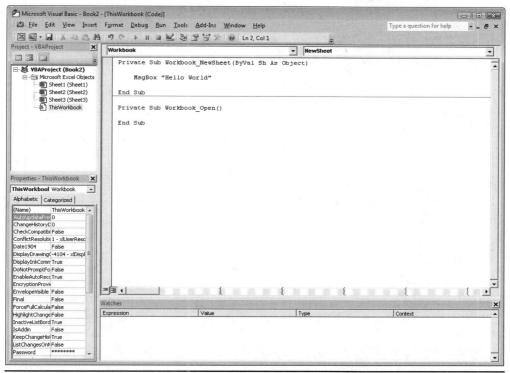

Figure 1-4   *Code to display "Hello World" message box using Workbook_NewSheet event*

Click the Worksheet icon in the Insert window and the "Hello World" message box will appear with an OK button on it, as shown in Figure 1-5.

You can see already that you can produce professional-looking interfaces on Excel with hardly any code!

This is a simple demonstration of adding code to an event. It would be extremely irritating if every time you added a new sheet to your workbook you got the message "Hello World," but fortunately there are more practical applications for adding code to events.

Events are being fired off all the time when things happen on an Excel spreadsheet. You can insert code to take action on a particular event, such as a user making changes to a worksheet, and each time the event happens, your code will be run.

However, you cannot do any editing in the code window until you click OK and the macro finishes running. This is because the focus of the code is on your message box window, and the focus cannot be moved anywhere else within Excel until the message box disappears.

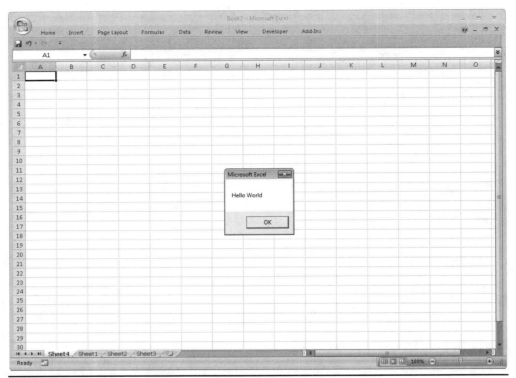

Figure 1-5 *Hello World message box on worksheet*

To stop this message box from appearing whenever a new sheet is loaded, delete the line MsgBox "Hello World" by pressing the DELETE key. Another way to prevent code from running is to turn it into a comment by putting the single quote (') character in front of the line: **' MsgBox "Hello World"**. This line will then turn green and will not be used. Comments are also used to place explanations and descriptions of your code inside a macro so that it can be understood at a later date.

More Exploring of the VBA Project Window

Going back to the Project Explorer and the tree showing the project (in the top left-hand corner of screen), there are also objects for each worksheet within the workbook. A new object should now be displayed in the tree for the worksheet you inserted in the last example. Every worksheet is a separate object and is represented as such in the Project tree.

Double-click any of these sheet objects, and a new code window will appear in the same way as for the workbook object. Again, the drop-down in the top-left corner shows (General), but you can click it to change it to Worksheet. Worksheets have different and fewer events than the **Workbook** object. Code can be inserted to execute when the sheet is activated or

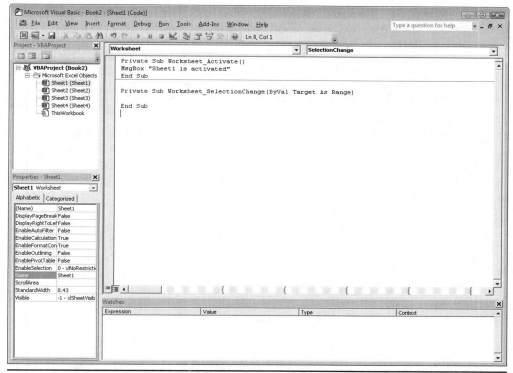

Figure 1-6   *VBA code to display a message box when Sheet1 is activated*

deactivated or when it is calculated. For example, you could enter the code shown in Figure 1-6, and each time Sheet1 is selected from the tab controls at the bottom of the Excel window, the message "Sheet1 is selected" will appear.

Saving Off Your Macro

You need to be able to save your code off along with the workbook file that you are working with. In Excel 2003, this was quite simple in that you either clicked the disk symbol on the toolbar or clicked File | Save on the menu bar in the VBE window.

Excel 2007 distinguishes between file types. Primarily, there is an Excel Workbook type and an Excel Macro Enabled Workbook type. When you create your initial workbook, it defaults to the standard Excel Workbook type. This means that when you create some VBA code and then try to save it, you will get an error message because the file is not Macro Enabled.

What you need to do when you first create the workbook is to immediately save it as the Excel Macro Enabled Workbook type. This will then identify your file as having macros and there will be no further problems saving your code.

Enabling the Developer Item in the Excel Menu

The Developer item in the Excel menu is used frequently within this book, and it is important that you have it displayed. When Excel 2007 is first installed, it is not shown by default.

To make it display, click the Excel Start button in the top left-hand corner of the worksheet screen and then click Excel Options at the bottom of the window that appears. Click Popular in the menu on the left-hand side of the Options window and check the Show Developer Tab in the Ribbon box. Click OK.

Variables, Arrays, Constants, and Data Types

Although the concept of having places to store data while the program is running is fairly straightforward variables, arrays, and constants have some fairly complicated rules. They are intrinsic to any program, so I have devoted a chapter to explaining about them.

Variables

Building up a structure of *variables* is a bit like building up a filing cabinet at home. You might have files for your job, insurance policies, taxation, and personal documents such as passports. These files can grow in size. Some may only hold a single document, such as an insurance policy, while others can carry quite a lot of information, such as a tax file.

The important thing is that each file has a particular category of document. You would not file your passport in with your tax papers, for example. You need to know which file holds which papers for quick and easy reference.

Think of a variable as being similar to a particular file holding a specific type of information. The variable may just be a single number or a piece of text that the program needs to hold and refer to while it is running. It could also be a whole array of information, almost like a spreadsheet. A spreadsheet has many cells that can hold information, and an array can be set up to have many cells or locations in exactly the same way.

A variable can have its value changed by the program when running, which is why it is called a variable. The same rules apply from the filing cabinet example, in that you do not mix the data types between the variables. If a variable has been defined as a certain type, it will not accept data specified as another type. For example, if you have defined a variable as an integer (whole number), you cannot put text into it, or if you put a floating point number (with decimal places) into an integer, you will lose the decimal places.

As your program runs, you often need somewhere to store data temporarily. In the past, macro programmers often stored this data on the spreadsheet itself. With VBA, you could do the same thing and write data to cells on the spreadsheet itself, but this would be inefficient and you, as the coder, would need a very good memory to organize where each piece of data on the spreadsheet was stored. Also, people do tend to change spreadsheets, and someone could easily delete or overwrite your variables, causing your program to crash or give incorrect results.

Instead, you can now use variables to store values while your code is executing. Within a procedure, you declare a variable using the **Dim** statement, supplying a name for the variable:

> **Dim** *variablename* [As type]

Variable names must follow these rules:

- ▶ They must begin with a letter.
- ▶ They must contain only letters, numbers, or the underscore character—no spaces!
- ▶ They must not exceed 40 characters.
- ▶ They must not be a reserved word (see the section "Reserved Words" at the end of this chapter).

The optional As type clause allows you to define the data type of the variable you are declaring. If you omit the type, it defaults to the Variant data type discussed in the next section.

```
Dim MyInteger as Integer
```

Implicit Declaration

You do not have to declare a variable before using it. You can just include the statement

```
TempVal=6
```

A variable will automatically be created for **TempVal** as a variant (default type), and it will have the value of 6.

However, a problem with doing this is that it can lead to subtle errors in your code if you misspell the name of the variable in a later statement. For example, if you refer to it as **temval** instead of **tempval**, you may know what you mean but VBA does not. It assumes that **temval** is a new variable and assigns it as such. The old variable, **tempval**, is still there but is no longer being used. You now have two different variables, although you think you only have one. This can lead to enormous problems that can take some time to straighten out in your code.

Explicit Declaration

To avoid the problem of misnaming variables, you can stipulate that VBA always generates an error message whenever it encounters an undeclared variable. To do this, you'll need to go to the declarations section of the code module. If you look at a module within the VB Editor window, you will see a heading called (General) in the top left of the module window and a heading called (Declarations) in the top right of the module window. Click (Declarations), and you will go straight to the declarations section. Do not worry if it appears that you are not typing into a defined section. Type the following statement. As soon as you type a declaration, a line will automatically appear underneath to show that it is within the declarations section.

```
Option Explicit
```

This prevents implicit declarations from being used. Now you have to define **TempVal**:

```
Dim TempVal
```

If you refer to **temval** during execution, an error message will be displayed stating that the variable has not been defined.

NOTE

Option Explicit works on a per-module basis — it must be placed in the declarations section of every code module you want it to apply to unless you define the variable as a global variable. A global variable is valid right across your project and can be used by the code in any module. See the later section "Global Variables."

Which method you use (implicit or explicit) depends on personal preference. Coding is often much faster using implicit because you do not have to initially define your variables before you use them. You can simply make variable statements, and VBA will take care of the rest. However, as discussed, this can lead to errors unless you have a good memory for variables you are using and have the experience to know exactly what you are doing. Implicit can also make it more difficult for someone else to understand your code. Using Option Explicit is the best practice and helps stop runtime errors.

Scope and Lifetime of Variables

If you declare a variable within a procedure, only code within that procedure can access that variable. The scope is local to that procedure. You will often need variables that can be used by several procedures or even the whole application. For these reasons, you can declare a variable at the local, module, or global level.

Local Variables

A *local* variable uses **Dim**, **Static**, or **ReDim** (arrays only) to declare the variable within a procedure. Several procedures can have a variable called **temp**, but because every variable is local to its procedure, they all act independently of each other and can hold different values. Local variables declared with the **Dim** statement remain in existence only as long as the procedure is executing. Local variables declared with **Static** remain in existence for the lifetime of the application. You may well wish to maintain a variable value throughout the application, and if you look at Chapter 18, you will see an example of how a static variable can make a difference to your code.

```
Dim TempVal
Static TempVal
```

You can also dimension a variable as an array of several elements, and even several dimensions. An array is almost exactly like a spreadsheet in concept. You can define an array with 10 elements so that it has 10 pigeonholes or cells to store information. You can also give it another dimension so that it is a 10 by 10 array and has 100 pigeonholes or cells to store your information. An array gives you tremendous flexibility over storing data—it is like poking the data into individual spreadsheet cells. For example, if you recursively searched a disk drive for all subdirectories on it, the way NT Explorer does, then you would need an array to store all the pathnames as they were found so that you could easily find and refer to them within your program.

```
Dim A()
ReDim A(10)
ReDim Preserve A(12)
```

To use **ReDim**, you must define the variable initially as an array (see the section "Arrays" later in this chapter). **Dim A(3)** creates a small array with 4 elements (0–3), so there are effectively 4 **A** variables. **ReDim A(10)** then makes it an 11-element array but loses all the data in it. **ReDim A(12) Preserve** makes a 13-element array but keeps all existing data. Note all subscripts start at 0 by default.

ReDim is useful when you need an array to store data but you do not know how many elements you will need. For example, if you are recursively searching directories, you have no idea how many will be on a disk device, so you start by specifying a small array of 10 elements. As this fills up, it can be resized using **ReDim** and **Preserve** to keep the data already in there.

Module-Level Variables

A *module-level* variable is declared in the declarations section of the module instead of an actual procedure on that module. Module-level variables use the same syntax as local variables, and are available to all procedures within that module but not to the rest of the application. Module-level variables remain in existence for the lifetime of the application and preserve their values.

Global Variables

Global variables are declared in the declarations part of a module with the **Global** statement, but they can be accessed by any code within the application. Global variables exist and retain their values for the lifetime of the application.

```
Global TempVal
```

Again, this would be placed in the declarations section of any module. Because you have specified that it is global, it can be accessed for any part of your code.

Name Conflicts and Shadowing

A variable cannot change scope while your code is running. However, you can have a variable with the same name in a different scope or module. You can have a global variable called **temp** and also a local variable in a procedure called **temp**. References to **temp** within the procedure would access the local variable **temp**, and references outside the procedure would access the global variable **temp**. In this case, the local variable *shadows* (that is, is accessed in preference to) less local variables. The only way to use the global variable over the local variable is to give it a different name. Shadowing can be confusing and can produce subtle errors that are difficult to debug. The best way is to use unique names for all variables.

The names of module-level and global variables can also cause conflicts with procedure names. A procedure (a subroutine) has global scope unless it is declared privately, as you will see in Chapter 3. A global variable cannot have the same name as any public procedure in any code module.

Static Variables

Variables also have a lifetime based on their scope. Module and global variables are preserved for the lifetime of the application, which means they hold their values while the application is executing until the user closes the application. Local variables declared with **Dim** exist only when the procedure is executing. When it stops, the values are not preserved and the memory is released. The next execution reinitializes the variables for the lifetime of the procedure. You should only use local variables to hold values that are being used during that procedure. If you expect to access them from other modules, they need to be global. However, you can use the **Static** keyword to declare and preserve a local variable:

```
Static Temp
```

You can make all local variables static by placing the **Static** keyword at the beginning of a procedure heading:

```
Static Sub Test_Static()
```

Data Types

A variable can be given a data type that determines the type of data it can store. This can have an effect on the efficiency of your code. If there is no data type, the default type is Variant.

Variant

A *variant* can store all kinds of data, whether it is text, numbers, dates, or other information. It can even store an entire array. A variant variable can freely change its type at runtime, whereas one that has been specified as, for example, a string cannot. You can use the function **VarType** to find out the type of data held by a variant:

```
Sub TestVariables()
stemp = "richard"
MsgBox VarType(stemp)
stemp = 4
MsgBox VarType(stemp)
End Sub
```

The message box will first display 8, which means that it is a string. It will then display 2, which means that it is an integer.

VBA always uses the most efficient means of storing data in a variant. As you can see from the preceding example, it automatically changes to suit the data stored in it.

Table 2-1 shows the return values for specific data types.

ReturnValue	Type
0	Variant
1	Null
2	Integer
3	Long
4	Single
5	Double
6	Currency
7	Date/Time
8	String
11	Boolean
17	Byte

Table 2-1   *VarType Return Values*

If you perform a mathematical operation on a variant that is not a numeric value, you will get a Type MisMatch error. This means that you are trying to put a data type into a variable not set up to hold that data type—a bit like banging a square peg into a round hole. In this case, it may be that you are trying to perform a mathematical operation on a variant holding a string of text.

You can use the **IsNumeric** function to test if the value of a variant is a number—it returns true or false (nonzero or zero).

```
Sub TestNumeric()
temp="richard"
MsgBox IsNumeric(temp)
End Sub
```

This will give the result False.

Date/Time Values Stored in Variants

Variant variables can also contain Date/Time values. This is a floating point number—the integer part represents the days since 31-Dec-1899, and the decimal part represents the hours, minutes, and seconds expressed as a proportion of 24 hours. For example, 37786.75 represents 14-June-2003 at 18:00. The difference between 31-Dec-1899 and 14-June-2003 is 37,786 days, and 0.75 of 24 hours is 18 hours.

Adding or subtracting numbers adds or subtracts days. Adding decimals increases the time of day; for example, adding 1/24 adds one hour. There are a number of functions for handling date and time, as explained in Chapter 5.

Note that the interpretation of day and month is dependent on the Regional Options settings within the Windows Control Panel. If you set your date to mm/dd/yy in Regional Options, this will be the default interpretation of day and month.

As you can use **IsNumeric** to determine if there is a numeric value, you can use the **IsDate** function to determine if there is a date value.

```
temp = "01-Feb-2002"
MsgBox IsDate(temp)
```

This will return True (nonzero).

Empty Value

A variant that has not had a variable assigned to it will have an empty value. This can be tested for using the **IsEmpty** function.

```
MsgBox IsEmpty(MyTest)
```

This will return True (nonzero) because temp has not been assigned a value.

Null Value

A variant can contain a special value of Null. The Null value is used to indicate unknown or missing data. Variables are not set to Null unless you write code to do this. If you do not use Null in your application, you do not have to worry about Null.

> **NOTE**
> *Null is not 0. This is an easy but incorrect assumption to make when you're starting to learn VBA.*

The safest way to check for a Null value in your code is to use **IsNull**. Other methods, such as the statement **Is Null**, may not give correct results.

```
Sub TestNull()
temp=Null
Msgbox IsNull(temp)
End Sub
```

The result will be True (nonzero).

Other Data Types

Why use data types other than Variant? Because Variant may not use the best data type for the purpose. If you want to create concise fast code, then you need other data types. For example, if you are doing lots of mathematical calculations on relatively small integer numbers, you can gain an enormous speed advantage by using the data type Integer instead of Variant. You can use Variant by default, but Variant will not necessarily assume that it is an integer being used. It could assume that it is a floating point number, in which case calculations will take far longer, although the same result will be produced.

There are also memory considerations to take into account. Each Double number takes up 8 bytes of memory, which may not seem like a lot. However, across a large array it can use a large amount of RAM, which would slow the process down. This will use up memory in the computer, which Windows could be using as virtual memory for its graphical display.

VBA Data Types

There are a number of data types that you can use in VBA. The details of these are set out in Table 2-2.

Numeric Types

If you only work with whole numbers, then you declare your variables as Integer or Long, depending on size. Mathematical operations are much faster and memory demands are less for these types.

Name	Description	Type-Declaration Character	Range
Integer	2-byte integer	%	−32,768 to 32,767
Long	4-byte integer	&	−2,147,483,648 to 2,147,438,647
Single	4-byte floating point number	!	−3.402823E38 to 1.401298E-45 (negative values) 1.401298E-45 to 3.402823E38 (positive values)
Double	8-byte floating point number	#	−1.79769313486232D308 to −4.94065645841247D-324 (negative values) 4.94065645841247D-324 to 1.79769313486232D308 (positive values)
Currency	8-byte number with fixed decimal point	@@	−922337203685477.5808 to 922337203685477.5807
Fixed Length String	String of characters— fixed length	$	0 to approximately 65,400 characters
Variable Length String	String of characters— variable length	$	0 to approximately 2 billion characters
Variant	Date/Time, floating point number, or string	None	Date Values: January 1, 0000 to December 31, 9999; numeric values: same range as double; string values: same range as string

Table 2-2   *Data Types Within VBA*

If you are working with fractions of numbers, then you use Single, Double, or Currency. Currency (fixed decimal point) supports up to 4 digits to the right of the decimal point and 15 digits to the left. Floating point (Single and Double) have larger ranges but can produce small rounding errors.

```
Dim temp as Integer
Dim temp as Long
Dim temp as Currency
Dim temp as Single
Dim temp as Double
```

String Types

If your variable will always contain text, you can declare it to be of type **String**:

```
Dim temp as String
```

You can then use string handling functions to manipulate it. You can take sections from it, search for a particular character, or turn it all into uppercase characters. For a more detailed description, see the section "Functions" in Chapter 5.

A string is of variable length by default. The string grows or shrinks according to the data in it. If you do not want this to happen, you can declare a fixed-length string by using **String** * size:

```
Dim temp as String * 50
```

This forces a string to be fixed at 50 characters in length. If your string is less than 50, it is padded with spaces. If it is greater than 50 characters, the excess characters are truncated and lost. So, although you do get control over the amount of memory being used because there is always a fixed length to each element, there is a risk of data loss if a user manages to input a longer string than you originally envisioned.

Arrays

Up to now I have discussed individual variables. You can set up a variable and give it a value such as a number or a string. A simple example is the name of an employee. You can set up a variable called **employee** and give it a string with the employee's name. However, what about other employees? Suppose you are writing a program that needs to refer to 26 employees. You would have a great deal of difficulty referring to them in your program using simple variables. You would have to do something like this:

```
Dim employee1 as String, employee2 as String, employee3 as
String,.......
```

This would be extremely cumbersome and inefficient. What would you do if new employees had to be added? Your program would no longer work!

Fortunately, a variable can be dimensioned as an *array*. All you need to specify is

```
Dim employee(25) as String
```

As mentioned previously, an array is effectively like a block of pigeonholes or cells in a spreadsheet that you can read and write data to by using the index of that array. You use the subscript number in brackets to indicate which element you are referring to. You can also **ReDim** the array at runtime to enlarge it if your program requires.

This example sets up a 26-element array numbered from 0 to 25, with 26 strings to put your names into. Each element can be referenced from your code by using the index number. A For..Next loop can easily be used to list out all names within the array:

```
Dim employee(25) as String
For n = 0 To 25
    employee(n) = Chr(n+65)
```

```
Next n
For n = 0 To 25
    MsgBox employee(n)
Next n
```

In this macro, you first dimension an array called **employee** as a string with 26 elements.

The first For..Next loop puts data into the array. The ASCII (American Standard Code for Information Interchange—see Appendix A) code for the letter *A* is 65, and this is added to the value of *n,* which starts at 0. The **Chr** function converts this into a character, which is inserted into the appropriate element of the array. On the first loop, the character *A* is inserted into the first element of the array because *n* is 0 at this point. The value of 65, which is the code for *A,* is added to it.

The second For..Next loop displays each element of the employee array in turn. When you run this example, it will give the letters *A* to *Z.*

Arrays follow the same rules as ordinary variables. They can be local, module, or global and can be any data type, including Variant. The size of the array in terms of elements is limited to an integer (in the range –32,768 to 32,767). The default lower boundary is always 0, but this can be altered by placing an Option Base statement in the declarations section of the module:

```
Option Base 1
```

All arrays in that module start at 1.

You can also specify the lower limit for an array by using the **To** keyword:

```
Dim temp (1 To 15) as String
```

Multidimensional Arrays

I have only discussed one-dimensional arrays, but you can have several dimensions to an array. Think of it as being like a spreadsheet. You have rows and columns that give a reference; you can also have several different sheets so that a cell reference is made up of the sheet name plus the cell column and row:

```
Dim temp(10,4) as String
```

If this were a spreadsheet, it would have 11 columns and 5 rows, a total of 55 pigeonholes or cells to place your data into and refer to it.

A three-dimensional array would be as follows:

```
Dim temp(10,4,3) as String
```

Imagining this again as a spreadsheet, it would have 11 columns and 5 rows, but they would span across 4 worksheets, giving a total of 220 pigeonholes. Bear in mind that each one of these elements can take a string up to 65,400 characters, and you begin to see how much memory can be used up by a simple array and how much data can be stored.

Dimensioning an array immediately allocates memory to it—this is an important consideration when planning your program. Taking up large chunks of memory can cause your program and Windows to run inefficiently. Because Windows itself is a graphical application, it uses large amounts of RAM (random access memory) to hold information. You may find that using a large array slows Windows right down, and other applications run more slowly and take longer to process information. This may be all right on your home computer, but a professional application needs to take this into account.

Further dimensions are possible, but these become complicated to manipulate and keep track of. Five dimensions is considered the safe maximum to use. If you go back to thinking of an array as like a series of spreadsheets, think how complicated a five-dimensional spreadsheet would be!

ReDim can still be used to resize the array, but you cannot use it to change the number of dimensions in the array, nor can you use it to change the type of the array—for example, from string to integer.

Dynamic Arrays

Sometimes you do not know how large an array needs to be. A good example is if you are recursively storing pathnames from a disk device in each array element. You do not know how many subdirectories there are and how long a branch will extend. You could set your array to 1,000 elements, taking up valuable memory in the process, and then find that you only needed 500 elements. Alternatively, there could be 2,000 subdirectory pathnames, so you would run out of room.

You create a *dynamic* array in exactly the same way as a normal array—using the **Dim** statement at the global, module, or local level or using **Static** at the local level. You give it an empty dimension list:

```
Dim temp()
```

You then use the **ReDim** statement within your procedure to resize the number of elements within the array. The **ReDim** statement can only be used within a procedure, and you cannot change the number of dimensions:

```
ReDim temp(100)
```

You could write code to check the number of values collected and then resize the array if it is getting close to the upper boundary. There are two functions that are helpful here when working with arrays—**LBound** and **UBound**. These are functions that can be used to return the upper and lower limits of the dimensions of an array by specifying the array number as a subscript:

```
Dim MyTemp(10)

MsgBox LBound(MyTemp)

MsgBox UBound(MyTemp)
```

LBound will return the value of 0; **UBound** will return the value of 10.

ReDim will automatically clear all values in the array unless you use the **Preserve** keyword:

```
ReDim Preserve temp(100)
```

Data already held in **temp** will now be preserved.

User-Defined Types

You can also define your own type of variable by using existing variable types using the **Type** keyword. This has to be entered in the declarations section of a module:

```
Type Employee
      Name as String
      Salary as Currency
      Years as Integer
End Type
```

This creates a new type called **Employee**, which holds information for Name, Salary, and Years of Service.

You can then use this type in exactly the same way as the built-in variable types. It is even automatically included in the drop-down lists within the VBA editor. You can set use these as normal variables, as seen in the following:

```
Dim temp as employee
temp.Name = "Richard Shepherd"
temp.Salary = 10000
temp.Years = 5
MsgBox temp.Name
MsgBox temp.Salary
MsgBox temp.Years
```

Note that the variable name has a list box showing the properties or fields for this data type as you type the variable name in within the code.

You can also create an array of this type and effectively use it as an object in its own right. Notice that after specifying the name of the array and the subscript index that is to receive the data, a dot is used so that Name appears as a property:

```
Dim temp(10) as employee
temp(0).Name = "Richard Shepherd"
```

Constants

Constants are, in effect, variables that do not change. They hold values that are used over again within your code and effectively provide shorthand for that particular constant value.

You use the same rules to create a constant as you do to create variables, but you cannot assign a new value to it from within your code as you can with a variable.

```
Const Path_Name = "C:\temp\"
```

This sets up a constant called **Path_Name**, and it always has the value C:\temp\. You can use this in your program every time you want to use that particular path.

There are also predefined constants within the Excel object model—you can see these by using the Object Browser, which is covered in Chapter 12. In the Excel object model, all constants begin with the letters "xl" to denote that they are part of the Excel object model—for example, **xlSaveChanges** or **xlDoNotSaveChanges**. The Object Browser also shows the actual value of the constant at the bottom of the browser window.

Reserved Words

You probably noticed that there are a number of keywords within VBA that make up the language—for example, **For**, **Next**, **Do**, and **Loop**. These cannot be used within your program for the purpose of naming variables, subroutines, or functions because they are *reserved words*. This means that they are part of the VBA language itself, and it would cause enormous confusion if you were allowed to go ahead and use these for random purposes within your own code. Fortunately, VBA checks what you are typing in instantly and puts up an error message—usually "Expected Identifier," which means that you have used a reserved word and VBA thinks you are entering it as program statement. Try entering

```
Dim Loop as String
```

Loop is, of course, part of VBA and is used in **Do** loop statements. It is impossible to enter this statement. Instantly an error message appears, and the line of code turns red to warn of a problem. Of course, you can ignore the warning, but as soon as you try to run the code you will get an error again. Try entering

```
Sub ReDim()
```

You will get an error message, and the code will turn red because **ReDim** is a keyword within VBA.

Strangely enough, you *can* use words from the Excel object model. You can call a subroutine Application or Worksheets, and it will work. However, this is not advised. I have seen problems of code not exiting cleanly when the application is closed down because it used words from the object model. It certainly causes confusion within VBA and should be avoided.

Generally, any VBA keyword or function cannot be used as a variable name, subroutine name, or function name.

Modules, Functions, and Subroutines

M odules are where you write your code. Functions and subroutines are the two different ways of creating a piece of working code.

Modules

Modules are code sheets that are specific to your application. They are not fired off directly by events on the spreadsheet, such as a new worksheet being added or a workbook being closed, but have to be called directly. They are a means of creating procedures in a general manner, rather than specifically running in an object like a workbook or worksheet. You can call them in a number of ways:

▶ Use a custom menu command or a custom toolbar command. See Chapter 11 for more on customizing toolbars.

▶ Insert a VBA control from the Control toolbox into the spreadsheet directly and attach your code to this; for example, you might enter code for a user's actions on a command button or a combo box.

▶ Click the Developer item in the menu bar and then click the Macros icon in the Code control of the Ribbon (left-hand side of ribbon). Select the macro name from the list and click Run. However, for a professional application this is not recommended. Uses will not want to have to select a macro from a list box where they have to know the macro name.

They will also need to have the Developer item showing on their Excel menu. Most users want things to happen in the most straightforward way possible, usually through clicking something once.

▶ Run the code from a UserForm. In Chapter 9, you will learn how to define your own forms, which can be used by the user to make selections and pick options. When the user clicks the OK button on the form, your macro runs and picks up the user preferences.

▶ Call your code from another macro. Code can form subroutines or functions that can then be used within other macros written on the same spreadsheet. For example, say you have to search a string of text for a particular character and you write a subroutine to do this, using a parameter to pass the text string to the subroutine. You can use this subroutine as a building block by calling it from anywhere else within other procedures in exactly the same way as you would a normal VBA keyword.

▶ Write your code as a function and call it directly by inserting the function into a cell, just as you would with the built-in functions in Excel. In the section "Writing a Simple Function," later in this chapter, you will learn how to write a simple spreadsheet function that can be used directly in a cell.

▶ Click directly on your code and press F5. This is for development work only. For example, if you are working on a subroutine in isolation, you may wish to run it only to see how it works.

All these methods are dealt with in further detail later on in the book.

A VBA project normally uses at least one module to store the necessary functions and subroutines known as procedures. To insert a new module, simply select Insert | Module from the VBE menu, and the new module will appear. Note that this contains only a general area initially. There are no events on it, as there were on the workbook and worksheet code sheets.

You can enter subroutines or functions here and make them public or private. The distinction between public and private is to decide whether other modules within the same workbook can access the procedure. If the code is private, it can only be used in the current workbook where it resides. If it is public, it can be used by any other procedure in any other module in the workbook. If you have a subroutine that you do not want to be used elsewhere in the code, make the subroutine private. The default is always public.

The Difference Between Subroutines and Functions

There are two types of code procedures: subroutines and functions, and on casual inspection they both appear to look the same. However, they actually are different.

A _subroutine_ is a piece of code that performs a set of actions or calculations or a combination of the two. It can form a "building block" within a program and may sometimes need to be repeated. It can be called by several different routines. The programmer has to write a subroutine only once, and it can be called from anywhere within the program as many times as needed. However, it does not directly return a value; if it performs a calculation, there is no direct way of finding the result. It can alter values of variables if you pass parameters using the ByRef methodology, and this is explained later in this chapter. It is called by inserting a **Call** instruction into the code, as shown here:

```
Sub Main()
     Call MySub         'Calls another macro/procedure called MySub
End Sub
```

You do not have to use the word **Call** to use the subroutine **MySub**. The following example also works:

```
Sub Main()
     MySub              'Calls another macro/procedure called MySub
End Sub
```

   A *function* is exactly like a subroutine except that it returns a value. Functions start with **Function** (instead of **Sub**) and end with **End Function** (instead of **End Sub**). This means that, generally speaking, functions should be called by using a variable, as discussed in Chapter 2, to accept the return value:

```
x=Now()
```

The variable **x** will contain the value of today's date. This is a very simple example of calling a built-in function.

   There are many other built-in functions that can also be used in this way. You cannot use the Excel formula functions, but many of them are already built into VBA as part of the language. Functions that you write can be used within spreadsheet formulas.

   Both subroutines and functions can have parameters or values passed to them. These are passed inside parentheses (more on this in the next section).

Writing a Simple Subroutine

A subroutine is different from a function in that it does not return anything directly and so cannot be used directly in the spreadsheet the way a function can. A subroutine is usually a building block that forms a piece of code that is going to be called many times, possibly from different points within your program. This is one of the great flexibilities of a subroutine. When it is called, the return address (from where the subroutine was called) is stored. When the subroutine finishes running, control is passed back to the return address. You can still pass parameters to it, but these are used internally within the code itself.

   Click back to Module1 and add the following code:

```
Sub Display(target)
     MsgBox target
End Sub
```

Note that this subroutine has an argument parameter for a variable called **target**. This is because you are going to call the subroutine from another procedure and pass a variable across.

A line is drawn to separate off the new subroutine, and the subroutine that you have written is automatically added to the drop-down in the top-left corner. Click the **This Workbook** object and return to the initial Hello World example from Chapter 1. On the **Workbook_Newsheet** event, add the following code:

```
Private Sub Workbook_NewSheet(ByVal Sh As Object)
'MsgBox "Hello World"
x = 3 * 5
MsgBox x
Call Display("my subroutine")
End Sub
```

Now, enter the Excel worksheet window and right-click one of the sheet tabs at the bottom left of the window. Click Insert in the context menu (pop-up window) and then click the Worksheet icon in the Insert window. You will see the message box showing 15 followed by a message box showing "my subroutine."

The **Call** command calls your subroutine and passes any required parameters to it. It then executes the code in the subroutine and returns to the next instruction following the **Call** statement. In this particular case, it passes the string "my subroutine" into the variable called **target**.

If the subroutine that you have written does not use parameters (arguments), you can run it from the code page by selecting Run | Run Sub/UserForm from the VBE (Visual Basic Editor) menu, pressing F5, or clicking the Run symbol on the toolbar. The cursor must be on the subroutine you intend to run. This is a useful way of testing the code you have written and seeing if there are any bugs in it.

Subroutines are a useful way of breaking large projects down into manageable pieces so that you do not end up with enormous, cumbersome routines. It is far easier to break a problem into constituent parts and work separately on each section, making sure you get that section working properly before moving onto other parts. The alternative is to write a large chunk of code, which inevitably leads to unnecessary duplication.

Writing a Simple Function

The object of this exercise is to create a function to accept two numbers, multiply them together, and return the result. The function will have the name **Multiply**. The following table cites the four main mathematical operators that you will use when writing functions and subroutines in VBA.

Add	+
Subtract	−
Multiply	*
Divide	/

The code for this function is as follows:

```
Function Multiply(a, b)

        Multiply = a * b

End Function
```

It should look like Figure 3-1. As with the subroutine, you must have at a bare minimum the function line and the end function line (header and footer). Notice that the function needs to be entered on to a module that you have inserted and not a module belonging to a worksheet or workbook.

The header introduces two parameters, **a** and **b**, by showing them in parentheses after the title of the function. A comma separates the two arguments. These arguments represent the two numbers to be multiplied—they could be called anything, as long as the variable name is consistent throughout the function.

The name of the function is **Multiply**, and this is used as a variable to return the answer. This is the only way to return the answer back to the routine that called the function.

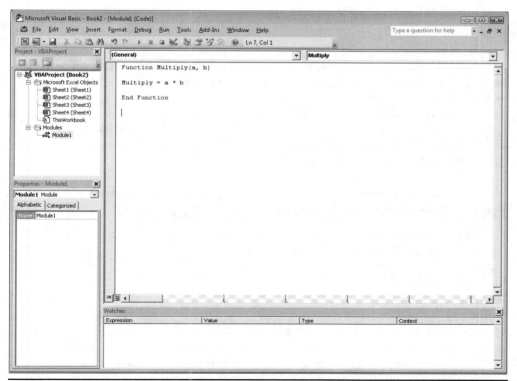

Figure 3-1   *Creating a simple multiply function*

Note that the name of the function now appears in the drop-down on the top right of the code window. This is because it is now an official function within both your VBA code and Excel.

You can now use this function in two ways: by calling it directly on the spreadsheet as a function or by using it within your VBA code. To call it directly on the spreadsheet, you do so in the same way that you would use any other function—for example, **SUM**. That's right, you have just written your first practical extension to Excel, and it's all your own work!

Click the spreadsheet and enter **=multiply(3,4)** into a cell. The answer 12 will appear in the cell. You can see how easy it is to write your own formula into Excel. The difficult calculation that you put together last week can now be turned into a custom function and used like any other Excel function.

Now, for the second way to use the function: calling it from within your VBA code. For the sake of simplicity, next you will call your new function from the same event that you called the Hello World example from.

Click the **ThisWorkbook** object and return to the initial Hello World example from Chapter 1. Turn the "Hello World" statement into a comment by putting a single quote (') character before it and enter the following code so that it looks like this:

```
Private Sub Workbook_NewSheet(ByVal Sh As Object)
     'MsgBox "Hello World"
     x = Multiply(3, 5)
     MsgBox x
End Sub
```

Note that when you type the word **Multiply** and open the brackets, VBA automatically displays the parameters it is expecting by name. By inserting the function into the code, you are forcing a call to that function using the parameters **3** and **5** to replace **a** and **b** in your function. The result is returned in the variable **x**.

Now got to the Excel worksheet and right-click one of the worksheet tabs at the bottom left. Click Insert in the context menu (pop-up menu) and then click the Worksheet icon in the insert window. A message box will appear with the answer of 15.

Public and Private Functions and Subroutines

VBA allows you to define your functions or subroutines as public or private using the keyword **Public** or **Private**. For example:

```
Private Sub PrivateSub()
End Sub
```

Any subroutines or functions that you create are public by default. This means that they can be used throughout the modules within your application, and spreadsheet users will find the subroutines available as macros by clicking Developer in the menu bar and then clicking the Macros icon in the Code control of the ribbon (left-hand side). They will also be able to access public functions in your code and will see them listed in the User Defined section if they click Formulas in the menu bar and then click Insert Function in the Function Library control of the ribbon (left hand).

There is one exception to this: UserForms. As discussed in Chapter 9, UserForms represent dialog forms and have their own modules. A public subroutine or function on a UserForm can be called from other modules within your code by referencing the form object—for example, **UserForm1.MysubRoutine**—but it will not appear in the macro or function list on the spreadsheet, and any function written on a UserForm cannot be used on the spreadsheet itself.

Also, if you create an Excel add-in, public procedures within that add-in can still be accessed by other modules by referencing the add-in object. This happens even if the code for the add-in is password protected. This can have advantages if you wish to write an add-in of your own procedures for use by other VBA programmers without letting them see how you did it! The disadvantage is that others can access your public procedures when you do not want them to. If the add-in is loaded, the public procedures within it are available to all modules.

Using private declarations, you can have procedures that have the same names but are in different modules. That procedure is private to that module and cannot be seen by other modules and, more importantly, cannot be seen and run by the spreadsheet user. This can cause confusion both for the programmer and for VBA. Which one does VBA choose to invoke if you call that procedure? Fortunately, VBA has a set of rules it uses for this. VBA first looks in the current module where the code is executing. If it cannot find a procedure of that name there, it then scans all modules for the procedure. Calls within the module where the private procedure is defined will go to that procedure. Calls outside that module will go to the public procedure.

Argument Data Types

When you specify arguments for a procedure, they always default to Variant, which is the default variable type in VBA. You can also declare your parameters as other data types, choosing from the data types you saw in the last chapter.

The advantage of declaring with data types is that they introduce a discipline to your code in terms of what information the procedure is looking for. If you do not specify a type but use the default Variant, then your procedure will accept anything, be it a number or a string. This could have unfortunate consequences within that procedure if you are expecting a string and a number gets passed across or vice versa. If you specify the parameter as a string, an error will occur if you do not pass a string:

```
Function Myfunction(Target as String)
```

This can also be useful if you are writing a custom spreadsheet function. When users enter your function into a cell, they must give the parameters according to the data type specified. If a string is specified, then they must put the value in quotes, or it must refer to a cell holding a text value.

Optional Arguments

You can make specific arguments optional by using the **Optional** keyword:

```
Function Myfunction (Target as String, Optional Flag as Integer)
```

In this example, the user has to specify the parameter **Target** as a string, but the parameter **Flag** will appear with square brackets around it and need not be specified. All optional parameters must come after the required ones.

Passing Arguments by Value

You can also use the **ByVal** or **ByRef** keyword to define how parameters are passed to your procedure. The important distinction is that ByVal takes a copy of the variable that is being passed and does not alter the original value of the variable within the subroutine or function. ByRef uses the original variable itself and any changes to the value that are made within the subroutine or function reflect through the entire scope of the variable. The ByRef methodology can often lead to bugs that are hard to track down. Your function may alter the value of your variable, but this may not be apparent when you are looking at the chain of your code.

It is generally accepted by programmers that ByRef is not a good idea unless you know exactly what you are doing.

```
Function MyFunction (ByVal Target as String)
```

The **ByVal** keyword ensures that parameters are passed by value rather than by a reference to a value from a variable. Passing a value by reference can easily allow bugs to creep into your code. To demonstrate this, if you pass by reference using a variable name, the value of that variable can be changed by the procedure that the variable is passed to—for example,

```
x = 100
z = Adjust(x)
Function Adjust(ByRef Target as Integer)
```

The variable **x** will be modified by what is going on within the function **Adjust**. However, if you pass by value, as shown here, only a copy of the variable is passed to the procedure:

```
x = 100
z = Adjust(x)
Function Adjust(ByVal Target as Integer)
```

If the procedure changes this value, the change affects only the copy and not the variable itself. The variable **x** will always keep its value of 100.

Normally, you would not expect a function to modify an argument, but it can happen and can lead to hard-to-find bugs within the code. To avoid these effects, use the declaration **ByVal**.

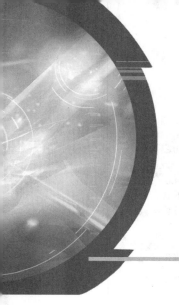

Programming Basics: Decisions and Looping

When writing programs, it's important to understand how programs make decisions and how they perform looping. Looping is the process of carrying out the same set of instructions until certain conditions are met.

Everyone is familiar with decisions. After all, you have to make them every day. For example when you wake up, which shirt do you decide to put on? You make this decision based on various facts such as what the weather is and what you are doing today. Your life would be very dull if you never had to make any decisions—think what it would be like if it was already decided what shirt you wore each day!

Programs also have to make decisions based on parameters that the program has access to. The computer program would also be very dull if it never made a decision. For example, if a program tries to load a workbook file and the file is not found, a decision needs to be made as to what to do next. Should the program simply display an error message and crash, or should it show some intelligence and alert the user that the file is missing and offer an alternative action?

Artificial intelligence is something that is frequently discussed in computing circles. By making your programs make decisions, you are introducing some primitive artificial intelligence into your program. Admittedly, it is your intelligence that goes into the code, but it tells the program what to do in the event of different circumstances happening. You are effectively writing a set of rules to deal with various situations.

Looping is also something everyone does daily without thinking about it. When you eat a meal, you perform the same routine of taking food from a plate and putting it into your mouth. Computer programs frequently loop around the same piece of code a number of times until a certain condition is met.

Decisions

Programs, unless they are extremely simple, usually have to make *decisions* according to data retrieved or input by the user. Decision making is one of the most important areas of programming, because it specifies what will happen when different events occur.

A good example of a common programming decision is IF something is true, THEN do *action1*, or ELSE do *action2*. In everyday life, this might be the statement "IF it is raining, THEN carry an umbrella, or ELSE (if the condition is not met and it is not raining) carry sunglasses."

Here is some sample code to show how the conditional If..Then..Else statement works and how it produces different results. Enter this in the module you created in Chapter 2 (this must be in a module that you have inserted yourself, not a sheet or worksheet module). See Figure 4-1 for an example of what your code window should look like.

```
Sub Test_If()
If Application.ActiveCell = 5 Then

     MsgBox "Cell is 5"
Else

     MsgBox "Cell is not 5"
End If
End Sub
```

This example refers to the active cell within the Excel application object with the line **Application.ActiveCell**, where the cursor is currently positioned. Click the worksheet and enter **5** in the current cell. Make sure that the cursor remains on that cell. Go back to your code window and press F5. You will get a message box saying that the cell is 5. Now go back to the spreadsheet and change the cell to another value or delete the value. Run the macro again and you will get the message box saying the cell is not 5.

Notice in Figure 4-1 that I have indented the code to separate the main parts of the conditional statement—this makes it easier to read and easier to debug because you can instantly see the groups of statements and where they start and finish. It is possible for If statements to be nested inside each other, so you can have an If statement within an If statement; this frequently happens in more complicated programs. (See the section "Looping," later in this chapter, for more on how this works.) It is convenient to be able to see at a glance where one If statement starts and ends. If there are others in between your start and stop point, you can frequently get lost when debugging code.

The End..If statement shows where the conditional statements finish, or you can put the entire If statement onto one line, as shown here, which then would not require an End..If:

```
If Application.ActiveCell = 5 Then MsgBox "Cell is 5"
```

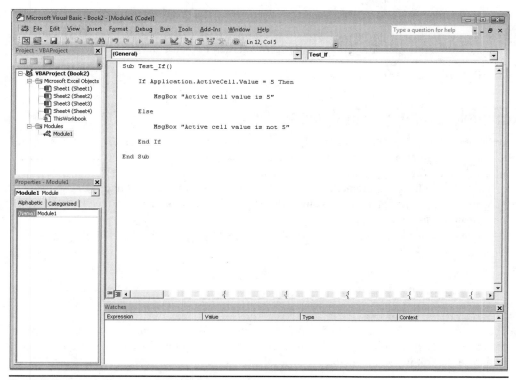

Figure 4-1   *Code for a conditional If statement*

If you have multiple instructions to be executed, you can place the statements on a single line if you separate each statement with a colon. However, this can become very difficult to read and debug and there are often several instructions to be carried out that preclude putting everything on one line.

Conditional operators that can be used are as follows:

Operator	Meaning
=	Both numbers or values are equal. This condition will also work for values, such as "dog" and "cat."
<	First value is less than second value.
>	First value is greater than second value.
<=	First value is less than or equal to second value.
>=	First value is greater than or equal to second value.
<>	First value is unequal to second value.

An expression such as **x=1** is evaluated as a Boolean value, that is, True or False or Non-zero or Zero. This means that you do not always have to use an operator—if you are only interested in whether a cell has a non-zero value in it, then you can use

```
If Application.ActiveCell Then MsgBox "Cell has a value"
```

Multiple Conditional Statements

In the preceding statements, I used only a single conditional statement in the form of **If x=1 Then...**. You can also use multiple conditional statements using a logical operator. For more information on logical operators, refer to Chapter 6.

Multiple conditional statements are straightforward and work almost like plain English. They use the operators **And** and **Or** and, for the purposes of this example, mean exactly what they mean in English.

If you have two conditions that you want to test, you write the If statement in the following form:

```
If x = 1 And y > 5 Then
     MsgBox "x=1 and y>5"
End If
```

The message box will be displayed only if both conditions (x = 1 and y > 5) are met. If, for instance, x > 1 but y has a value of 4, the message box will not be displayed. Similarly, you could use the following statement:

```
If x = 1 Or y > 5 Then
     MsgBox "x=1 or y>5"
End If
```

In the case of the preceding **Or**, the message box will be displayed if either one of the conditions is met. For example, if x = 1 or y > 5, the message box will be displayed. Therefore, x could be 0 and y could be 6, or x could be 1 and y could be 4, and the message box would still be displayed in either case.

You can put in several **And**s or **Or**s within the condition, although it gets complicated with more than three. It all depends on what you are trying to achieve in your decision statement and what the procedure is trying to do. You may be writing something very simple such as **If x=1 Then**, or you may be working on a more complicated conditional statement.

Select Case Statements

Another statement available in VBA for conditional processing is the **Select Case** statement. If you have a variable and you want different actions to occur depending on the value of that variable, you can use a series of If statements as follows:

```
If x=1 then MsgBox "x=1"
If x=2 then MsgBox "x=2"
If x=3 then MsgBox "x=3"
```

However, this is a good example of where a **Select Case** statement makes the code much cleaner:

```
x = 23
Select Case (x)

    Case (1)
        MsgBox "x=1"
    Case (23)
        MsgBox "x=23"

End Select
```

The **Select Case** statement provides a simple means to interrogate a specified variable and take action accordingly. The statement **Select Case (x)** defines the variable to be interrogated as **x** and is the start of the block of code for this procedure. **Case (1)** gives the action for if the value is 1—show a message box showing "x=1." **Case (23)** gives the action for if the value is 23—show a message box showing "x=23." Because **x** has been set to **23** at the start of the code, the message box will show "x=23."

You can also include the statements **To** and **Is** in the **Case** statement:

```
Sub Test_Case (Grade)
    Select Case Grade
        Case 1
            Msgbox "Grade 1"
        Case 2, 3
            Msgbox "Grade 2 or 3"
        Case 4 To 6
            Msgbox "Grade 4, 5 or 6"
        Case Is > 8
            MsgBox "Grade is above 8"
        Case Else
            Msgbox "Grade not in conditional statements"
    End Select
End Sub
```

Looping

Without looping facilities, programs would be extremely tedious and difficult to maintain. *Looping* allows a block of code to be repeated until a condition or a specified value is met. Suppose, for example, you wanted to display the numbers from 1 to 5. You could write the program as follows:

```
MsgBox "1"
MsgBox "2"
```

```
Msgbox "3"
Msgbox "4"
MsgBox "5"
```

This would work, but it is very inefficient and does not make use of the functionality of VBA. If you wanted to display more numbers, you would have to write more code. If you wanted to display all the numbers up to 1,000, it would require you to add an additional 995 lines of code!

For..Next Loops

This code can be reduced and made easier to maintain by using the For..Next looping statement as follows:

```
For n = 1 to 5
     MsgBox n
Next n
```

The message box will appear five times showing the values of **n** from 1 to 5.

The variable used can be anything—although I used **n** here, it could be a word such as **num**, but it must be consistent throughout the looping process. You could not use **For n = 1 to 5** and then try to use an index called **m**. If you changed the line "Next n" to "Next m," you would get an error because it does not match your original loop. Also, you must not use a reserved word for the variable name. You can put as many instructions as necessary between For and Next and even call subroutines or functions. The start and end values in the For..Next loop can also be different—they do not have to start at 1 or end at 5.

Step gives extra functionality. You may have noticed that the variable **n** is incremented by 1 each time in the loop—this is the default. You can change this behavior by using the **Step** option. **Step** allows you to specify the size of the increment and also the direction by using the following code:

```
For n = 3 to 12 Step 3


     MsgBox n
Next n
```

You will get the results 3, 6, 9, and 12, because it works in increments of 3.

To see how **Step** works backward, try this example:

```
For n= 10 to 1 Step -1
     MsgBox n
Next n
```

You will get the results 10, 9, 8, 7, 6, 5, 4, 3, 2, and 1.

For..Next loops are ideal for reading across column numbers or row numbers. You can use a For..Next loop to automatically increment a row number in a cell address.

For..Next loops can also be nested inside each other. For example, if you want to look at each value in a spreadsheet, you can use one For..Next to go across the columns and a second For..Next to go down the rows.

Following is an example that loops through values for **n** and **m**. Notice the indentation of the code; it makes the nesting of the For..Next clear. The **m** loop has been nested inside of the **n** loop so that it will perform the first **n** value, then all values of **m**, then the next **n** value, then all values of **m** again. Indenting helps prevent you from getting lost in your code when you look at it in a month's time.

```
Sub test_loop()
  For n = 1 To 4

    For m = 1 To 5

      MsgBox "n= " & n
      MsgBox "m= " & m
    Next m
  Next n
End Sub
```

For Each Loops

The For Each loop is very similar to a For..Next loop, but it is specifically for use on collections or arrays. For Each allows you to step through each item within the collection or array. You do not use an index (such as **n** in the previous example) because it automatically moves through each item within the collection. This is very useful if you need to search through a collection for a certain object and then delete it because the position in the collection after deletion is maintained in your loop. If you use a For..Next loop with an index and delete the object, the index will be moved up one and your routine will go through one loop too many, causing an error message.

The following example displays worksheet names using a For Each loop:

```
Sub ShowName()
    Dim oWSheet As Worksheet
    For Each oWSheet In Worksheets
        MsgBox oWSheet.Name
    Next oWSheet
End Sub
```

Do Until Loops

The **Do Until** loop keeps looping until a specified condition is met. Often this means waiting for a variable to contain a particular value. When the condition is met, the loop stops, and the program continues executing on the next instruction after the loop. You can also use a While statement so that while a certain condition is met, the code will carry on looping. Here is a simple example:

```
Sub test_do()
x = 0
Do Until x = 100
    x = x + 1
Loop
MsgBox x
End Sub
```

First a variable **x** is set to the value 0. The condition of x=100 is then supplied as the criterion for when the **Do** loop should stop. The variable (**x**) is then incremented by 1 each time through the loop, so it loops 100 times until x=100. At this point, it displays a message box giving the value of **x** that is 100.

While..Wend Loops

Finally, there is the While..Wend loop. This continues to loop while a specified condition is true. It stops as soon as the condition is false. Here is a simple example that is very similar to the previous Do Until loop:

```
Sub test_do()
x = 0
While x < 50
    x = x + 1

Wend
MsgBox x
End Sub
```

Again, a variable, **x**, is set to 0. The condition that **x** must be less than 50 is supplied, and **x** is incremented by 1 each time the loop is run. When x=50, it is no longer less than 50, so a message box is displayed showing the value of **x** at 50.

Early Exit of Loops

Under some circumstances, you may want your procedure to exit a loop early before it has worked all the way through and satisfied its criteria. An example might be where you are searching for a particular string of characters within an array. You may have 25 instances of that string to look through, but once the procedure has found what it is looking for, there is no point in further looping until the final condition is met. You could have an array of several thousand records that you are searching through, and a lot of time could be wasted in carrying on to the bitter end when the instance has already been found. In the case of a

For..Next loop, the value of the index is also preserved, which means that you can use it to locate where your condition was correct. Here is an example:

```
Sub test_exit()

    For x = 1 To 100
        If x = 50 Then
            Exit For
        End If
    Next x
    MsgBox x
End Sub
```

You exit a loop by using an **Exit For** statement in a For..Next loop or a For Each loop. You use an **Exit Do** within a Do Until loop. In the case of a For..Next loop, the value of the index is preserved. If the loops are nested, your code will only exit from the loop it is actually in. It will not exit from the outer loop unless you put another **Exit** statement in. The statement **Exit Do** and **Exit For** will stop execution of the loop and go on to the next instruction after the end of that loop.

5

Strings, Functions, and Message Boxes

This chapter covers how to handle strings of text, how to use the built-in functions of VBA, and how to design professional message boxes.

Strings

If you already use Excel frequently, you will know that a string is not something that you cut off from a ball of string and use around the house, but a stream of consecutive characters. They are not limited to the alphabet but can be any character within the character set (0 to 255). This covers all alphanumeric and control characters. These can be different according to what language code page you are using, but there are still only 256 characters. A string is useful for displaying a message to the user or providing a caption. A string could be "Richard", or it could be "1234".

VBA provides a number of functions for concatenating (joining) strings together, removing sections, searching, and changing case (to upper- or lowercase). For example, if you have a string "Your answer" and another " is wrong", you can join these together into one string: "Your answer is wrong". You can also use a function to change the entire string to uppercase characters so that it reads "YOUR ANSWER IS WRONG", or you can search for a particular word or set of characters within the string.

Concatenation

Concatenation is how you join strings together, generally using the & sign. It is extremely useful when you want to display messages. Suppose you are writing a program to display the number of worksheets in a workbook. Your program counts up the worksheets and stores the number in a variable. You could easily display the variable to the user, but what would it mean to that user?

When writing software, you want a clear message displayed to the user, such as, "There are n worksheets within the workbook." You do this by concatenating the string "There are", the variable **n** (which contains the number of worksheets), and the string "worksheets within the workbook". You can also introduce code that changes the first string to read "There is" when **n** has a value of 1, so that it is always grammatically correct.

```
MsgBox "There are " & n & " worksheets within the workbook"
```

Consider the simple example of a For..Next loop from the section titled "Looping" in Chapter 4. The code is as follows:

```
For n = 1 to 5
     MsgBox n
Next n
```

The message box gives the value of **n** as it increments, but it is just a message box with a number and does not provide the number any meaning. By adding a string, you can make a more user-friendly message:

```
For n = 1 to 5
     MsgBox "The value of n is " & n
Next n
```

The message box will now show the text "The value of n is 1." This will be displayed five times in all with the value of **n** incrementing each time. Don't forget to leave a space after the word "is," or your message will look peculiar and may be difficult to read.

There is no limit to how many strings and values you can concatenate in this way. Note that, although **n** is numeric, VBA automatically turns it into a character string for concatenation.

Splitting Strings

You may need only a part of a string in your code. For example, say you have a two-figure reference number at the beginning of the string that you need to use elsewhere in your program, but you wish to show only the name:

```
"12Richard"
```

To pull out the name only, you can use the **Mid** command:

```
x=Mid("12Richard",3)
```

This code will start at the third character and continue to the end of the string and place the result in the variable **x**, which will then contain the string "Richard". The **Mid** command has an optional length parameter so that you can specify the length of your substring. If you leave this out, you will get everything from your start point to the end of the string.

Note that in all these functions you can also use a variable that contains a string:

```
temp="12Richard"

x=Mid(temp,3)
```

You can also use this command to extract the number portion of the string at the front:

```
x=Mid("12Richard",1,2)
```

This code will start at the first character and take the next two characters from the string and place them in the variable **x**, which will contain a string with the value of 12, although this is not actually a number but a string. VBA is quite forgiving—if you want to do further calculations with this, you do not need to change it back to a number.

However, if you are putting it back into a spreadsheet cell, you may need to change it to a number from a formatting point of view. You do this by using the **Val** function:

```
Dim iValue as Integer
iValue = Val("12")
```

The variable **iValue** will then be an actual number rather than a string.

VBA also includes **Right** and **Left** string functions. The **Left** function can also be used to separate the number 12:

```
x=Left("12Richard",2)
```

The variable **x** will have the value 12.

If the **Right** function is used, **x** will have the value rd:

```
x=Right("12Richard",2)
```

The **Left** and **Right** functions grab from the side of the string, as indicated by the function name.

VBA also contains functions to change the case of a string, as discussed next.

Changing the Appearance of Strings

Ucase changes everything in the string to uppercase:

```
x=UCase("Richard")
```

The variable **x** will have the value RICHARD.

LCase changes everything to lowercase:

```
x=LCase("Richard")
```

The variable **x** will have the value richard.

In both of these examples, any nonletter characters such as numbers will be left as they are.

Searching Strings

There is also a function to search a string for a specified substring. This function is called **Instr**, which stands for "in string." The syntax for this is fairly complicated because two of the arguments are optional:

```
InStr([start, ]string1, string2[, compare])
```

Start is an optional parameter and shows where in the string the search should start from. If it is omitted, the search starts from position 1. **Start** must not contain a null value, and if **Start** is used then the **Compare** parameter must be used.

String1 is the string being searched (for example, "Richard Shepherd"). **String2** is the string being sought (for example, "shepherd").

Compare is the technique used to compare the strings. The possible values are **vbBinaryCompare** and **vbTextCompare**. In simple terms, this determines whether the search is case sensitive or not. Binary compare uses the actual binary value, so *A* equals *A*, but *A* does not equal *a*. Text compare ignores case, so *A* will equal *a*. A null value here will produce an error. The default for **Compare** is binary, which means it is case sensitive.

Table 5-1 lists the values the **Instr** function produces. Here is a simple example:

```
x=Instr("Richard Shepherd","Shepherd")
```

This will give the answer of 9.

Note that the default compare flag is binary/case sensitive:

```
x = Instr("Richard Shepherd","shepherd")
```

Value Returned by Instr	Meaning
0	**String1** is zero length
Null	**String1** is null
Start Value	**String2** is zero length
Null	**String2** is null
0	**String2 not found**
Position	Position of **String2** within **String1**
0	Start is greater than length of **String1**

Table 5-1 *Values of the Instr Function*

This will give the answer 0 because the string "shepherd" is not found due to the difference in case. The following will give the answer 9:

```
MsgBox InStr(1, "Richard Shepherd", "shepherd", vbTextCompare)
```

The next example uses the two optional parameters. Notice the use of start position:

```
MsgBox InStr(10, "Richard Shepherd", "shepherd", vbTextCompare)
```

This will give the result 0 (string not found) because the start search position is after where the search string is found.

The **InstrRev** function can be used to do a reverse search through a string.

Functions

This section is intended to give an overview of the most commonly used functions in VBA. There are many others available, but you will find that these are the major ones used.

Len

Len returns the number of characters in a string. The following will return the value of 3:

```
MsgBox Len("abc")
```

This example will return the value 8:

```
Msgbox Len("shepherd")
```

This function is useful in conjunction with the string handling commands. For example, if you want the last four characters of a string that is variable in length, you would need to know the string's length.

Abs

Abs stands for *absolute value* and returns a value of the unsigned magnitude. The following examples both will give the value of 1:

```
MsgBox Abs(1)
MsgBox Abs(-1)
```

Int

Int is short for *integer* and rounds a number to the previous integer. It does not round to the nearest whole number. This will give the value of 1:

```
MsgBox Int(1.2)
```

The following will also give the value of 1 despite being so close to 2:

```
MsgBox Int(1.99)
```

Sqr

Sqr returns the square root of a number. This example will result in the value 2:

```
MsgBox Sqr(4)
```

The following will result in the value 1.732:

```
MsgBox Sqr(3)
```

The following will give the value 10:

```
MsgBox Sqr(100)
```

Asc

Asc gives the ASCII (American Standard Code for Information Interchange) code for a given character. Values are from 0 to 255. The following will give the value of 65:

```
MsgBox Asc("A")
```

The following will give the value of 105:

```
MsgBox Asc("i")
```

Note that this only works on the first character of the string:

```
Asc("richard")
```

This will give 114, as this is the ASCII code for 'r'.

Chr

Chr is the reverse of **Asc**; it takes an ASCII code number and converts it to a character. This example will give the string "A":

```
MsgBox Chr(65)
```

The following will give the string "i":

```
MsgBox Chr(105)
```

Because this deals with the entire character set, it also includes nonprintable characters. For example, ASCII code 13 is a carriage return, which can be useful if you want to force a carriage return on something like a message box:

```
MsgBox "This is " & Chr(13) & "a carriage return"
```

Conversion Functions

Conversion functions are used to convert a value from one format to another. An example would be converting a numeric value into a string or converting the string back into a numeric value. These functions are extremely useful for switching values between various formats. For example, you may have a four-figure number where you want the second digit on its own. One of the easiest ways to do this is to convert the number into a string and then use the **Mid** function to separate out that digit. You can then convert it back to a numeric for the purposes of performing further calculations.

CStr

Cstr converts a value to a string. The following example will produce the string "1234":

```
Cstr(1234)
```

CInt

CInt converts a value or a string to an integer (2 bytes). There are no decimal places shown. Both of the following examples will give the value 123:

```
CInt (123.45)
CInt("123.45")
```

CInt does not work like the **Int** function but instead rounds to the nearest whole number instead of rounding down. If there are any nonnumerical characters in the expression, you will get a Type Mismatch error.

CLng

CLng converts a value or a string to a long integer (4 bytes). There are no decimal places shown. Both of the following examples will return the value 123456789:

```
CLng(123456789.45)
CLng("123456789.45")
```

Note that **CLng** does not work like the **Int** function but rounds to the nearest whole number instead of rounding down. If there are any nonnumerical characters in the expression, you will get a Type Mismatch error.

CDbl

CDbl converts a value or a string to a double-precision floating point number (eight bytes) where decimal places are allowed:

```
CDbl("123.56789")
```

This will return the value 123.56789.

If there are any nonnumeric characters in the expression, you will get a Type Mismatch error.

Val

Val converts a string to a value. It is more forgiving than **CInt** or **CLng** because it will accept nonnumeric characters:

```
Val("123")
```

This will give the value 123. The following will give the value 123.45:

```
Val("123.45")
```

The next example will give the value 12:

```
Val("12richard")
```

The following will give the value 0, meaning there are no numeric characters to evaluate:

```
Val("richard")
```

Format Function

The **Format** function is one of the most useful and complex functions within VBA. It allows you to format numbers to a chosen output format, similar to the way Excel formats a cell, where you can select from a number of options designating how a number will appear in a cell.

The **Format** function does exactly the same thing as formatting a number or a date within a cell in a spreadsheet, except it does so from within the code itself. If you wish to display a number in a message box or on a user form, this function is very useful for making it readable, particularly if it is a large number:

```
MsgBox Format(1234567.89, "#,###.#")
```

This will give the displayed result 1,234,567.9.

In the format string, each # represents a digit placeholder. The comma indicates that commas are used every three numeric placeholders. Only one numeric placeholder is shown after the decimal point, which means that the number is shown rounded to one decimal place.

You can also use the predefined format names as the format string, as shown in Table 5-2. This example uses the format "Currency":

```
MsgBox Format(1234567.89, "Currency")
```

This will give the displayed result of $1,234,567.89, depending on the currency symbol in the Windows settings. Other settings could be a pound sign for England or a euro sign for Europe.

There are a number of characters that can be used to define a user-defined format, as shown in Table 5-3.

Format Name	Description
General Number	Display the number as is.
Currency	Display the number with currency symbol. Use thousand separator. Enclose in brackets if negative. Display to two decimal places.
Fixed	Display at least one digit to the left and two digits to the right of the decimal point.
Standard	Display number with thousand separator. Display to two decimal places.
Percent	Display number multiplied by 100 with a percent sign (%) appended after. Display to two decimal places.
Scientific	Use standard scientific notation.
Yes/No	Display No if number is 0; otherwise, display Yes.
True/False	Display False if number is 0; otherwise, display True.
On/Off	Display Off if number is 0; otherwise, display On.

Table 5-2   *Predefined Formats*

Character	Description
Null String	No formatting.
0	Digit placeholder. Displays a digit or a zero. If there is a digit for that position, then it displays the digit; otherwise, it displays 0. If there are fewer digits than zeros, then you will get leading or trailing zeros. If there are more digits after the decimal point than there are zeros, then the number is rounded to the number of decimal places shown by the zeros. If there are more digits before the decimal point than zeros, these will be displayed normally.
#	Digit placeholder. This displays a digit or nothing. It works the same as the preceding zero placeholder, except that leading and trailing zeros are not displayed. For example, 0.75 would be displayed using zero placeholders, but this would be .75 using # placeholders.
.Decimal point.	Only one permitted per format string. This character depends on the settings in the Windows Control Panel.
%	Percentage placeholder. Multiplies number by 100 and places % character where it appears in the format string.
,	Thousand separator. This is used if 0 or # placeholders are used and the format string contains a comma. One comma to the left of the decimal point means to round to the nearest thousand (e.g., ##0,). Two adjacent commas to the left of the thousand separator indicate rounding to the nearest million (e.g., ##0,,).
E- E+	Scientific format. This displays the number exponentially.
:	Time separator—used when formatting a time to split hours, minutes, and seconds.
/	Date separator—this is used when specifying a format for a date.
- + £ $ ( )	Displays a literal character. To display a character other than listed here, precede it with a backslash (\).

Table 5-3   *User-Defined Formats*

The format string can have up to four sections separated by semicolons (;). These are so that different formats can be applied to different values, such as to positive and negative numbers. For example, you may wish to show brackets around a negative value:

```
MsgBox Format(-12345.67,"$#,##0;($#,##0)")
```

The following table provides section details depending on the number of sections included.

Section	Details
One section only	Applies to all values
Two sections	First section for positive values, second section for negative values
Three sections	First section for positive values, second section for negative values, third section for zeros
Four sections	First section for positive values, second section for negative values, third section for zeros, fourth section for null values

There are also predefined date and time formats, as shown in Table 5-4. These are controlled by the time and date settings in the Windows Control Panel.

There are a number of characters that you can use to create user-defined date and time formats, as listed in Table 5-5.

Here is an example of formatting the current time to hours, minutes, and seconds:

```
MsgBox Format(Now(), "hh:mm:ss AM/PM")
```

Format Name	Description
General Date	Display a date and / or time. For real numbers, display date and time. Integer numbers display time only. If there is no integer part, then display only time.
Long Date	Displays a long date as defined in the international settings of Windows Control Panel.
Medium Date	Displays a date as defined in the short date settings of Windows Control Panel, except it spells out the month abbreviation.
Short Date	Displays a short date as defined in the International settings of the Windows Control Panel.
Long Time	Displays a long time as defined in the International settings of the Windows Control Panel.
Medium Time	Displays time in 12-hour format using hours, minutes, and seconds and the AM/PM format.
Short Time	Displays a time using 24-hour format, e.g., 18:10.

Table 5-4   *Predefined Date and Time Formats*

There are a number of characters that you can use to create a user defined format.

Character	Meaning
c	Displays the date as ddddd and the time as ttttt.
d	Displays the day as a number without leading zero.
dd	Displays the day as a number with leading zero.
ddd	Displays the day as an abbreviation (Sun–Sat).
dddd	Displays the full name of the day (Sunday–Saturday).
ddddd	Displays a date serial number as a complete date according to Short Date in the International settings of the windows Control Panel.
dddddd	Displays a date serial number as a complete date according to Long Date in the International settings of the Windows Control Panel.
w	Displays the day of the week as a number (1 = Sunday).
ww	Displays the week of the year as a number (1–53).
m	Displays the month as a number without leading zero.
mm	Displays the month as a number with leading zeros.
mmm	Displays month as an abbreviation (Jan–Dec).
mmmm	Displays the full name of the month (January–December).
q	Displays the quarter of the year as a number (1–4).
y	Displays the day of the year as a number (1–366).
yy	Displays the year as a two digit number.
yyyy	Displays the year as four digit number.
h	Displays the hour as a number without leading zero.
hh	Displays the hour as a number with leading zero.
n	Displays the minute as a number without leading zero.
nn	Displays the minute as a number with leading zero.
s	Displays the second as a number without leading zero.
ss	Displays the second as a number with leading zero.
ttttt	Displays a time serial number as a complete time.
AM/PM	Uses a 12-hour clock and displays AM or PM to indicate before or after noon.
am/pm	Uses a 12-hour clock and uses am or pm to indicate before or after noon.
A/P	Uses a 12-hour clock and uses A or P to indicate before or after noon.
a/p	Uses a 12-hour clock and uses a or p to indicate before or after noon.

Table 5-5   *Date/Time Formats*

Character	Definition
@	Character placeholder. Displays a character or a space. If there is a character, then it is displayed; otherwise, a space is displayed.
&	Character placeholder. Display a character or nothing. If there is a character, then display it; otherwise, display nothing.
<	Force lowercase.
>	Force uppercase.
!	Force placeholders to fill from left to right.

Table 5-6   *Additional Format Characters*

Date formats, like number formats, can use sections. One section only applies to all data; two sections means that the first section applies to all data and the second to zero-length strings and null. For examples, look at the following table:

Format String	Definition
mm/dd/yy	01/03/03
dd-mmm-yyyy	01-Mar-2003
hh:mm	a.m./p.m.

You can also use the certain characters within your format string to create formatting, as shown in Table 5-6.

Some examples of the use of the **Format** function on numbers and strings are shown here:

```
MsgBox "This is " & Format("1000", "@@@,@@@")
MsgBox "This is " & Format("1000", "&&&,&&&")
MsgBox Format("richard", ">")
```

Date and Time Functions

There are a number of functions dealing specifically with date and time, and these are included in this section.

Now

The **Now** function returns the current date and time:

```
MsgBox Now
```

This displays the short date and time formats from the Windows Control Panel.

Date

Date returns the current date in short format as defined in the Windows Control Panel:

```
MsgBox Date
```

Time

The **Time** function returns the current system time:

```
MsgBox Time
```

DateAdd

DateAdd allows the addition and subtraction of a specified time interval to a date. The syntax is as follows:

```
DateAdd (interval, number, date)
```

Interval is a string that expresses the interval of time you want to add.
    The following table provides a list of interval types:

Time Period	Interval
Year	Yyyy
Quarter	Q
Month	M
Day of Year	Y
Day	D
Weekday	W
Week	Ww
Hour	H
Minute	N
Second	S

Number is a numeric that determines the number of intervals you want to add. A negative value is allowed and will cause subtraction from the date.
    Date is the date being added to or the name of a variant containing the date. This example will add one month to January and return 1-Feb-03:

```
MsgBox DateAdd ("m",1,"1-Jan-03")
```

The following will add two weeks and return 15-Jan-03 (depending on your date format):

```
MsgBox DateAdd ("ww",2,"1-Jan-03")
```

The following will subtract two days from 1 January 2003 and return 30-Dec-02:

```
MsgBox DateAdd ("d", -2, "1-Jan-03")
```

DateDiff

The **DateDiff** function returns the number of time intervals between two specified dates:

```
DateDiff (interval, date1, date2)
```

Interval is a string expression based on the following table to show the type of interval, the **date1** string indicates the start date, and **date2** the end date.

Time Period	Interval
Year	yyyy
Quarter	q
Month	m
Day of Year	y
Day	d
Weekday	w
Week	ww
Hour	h
Minute	n
Second	s

The following is an example of **DateDiff**:

```
MsgBox DateDiff("m", "1-jan-03", "15-mar-03")
```

This will return the result 2 because there are two months between 1-jan-03 and 15-mar-03. Note that it rounds to the lower month. If **date2** was 30-mar-03, it would still return 2. Only when **date2** is 1-apr-03 will it return 3.

DatePart

The **DatePart** function returns a specified part of a given date:

```
DatePart (interval, date)
```

Interval is the time period based on the following table, and date is the date you want to inspect.

Time Period	Interval
Year	yyyy
Quarter	q
Month	m
Day of Year	y
Day	d
Weekday	w
Week	ww
Hour	h
Minute	n
Second	s

The **DatePart** syntax is as follows:

```
MsgBox DatePart("q", "1-mar-03")
```

This will return the result 1 because 1-Mar-03 is in quarter 1.

The following will return the result 3 because March is the third month:

```
MsgBox DatePart("m", "1-mar-03")
```

DateSerial

DateSerial returns the date serial for a specific year, month, and day entered as integers. The date serial is the actual number representing that date:

```
DateSerial (year, month, day)
```

where **year** is a number between 100 and 9999 or a numeric expression; **month** is a number between 1 and 12 or a numeric expression; and **day** is a number between 1 and 31 or a numeric expression.

For example, the following will return the value 37686, which is the date 6-Mar-2003:

```
MsgBox CDbl(DateSerial(2003, 3, 6))
```

You need to use **CDbl** (convert to double) in this code, or the message box will display the date as per the format in the Windows Control Panel rather than as an actual number.

DateValue

This function converts a date into a value. For example, the following will return the value 37686, which is the date 6-Mar-2003:

```
Msgbox CDbl(DateValue("06-Mar-2003"))
```

You need to use **CDbl** (convert to double) in this code or the message box will display the date as per the format in Windows Control Panel rather than as an actual number.

Day

This will return an integer between 1 and 31, representing the day of the month for the date expression given, as seen here:

```
Day (dateexpression)
```

Dateexpression can be a date string or it can be a numeric expression representing a date.

Both of the following return the value 6 for the sixth day of March because they represent the same date:

```
Msgbox Day(37686)
Msgbox Day("6-Mar-2003")
```

Hour

Hour returns an integer between 0 and 23 representing the hour of the day for the date expression:

```
Hour(dateexpression)
```

An example of a **dateexpression** could be "31-Dec-2002 12:00" or could be a time without the date, such as "09:00":

```
MsgBox Hour("17:50")
```

This will return a value of 17 for the seventeenth hour.

The following will return a value of 16 because 4:30 in the afternoon is the sixteenth hour:

```
MsgBox Hour("6-Mar-2003 4:30pm")
```

The following will return the value of 11; 11 divided by 24 is equal to .458333, which is the time value for 11:00 A.M.:

```
MsgBox Hour(11 / 24)
```

Month

Month returns an integer between 1 and 12, based on the date expression:

```
Month (dateexpression)
```

An example of a **dateexpression** could be "31-Dec-2002 12:00" or could be a time without the date, such as "09:00."

The following will both return the value of 3 because both date expressions represent 6-Mar-2003:

```
Msgbox Month(37686)
Msgbox Month("6-Mar-2003")
```

Second

The **Second** function returns an integer between 0 and 59 based on the **timeexpression** representing the seconds of a minute:

```
Second(timeexpression)
```

An example of a **timeexpression** could be "31-Dec-2002 12:00" or could be a time without the date, such as "09:00."

The following will return the value 48:

```
Msgbox Second("4:35:48pm")
```

Minute

The **Minute** function returns an integer from a time expression representing the actual minute of that time.

```
Msgbox Minute(11.27 / 24)
```

This will return the value 16, since 11.27 is 11:16:12 A.M. This may look confusing because we are dealing with decimal parts of an hour. The expression 11.27 is a decimal of an hour, so .27 is just over a quarter of an hour.

Following are two examples of the **Minute** function:

```
Msgbox Minute("4:35pm")
Msgbox Minute(11.25 / 24)
```

Year

The **Year** function returns an integer from a date expression representing the actual year value of that date:

```
Msgbox Year(37686)
Msgbox Year("6-Mar-2003")
```

Weekday

The **Weekday** function returns an integer between 1 (Sunday) and 7 (Saturday) that represents the day of the week for a date expression:

```
Weekday (dateexpression)
MsgBox WeekDay("6-Mar-2003")
```

This will return the value 5, which is Thursday.

This function can be useful if you want a date to always default to a particular day of the week. For example, if you always want a date to show the week ending Friday for the current week, you could use the following formula:

```
MsgBox Now - WeekDay(Now) + 6
```

The **Weekday** function starts from Sunday, so it reduces **Now** back to the last Sunday and then adds 6 to get to Friday. You can also use it to calculate the number of working days between two dates:

```
For n = DateValue("1-Jan-03") To DateValue("18-Jan-03")

    If Weekday(n) <> 1 Or Weekday(n) <> 7 Then

    WorkDay = WorkDay + 1

    End If
Next n

MsgBox WorkDay
```

WorkDay will return the value of 13, which is the number of working days between the two dates.

SendKeys Command

The **SendKeys** command is not exactly a function but rather a command statement. A command statement like this can be used in a function or a subroutine. It allows you to command another application by sending keypresses to it, exactly the same as if you were typing at the keyboard into that application. It effectively simulates keypresses on the keyboard and can be used for low-level automation of programs that do not support OLE automation.

All the applications in the Microsoft Office Suite support OLE automation in that you can load in a reference to a particular object model and then manipulate that application from inside your code. See Chapter 14 on how to use other Microsoft applications from within your code.

Other applications do not support this; a good example is the calculator application that is supplied with Microsoft Windows. There is no access to an object model, but you can use **SendKeys** to manipulate it.

SendKeys sends one or more keystrokes to the active window as if they had been entered at the keyboard:

```
SendKeys keytext [,wait]
```

In this example, **keytext** is the string of keys to be sent to the active window; **wait** is a Boolean value (True or False). If **wait** is True, then the keys must be processed first before control is returned to the procedure. If **wait** is False, then control is returned to the procedure immediately after the keystrokes are sent. If **wait** is omitted, then False is assumed as the default.

The value of **wait** can be extremely important when sending keys to another application. If the application is running quickly, it may have moved on in execution by the time the key statement comes across, so the **SendKeys** statement gets ignored. You set **Wait** to True so that the keystrokes are processed first, preventing the application from moving on ahead.

Generally, the keyboard keys themselves are used in the **SendKeys** statement most of the time. For example,

```
SendKeys "A123"
```

sends A123 to the current window.

Of course, this is assuming you have the relevant application running and that it is the active window!

Two other commands will help with this. The first is the **Shell** function. This allows your code to launch another application and transfer control to it:

```
Shell (commandstring [,windowstyle])
```

The **commandstring** is the command line to call the application. If you look at the properties of the shortcuts on your desktop, you will see that there is a text box called Target that holds the pathname and filename of the application plus any necessary parameters. This is used as the **commandstring**.

The **windowstyle** parameter dictates how the application will be opened, whether it will be opened as a normal window and icon or hidden.

Before you can send your keypresses to the application, you need to open it. Here is an example opening the Windows Calculator:

```
x = Shell("calc.exe",1)
```

This opens the Windows calculator application in a standard window with focus. As it is then the active window, you can use **SendKeys** to send keypresses to it.

The other command to use before you send keys is **AppActivate**. If the application is already loaded, you do not need to use the **Shell** function to load it in again, but you do need to switch the focus over to that application so that it can send the keys. This allows your code to activate another application already loaded by use of the title in the header bar:

```
AppActivate "Microsoft Word"
```

In this way, you can perform simple automation of other applications:

```
Sub test_sendkeys()

x = Shell("calc.exe")

For n = 1 To 10

  SendKeys n & "{+}", True

Next n

MsgBox "Press OK to close calculator"

AppActivate "calculator"

SendKeys "%{F4}", True

End Sub
```

In this example, the Windows calculator is loaded, and then a For..Next loop makes it add up the numbers from 1 to 10.

The message box will appear on the Excel application, because that is where the code is running from. The Excel icon will flash on the Windows toolbar. Select Excel and click OK, and the calculator will close.

The plus sign (+), caret (^), percent sign (%), tilde (~), and parentheses (( )) have special meanings to **SendKeys**. To specify one of these characters, enclose it in braces ({ }). For example, to specify the plus sign, type **{+}**. Brackets ([ ]) have no special meaning to **SendKeys**, but you must enclose them in braces.

To specify special characters that aren't displayed when you press a key, such as ENTER or TAB, and keys that represent actions rather than characters, use the codes shown in Table 5-7.

To specify keys combined with any combination of the SHIFT, CTRL, and ALT keys, precede the key code with one or more of the following codes:

Key	Code
SHIFT	+
CTRL	^
ALT	%

Key	Code
BACKSPACE	{BACKSPACE}, {BS}, or {BKSP}
BREAK	{BREAK}
CAPS LOCK	{CAPSLOCK}
DEL or DELETE	{DELETE} or {DEL}
DOWN ARROW	{DOWN}
END	{END}
ENTER	{ENTER}or ~
ESC	{ESC}
HELP	{HELP}
HOME	{HOME}
INS or INSERT	{INSERT} or {INS}
LEFT ARROW	{LEFT}
NUM LOCK	{NUMLOCK}
PAGE DOWN	{PGDN}
PAGE UP	{PGUP}
PRINT SCREEN	{PRTSC}
RIGHT ARROW	{RIGHT}
SCROLL LOCK	{SCROLLLOCK}
TAB	{TAB}
UP ARROW	{UP}
F1	{F1}
F2	{F2}
F3	{F3}
F4	{F4}
F5	{F5}
F6	{F6}
F7	{F7}
F8	{F8}
F9	{F9}
F10	{F10}
F11	{F11}
F12	{F12}

Table 5-7 *Special Keys Not Normally Displayed*

To specify that any combination of SHIFT, CTRL, and ALT should be held down while several other keys are pressed, enclose the code for those keys in parentheses. For example, to specify to hold down SHIFT while E and C are pressed, use **+(EC)**. To specify to hold down SHIFT while E is pressed, followed by C without SHIFT, use **+EC**.

If you use **SendKeys** to drive another application, be aware that the keyboard is still active and can have disastrous results if it is touched while **SendKeys** is running.

Some years ago, I wrote a **SendKeys** program for a major bank in the UK to work with a time-recording application. The program ran overnight and generated timesheets for use on Friday morning. One Friday morning, there were no timesheets, and the program had gone haywire. The reason for this was that during the evening, a cleaner had been dusting and managed to hit the RIGHT ARROW key on the keyboard, throwing out my careful sequence of keystrokes. This meant that instead of going down one particular column, it went down the next one, and the keystrokes had no effect. After that incident, when the program was run on a Thursday evening, the keyboard was always placed behind the monitor out of harm's way.

SendKeys is not the most elegant way of doing things, but in this particular case it was the only way available given the application involved. With thousands of users on the application, there was immense pressure on the server on a Friday morning with people logging on and generating timesheets, which led to the server going down and a lot of unhappy project managers. The SendKeys option saved the day in this particular case and allowed the timesheets to be generated overnight. Managers were pleased and the servers stayed up!

Message Boxes

In many of the examples in this book I have used the **MsgBox** function to communicate results to the user. You can write code to place the result into a particular cell on the spreadsheet, but the message box is an extremely easy way to send data back to the user. It only needs one command, and the line of text that you wish to display to provide a professional-looking message box onscreen. So far it has only been used in its simplest form:

```
MsgBox "Hello World"
```

Figure 5-1 shows the result of this. It does look slightly different from the message boxes that you see in other programs. The caption in the title bar says "Microsoft Excel." In addition, there is no icon and there is only one option button.

You can very easily customize the message box's title bar and icon to suit your needs.

```
MsgBox "Hello World", vbInformation
```

This will cause the message box to look more professional, with a proper icon and a meaningful title. When you typed this line of code, you probably noticed that when you get

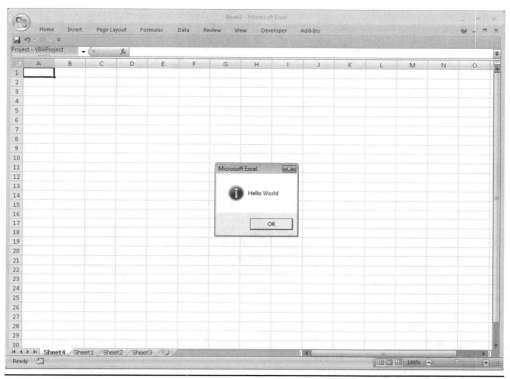

Figure 5-1   *A simple message box*

to the **type** parameter, you get a nice list box showing all your options. There are four icons you can use depending on circumstances, as shown in the following table:

Constant	Definition
vbCritical	Stop. A white cross on a red circular background. Use this to tell users they are attempting to do something that they should not.
vbExclamation	Exclamation mark. Use this as a warning, for example, "This may lead to loss of data."
vbInformation	Information sign. Use this to indicate that the message box is supplying information that the user may find useful at this point in the program.
vbQuestion	Question mark. Usually associated with multiple buttons, for example, "Are you sure you wish to take this action: Yes or No?"

This is all quite straightforward, but what happens if you want to add more or different buttons, such as Yes and No? Microsoft has built in a number of constants to allow for different button combinations and icons. These are detailed in Table 5-8.

Constant	Value	Description
vbAbortRetryIgnore	2	Displays Abort, Retry, and Ignore Buttons.
vbCritical	16	Displays Stop icon—white cross on a red circle.
vbDefaultButton1	0	First Button is default button.
vbDefaultButton2	256	Second Button is default button.
vbDefaultButton3	512	Third Button is default button.
vbDefaultButton4	768	Fourth Button is default button.
vbExclamation	48	Displays Exclamation icon.
vbInformation	64	Displays Information icon.
vbOKCancel	1	Displays OK and Cancel buttons.
vbOKOnly	0	Displays OK button only.
vbQuestion	32	Displays Question icon.
vbRetryCancel	5	Dispays Retry and Cancel Buttons.
vbYesNo	4	Displays Yes and No buttons.
vbYesNoCancel	3	Displays Yes, No, and Cancel buttons.

Table 5-8   *Constants for Message Boxes*

Following is an example of the message box with Yes and No buttons and a defined caption:

```
MsgBox "Test message", vbYesNo, "My message"
```

You can combine icon and button constants with the **Or** operator:

```
x = MsgBox("Test Message", vbAbortRetryIgnore Or vbCritical)
```

This will display a message box with the Abort, Retry, and Ignore buttons and a Critical message icon.

Displaying the buttons is relatively easy, but how do you detect when the user clicks a particular button? You still need to write code to deal with the button that has been clicked. You do this by collecting the response in a variable:

```
x = MsgBox ("Test Yes No",vbYesNo,"Test")
Msgbox x
```

Note that in this instance you use **x =** and put parentheses around the parameters. Without the brackets, you will get an error because you are calling a function, which needs the parentheses to show the parameters.

This example will show a two-button message box (Yes and No). If Yes is clicked, the following message box will show 6 (**vbYes**). If No is clicked, the message box will show 7 (**vbNo**). You can then write your code to specify what will happen according to which action is taken:

```
If x = vbYes Then Action1 Else Action2
```

The following table lists the return values for a message box:

Constant	Value	Description
vbOK	1	OK button clicked
vbCancel	2	Cancel button clicked
vbAbort	3	Abort button clicked
vbRetry	4	Retry button clicked
vbIgnore	5	Ignore button clicked
vbYes	6	Yes button clicked
vbNo	7	No button clicked

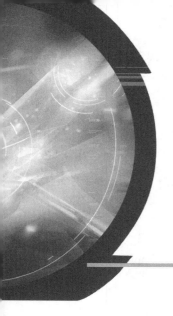

Operators

Operators perform mathematical functions, comparison functions, or logical operations between two numbers or numerical expressions within your program. A simple example of an operator is the plus (+) or minus (–) sign. You will have already come across many operators when using spreadsheet formulas.

Operators have orders of precedence that determine the order in which the calculations take place. Within individual categories (arithmetic, comparison, and logical), operators are evaluated in the order of precedence as shown in the following table from the top down:

Arithmetic	Comparison	Logical
Exponentiation (^)	Equality (=)	Not
Negation (–)	Inequality ()	And
Multiplication and division (*, /)	Less than (<)	Or
Integer division (\)	Greater than (>)	Xor
Modulo arithmetic (Mod)	Less than or equal to (<=)	Eqv
Addition and subtraction (+, –)	Greater than or equal to (>=)	Imp
String concatenation (&)	Like / Is	

These orders of precedence can be changed by using parenthesis (brackets) within the formula, in the same way that you can in Excel formulas. The formulas within the innermost nested set of parentheses will always be evaluated first.

The use of brackets to change the order of precedence can end up giving different results than you expect, so it is important to understand how they work. Try the following code examples in a subroutine on a module:

```
MsgBox (10 + 6) / 3
```

This gives the answer 5.3333.

```
MsgBox 10 + 6 / 3
```

This gives the answer 12.

In the first example, the brackets force **10 + 6** to be evaluated first before division by 3. In the second example, the division of **6 / 3** takes precedence followed by the addition of 10.

Arithmetic Operators

These are the operators that do the arithmetical work, such as plus (**+**), minus (**−**), multiply (*****), and divide (**/**).

* Operator

This signifies the multiplication of two numbers.

```
MsgBox 6 * 3
```

This gives the answer 18.

The numbers can be any numeric expressions. The data type of the result is that of the most precise operand ranging from Integer (least precise), Long, Single, Double, Currency (most precise). See Chapter 2 for more details on these data types. If one operand is Null, then the result will be Null.

+ Operator

This adds two numbers or expressions together.

```
MsgBox 4 + 2
```

The answer will be 6.

This operator can both add numbers and concatenate strings. String concatenation can cause confusion, so it is best to use the **&** operator for this purpose because you cannot always determine if string concatenation will occur with **+**. See the example at the end of this section showing how string concatenation can be affected by use of the **+** operator.

The numbers can be any numeric expressions. The data type of the result is that of the most precise operand ranging from Integer (least precise), Long, Single, Double, Currency (most precise). If one operand is Null, then the result will be Null.

Here are some general rules of addition and concatenation:

► Add if both operands are numeric.

► Concatenate if both operands are strings.

► Add if one operand is numeric and the other is a variant (not Null).

► Concatenate if one operand is a string and the other is a variant (not Null).

A Type Mismatch error occurs if one operand is numeric and the other is string, as shown here:

```
MsgBox 1 + " Richard"
```

Note this does not happen if you use the **&** operator to concatenate, as shown here:

```
MsgBox 1 & " Richard"
```

– Operator

This subtracts one number from another or shows a negative value. The following will give an answer of 2:

```
MsgBox 6 - 4
```

The following will display –5:

```
MsgBox -5
```

The numbers can be any numeric expressions. The data type of the result is that of the most precise operand ranging from Integer (least precise), Long, Single, Double, Currency (most precise). If one operand is Null, then the result will be Null.

/ Operator

This divides two numbers and returns a floating point result.

```
MsgBox 6 / 3
```

The result is 2. If there were a remainder, it would be displayed as decimal places.

The numbers can be any numeric expressions. The data type of the result is that of the most precise operand ranging from Integer (least precise), Long, Single, Double, Currency (most precise). If one operand is Null, then the result will be Null.

\ Operator

This divides two numbers and returns an integer result.

```
Msgbox 6 \ 4
```

The answer is 1.

The numbers can be any numeric expressions. The data type of the result is Integer or Long. If one operand is Null, then the result will be Null.

^ Operator

This raises a number to the power of an exponent.

```
MsgBox 2 ^ 3
```

The answer is 8 (2 to the power of 3).
   The operands can be any numeric expression.

Mod Operator

This divides two numbers and returns only the remainder.

```
MsgBox 6 Mod 4
```

This returns 2, which is the remainder of 6 divided by 4.
   This is often used when testing to see if a number is odd or even. If the modulus is True (nonzero) when divided by two, then the number is odd.

Comparison Operators

Comparison operators compare two expressions, as you found out in Chapter 4 when we discussed making decisions in VBA.

```
MsgBox 3 > 1
```

This returns True because 3 is greater than 1.
   Comparison operators always return a Boolean value of True or False except when Null is included, in which case the result is always Null. Here is a list of comparison operators:

Operator	Meaning
<	Less than
<=	Less than or equal to
>	Greater than
>=	Greater than or equal to
=	Equal to
<>	Not equal to

   If both expressions are numeric, then a numeric comparison is performed. If they are both string expressions, then a string comparison is performed. If one is numeric (the variable is a numeric type containing a number) and one is a string (a variable containing a string of characters), then a Type Mismatch error will occur.

Concatenation Operator

This concatenates two operands together.

```
MsgBox "Richard " & "Shepherd"
```

This gives the result "Richard Shepherd." Note that a space was left at the end of "Richard " to give the space in the final string.

You can also concatenate numbers and strings, but remember that the result will be a string. The following gives the result "12 Twelve":

```
Msgbox 12 & " Twelve"
```

While this works because VBA is intelligent enough to work out that you are combining a number and a string and converts the number (12) to a string, it is not best practice to concatenate two different data types without converting them to the same data type.

The following gives the result 34, but as a string, not a number:

```
Msgbox 3 & 4
```

Logical Operators

These perform a logical bit-by-bit conjunction on two expressions. They use pure binary math to decide the result.

And Operator

This works on the basis that both values have to be True (nonzero). The value of True in VBA is actually −1. The following will give the result False because both values have to be True for an overall True value when the **And** operator is used:

```
Msgbox True And False
```

Numbers can also be **And**ed together. This is done on a binary basis. The top row of the following table represents the value of each binary bit going from bit 7 to bit 0. The two rows below it represent the binary equivalents of the numeric numbers on the right of the table (column n). The final row shows both the binary and numeric equivalents when the two numbers are **And**ed together. Each bit pair uses an **And** operator to achieve the final result on the bottom row.

128	64	32	16	8	4	2	1	n
0	1	0	1	0	1	0	0	84
1	0	0	1	0	0	0	1	145
0	**0**	**0**	**1**	**0**	**0**	**0**	**0**	**16**

Each column of this table shows a binary bit based on an eight-bit number. The bit values are shown in bold across the top. The right-hand column (*n*) contains the actual decimal values.

Bits are counted from the right to left, starting at bit 0 and ending at bit 7 for a single-byte number. Notice that the values of each bit increase in powers of 2. Bit 0 is represented by the value of 1, and bit 7 is represented by the value of 128. The first number is 84, so bit 6, bit 4, and bit 2 are all set. If you add 64 + 16 + 4, this comes to 84. The second number is 145, so bit 7, bit 4, and bit 0 are set. If you add 128 + 16 + 1, this comes to 145.

When a logical **And** is done on the two numbers, the result is 16. This is because the only bit where both numbers have a value is bit 4. This can be shown with the following example:

```
MsgBox 84 And 145
```

This will give the result of 16.

This strange binary arithmetic is generally used for testing whether bits are set within a number or for masking purposes. Masking sets the values of certain bits to True or False within a number. To do this, a "mask" number is **And**ed with the target number and the bit in the mask will be set to the mask value. For example, if you want bit 7 to be set to 1, then you **And** your target number with 128 (bit 7 value) and bit 7 in the target number is then set to True, regardless of what values the other bits have.

Also, for example, you could have a variable that uses eight bits to hold various information on something, almost like properties. Each bit may represent a certain setting. If bit 4 represents a certain value and you want to see if it is set, all you do is **And** it with 16, which is the binary number for bit 4. If the bit is set, it will give a value of 16; otherwise, it will give a value of 0. This acts totally independently of values that the other bits are set to.

Not Operator

The **Not** operator performs a logical **Not** on two numbers or expressions. It basically inverts the bits within a number. If a bit is set to 0, then it becomes 1; and if it is set to 1, it becomes 0.

```
MsgBox Not (2 = 3)
```

This will give the result True because 2 does not equal 3 (which is False), but the Not statement then inverts the bits and makes it True.

Or Operator

This works on the basis that either two values can be True (nonzero) or one can be True and the other False (zero). The following returns True because one of the values is True:

```
MsgBox True Or False
```

The following returns False because there is no True value:

```
MsgBox False Or False
```

It works on binary arithmetic on the basis that 1 and 1 make 1, 1 and 0 make 1, 0 and 1 make 1, and 0 and 0 make 0.

The top row of the following table represents the value of each binary bit going from bit 7 to bit 0. The two rows below it represent the binary equivalents of the numeric numbers on the right of the table (column n). The final row shows both the binary and numeric equivalents when the two numbers are **Or**ed together. Each bit pair uses an **Or** operator to achieve the final result on the bottom line.

128	64	32	16	8	4	2	1	n
0	1	0	1	0	1	0	0	84
1	0	0	1	0	0	0	1	145
1	**1**	**0**	**1**	**0**	**1**	**0**	**1**	**213**

Each column of the preceding table shows a binary bit based on an eight-bit number. The bit values are shown in bold across the top. The right-hand column contains the actual decimal numbers.

Bits are counted from right to left, starting at bit 0 and ending at bit 7 for a single-byte number. Notice that the values of each bit increase in powers of 2. The first number is 84, so bit 6, bit 4, and bit 2 are all set. If you add 64 + 16 + 4, this comes to 84. The second number is 145, so bit 7, bit 4, and bit 0 are set. If you add 128 + 16 + 1, this comes to 145.

When a logical **Or** is done on the two numbers, the result is 213 (128 + 64 + 16 + 4 +1). This can be shown using the following VBA example:

```
MsgBox 84 Or 145
```

This will give the result of 213.

The **Or** operator is often used for masking purposes in graphics and also for combining two parameters. In Chapter 5, I discussed the message box you had to combine with **vbExclamation** and **vbYesNo** in order to get the correct icon and the correct buttons on the message box. Using a simple **+** operator to add **vbExclamation** and **vbYesNo** together will result in the wrong value being set for the required flag. It is only by using **Or** that the correct result is achieved.

You also see use of **Or** in If statements, as in Chapter 4:

```
If  x = 1  Or  y = 1 Then
```

Xor Operator

Xor is very similar to **Or**, except that True and True make False. Only True and False make True, but there must be one True and one False. **Xor** stands for *Exclusive Or*—both values cannot both be True or False. The following gives the value True:

```
MsgBox True Xor False
```

The following gives the value False:

```
MsgBox True Xor True
```

The **Xor** operator works on binary arithmetic on the basis that 1 and 1 make 0, 1 and 0 make 1, 0 and 1 make 1, and 0 and 0 make 0.

The top row of the following table represents the value of each binary bit going from bit 7 to bit 0. The two rows below it represent the binary equivalents of the numeric numbers on the right of the table (column *n*). The final row shows both the binary and numeric equivalents when the two numbers are **Xor**ed together. Each bit pair uses an **Xor** operator to achieve the final result on the bottom line.

128	64	32	16	8	4	2	1	*n*
0	1	0	1	0	1	0	0	84
1	0	0	1	0	0	0	1	145
1	**1**	**0**	**0**	**0**	**1**	**0**	**1**	**197**

Each column of the preceding table shows a binary bit based on an eight-bit number. The bit values are shown in bold across the top. The right-hand column contains the actual numbers.

Bits are counted from the right to left, starting at bit 0 and ending at bit 7 for a single-byte number. Notice that the values of each bit increase in powers of 2. The first number is 84, so bit 6, bit 4, and bit 2 are all set. If you add 64 + 16 + 4, this comes to 84. The second number is 145, so bit 7, bit 4, and bit 0 are set. If you add 128 + 16 + 1, this comes to 145.

When a logical **Xor** is done on the two numbers, the result is 197 (128 + 64 + 4 +1). This can be shown with the following VBA example:

```
MsgBox 84 Xor 145
```

This will give the result of 197. This result has an interesting property. If you **Xor** the result with one of the numbers used, you will get the other number that was used to create the result. The following will return the value 145:

```
MsgBox 84 Xor 197
```

The following will return the value 84:

```
MsgBox 145 Xor 197
```

This operator is often used in simple encryption routines. You use a string of random characters. The string you want to encrypt is then **Xor**ed character by character against your random string. This produces another apparently random string with no discernible pattern in it (and patterns are what code breakers look for).

To decrypt the string, all you have to do is **Xor** character by character against the original random string.

Other Operators

There are a number of other operators that can be used within Excel VBA.

Is Operator

Is compares two object reference variables to see if they are the same. The following returns True because the two expressions are both the same—sheet1 is the same as sheet1:

```
MsgBox Worksheets(1) Is Worksheets(1)
```

The following returns False because the two expressions are not the same:

```
MsgBox Worksheets(1) Is Worksheets(2)
```

Here, sheet1 is not the same as sheet2 because it has a different name. There may be other differences, but if the two sheets are totally new, the name will be the only difference.

Like Operator

Like compares two string expressions that are similar to each other to see if they match a pattern. They may have the first few characters the same or may simply be in uppercase and lowercase.

```
Option Compare Text
Sub test()
     MsgBox "RICHARD" Like "richard"
End Sub
```

If the **Option Compare** statement in declarations is set to Text, then this will return True. If it is set to **Binary**, then it will return False. This works in the same way as the **Compare** parameter used in the **Instr** function in Chapter 5, in that it sets whether a binary or a text compare (case sensitive) will happen.

You can use wildcard characters. A ? denotes a single character and a * denotes a string of characters. It is exactly the same as doing a file search when you use wildcard characters. A table of pattern characters is shown here:

Character	Meaning
?	Any single character
*	Zero or more characters
#	Any single digit (0–9)
[charlist]	Any single character in charlist
[!charlist]	Any single character not in charlist

The following examples will return True:

```
MsgBox "RICHARD" Like "ri?hard"
```

```
MsgBox "RICHARD" Like "ric*"
```

Debugging

Whenever you write code, there is a chance that bugs will exist that can cause a program failure, the program to hang, or simply unexpected results. In my opinion, this is the area that sorts out the true analytical programmers from people who just type in code and hope it will work.

There have been many reports written on "computer rage," where users of an application get upset because the results are different from what they expected. All I can say to those people is wait until you work on code for an application like Excel! You will then realize how straightforward and well put together this application is. Once you have tried your hand at fixing a few bugs in what appears to be a simple program, you will appreciate what goes on behind the scenes when you make a menu selection or press an OK button.

Types of Errors

Errors occur very easily when you are writing code. This section gives you examples of the types of errors you can expect to see.

Compile Errors

Compile errors result from incorrectly constructed code. You may have used a property or method that does not exist on an object, or put in a For without a Next or an If without an End If.

When you run code, the compiler goes through the code first and checks for these types of errors. If any are found, the code will not be run but an error message will be displayed referring to the first error found. Note that there could be several compile errors in a procedure, but only the first one will be flagged. You might correct the error and think,

"I've fixed it now," and then rerun the procedure, and up comes another one! This can be very frustrating to fix, but the real answer is to obey the rules of coding in the first place.

These are the types of errors that appear when the code is compiled, and they are often referred to as design-time or compile-time errors.

Runtime Errors

These are errors that occur when your program is running. You could, for example, try to open a file that does not exist, or attempt a division by zero. These would create an error message and halt execution of the program. They would not show up at compile time because they are not breaking any programming rules, but they will cause the code not to run.

Logic Errors

Logic errors occur when your application does not perform the way you intended. The code can be valid and run without producing any errors, but what happens is incorrect. For example, the user could have two workbooks open, each with a Sheet1 worksheet in them. You write code in a module referring to Sheet1 but not specifying which workbook collection it resides in. A case of faulty logic!

These are by far the most difficult errors to locate. They can require a lot of painstaking searching to find, even using all the debugging tools at your disposal. It is very easy to keep looking at a few lines of code and thinking, "There is nothing wrong with this, it should give the right answer." It is only by looking at each line in turn that you can see what is going wrong, and usually, when the problem hits you in the face, you will suddenly realize what a simple mistake it was. You may also find a situation that you did not envision when you designed your code.

Design Time, Runtime, and Break Mode

When working on an application in VBA, there are three modes that you can be in:

▶ **Design time**   When you are working on the code for the application or designing a form.

▶ **Runtime**   When you run your code or your form. The title bar of the VBA screen will contain the word "running," and at this point you can view code but you cannot change it.

▶ **Break**   If you press CTRL-BREAK during runtime, it will stop execution of your code. You can also insert a breakpoint by pressing the F9 Key. Pressing it again removes it. You can insert a breakpoint from the VBE menu by selecting Debug | Toggle Breakpoint. A dialog will be displayed with the error message, "Code execution has been interrupted" as well as several buttons. Clicking the Debug button will take you into the code window.

When you click Debug, you go into instant watch mode, also known as debug mode. You'll be able to see your code and the line it has stopped at will be highlighted in yellow. This is the line that is causing the problem. You can place your cursor on any variable that is in scope, and it will give you the value of it instantly. You can also move the point of execution by dragging the yellow arrow to the line of code to be executed.

Try this simple program:

```
Sub TestDebug()
x = 2
Do Until x = 1
    x = x + 1
Loop
End Sub
```

When you run this, the program never finishes because **x** will never equal 1. Press CTRL-BREAK, and the error window will appear. Click Debug, and you will be in instant watch mode in the code window. Move your cursor across any instance of **x** and its value will appear (see Figure 7-1).

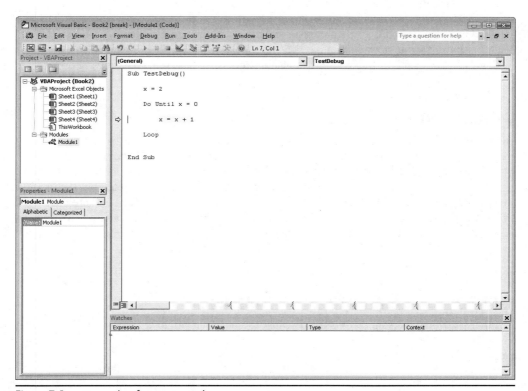

Figure 7-1 *Example of instant watch*

You can restart your code by clicking the Run symbol on the toolbar (the triangle symbol pointing to the right) or pressing F5; it will start from the point where it was stopped. You will notice a yellow arrow on the left of the code that indicates the current execution point. Try dragging the yellow arrow to a new start point, such as **x = 2**, and then rerun the code. This is useful if you want to restart a loop or an If condition after you have changed code due to a bug.

Breakpoints

You can add a breakpoint into your code so that your code will halt at that line. You can then use step commands to move through one line at a time and use instant watch to examine variables as the code steps through.

Breakpoints can be toggled on and off by using F9 or by selecting Debug | Toggle Breakpoint from the menu. They appear as a solid brown circle in the leftmost column of the code window.

If you run the preceding loop example and place a breakpoint on the **Loop** statement, you will see that every time you click the Run symbol or F5, it stops on the **Loop** statement.

You can step through the program one line at a time by clicking F8 or by using Debug | Step Into (F8) from the code menu. Other options allow you to Step Over (SHIFT-F8), Step Out (run program normally), or Run to Cursor (run code down to where the cursor is). While you are stepping through a program, you can still use your cursor to examine values.

You can also open a Debug window to watch expressions and see what they are doing.

Using Stop Statements

Entering a **Stop** statement in your code is the same as entering a breakpoint, except it is in your code. When VBA encounters a **Stop** statement, it halts execution and switches to break mode. Although **Stop** statements act like breakpoints, they are not set or cleared in the same way.

If you set breakpoints using F9, when you leave your project and then reload it, the breakpoints are all cleared. However, **Stop** statements form part of the code and are only cleared when you delete them or put a single quote (') character in front to change them into a comment. Make sure that once you have your code working properly, you remove all **Stop** statements.

Running Selected Parts of Your Code

If you know where the statement is that is causing an error, a single breakpoint will locate the problem. However, it's more likely that you will only have a rough idea of the area of code causing the problem.

You can insert a breakpoint where you want to start checking the code and then single-step the procedure to see what each statement is doing. You can also skip a statement or start execution from a different place.

Single Stepping

Single stepping allows you to execute one statement at a time. You can place your cursor on variables anywhere in the code to see the state of variables, and you can also use the Debug window to view values of variables.

You can single-step by using Debug | Step Into from the menu or pressing F8. You can also run the code to the position of the cursor. Click the mouse on a line of code and then press CTRL-F8. The code will only execute as far as where you have clicked the mouse. Note the cursor must be on an executable line of code, not a blank line. You can also step between individual statements if they are on the same line but separated by the : character.

```
temp = 4: If temp = 3 Then Exit Sub
```

Procedure Stepping

If you have a subroutine or function that is being called, you may not wish to step through the whole procedure line by line. You may have already tested it and be satisfied with its performance. If you use F8 to step through (Single Step), you will be taken all through the subroutine's code one step at a time. This could be extremely time-consuming for something that you know already works. If you use SHIFT-F8 (Step Over), then your subroutine will be treated as a single statement but without stepping through it.

Call Stack Dialog

The Call Stack dialog, shown in the following illustration, displays a list of active procedure calls—that is, calls that have been started but not completed. You can display this dialog by using CTRL-L, but it is only available in Break mode. It can help you trace the operation of calls to procedures, especially if they are nested where one procedure then calls another procedure.

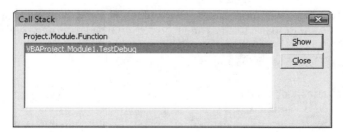

The earliest active procedure call is shown at the top of the list, and any subsequent procedure calls are added to the top, as shown in Figure 7-2. By highlighting the procedure in

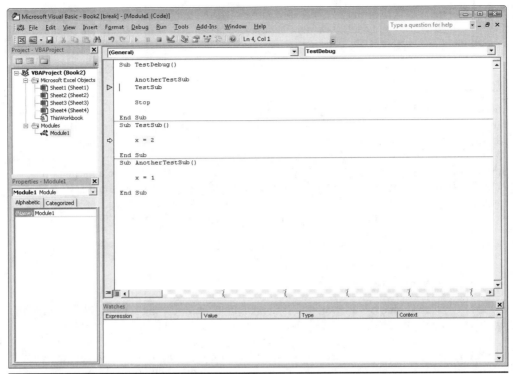

Figure 7-2   *How to call a subroutine and show which procedure called it*

the figure and clicking Show, you can view the statement calling that procedure. This is highlighted with a green arrow.

The Debug Window

The Debug window allows you to set a watch on specific variables or properties to see what values they hold as your program executes. This will aid you in debugging by allowing you to analyze a variable or property that has an incorrect value and determine where the problem is coming from.

You can set the Debug window, as shown in Figure 7-3, by using Debug | Add Watch from the menu.

You enter the variable or expression that you wish to monitor in the Expression box. For example, if you have a variable **x** and you wish to keep track of the value of it, you enter **x** into the box. The context details are entered automatically, although they can be amended. You can also specify whether you want the code to break when the value of the variable is True (nonzero) or when the value changes.

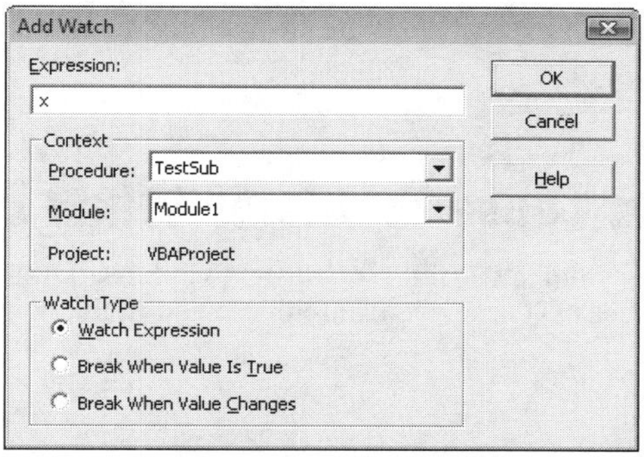

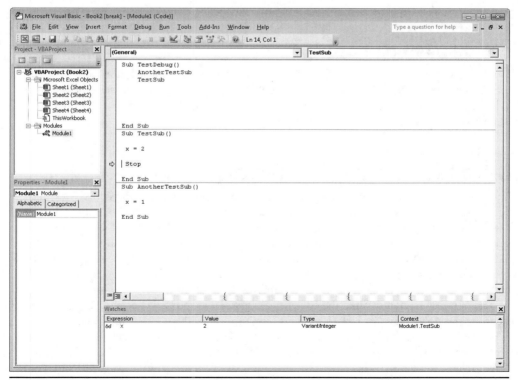

Figure 7-3   *Adding a watch on a variable*

Click OK, and the Debug window will appear with details of your variable in it, as shown in Figure 7-4.

When the program reaches a breakpoint, the value in the Debug window is updated. As you step through, it will also be updated. You can delete a watch expression by highlighting the expression in the watch window, clicking it, and then pressing the DELETE key.

Figure 7-4   *Monitoring the value of a variable from within a watch window*

You can also edit the watch expression by right-clicking the selected expression and selecting Edit Watch.

Events That Can Cause Problems When Debugging

Certain events in windows can pose problems for the debugger. They can complicate and confuse the debugging process. These events are discussed in the next sections.

Mouse Down

Mouse down is the event fired off when the user presses any mouse button down. This is before the button comes back up. If you break the code at this point, you will not get a mouse up event. A mouse up event occurs only when you press the mouse button again and release it.

Key Down

Key down is the event fired off when the user presses any keyboard key down. This is before the key comes back up. If you break the code at this point, you will not get a key up event. A key up event occurs only when you press the key again and release it.

Got Focus/Lost Focus

This event occurs when a user clicks your form or a particular control on the form to get the focus on that control. If you break the code at this point, you may get inconsistent results. Whether you do or not depends on whether your control had the focus at the point that the BREAK key was pressed.

Using Message Boxes in Debugging

There are methods besides those discussed already that can isolate bugs in code. They may be considered somewhat crude, but they do work. For example, message boxes are always useful for letting you know what is going on. They can display the value of a variable or even several variables by concatenating them together. They are extremely useful when you have a large procedure and you do not know the region the bug is in. For example, a large piece of code appears to run but hangs and will not respond to CTRL-BREAK. Perhaps it ran perfectly up to now but has hit certain circumstances that cause it to hang.

The question is, how far into the code do you get before the issue occurs? You could try stepping through it, but this is very time-consuming if it is a large procedure. Placing message boxes at strategic points throughout the code will give you an idea of where it stops. Make sure all the message boxes display something meaningful, such as "Ok1," "Ok2," and "Ok3." You can then see what stages the program has covered before it hangs. Be sure you clear all the extra message boxes out once you have found the bug! You can also concatenate variables together.

```
Sub test_for()
For n = 1 To 4
    For m = 2 To 8

        MsgBox m & " xxxxx " & n

    Next m

Next n

End Sub
```

This message box will display the values of **m** and **n** separated by a line of x's. The purpose of the x's is to prevent null values or spaces being hidden. Although it would not happen in this example, variables can sometimes end up with Null values or be spaces if they are string variables, in which case you would only see one number appearing, and how would you know whether it is the value of **m** or **n**? The row of x's distinguishes this.

   If you want a continuous readout of variables while the program is running, there are ways to get one. Debug does not offer this option, but with a little ingenuity it can be accomplished. You can change the caption properties on both the **Application** object (spreadsheet) and a **UserForm** object using code. This assumes that you have already defined **UserForm1**. See Chapter 9 for how to create a user form for use with VBA. If you are uncertain how to define a user form, leave out that line of the example.

```
Sub test_for()

For n = 1 To 4

    For m = 2 To 8

        Application.Caption = n & " xxxx " & m

        UserForm1.Caption = n & " xxxx " & m

    Next m

Next n
End sub
```

This will display the variables in the caption of the window as the program is running. Depending on how fast the variables change and how long the procedure is, you will be able to see patterns occurring and see what is happening live at each stage. In terms of patterns, you will be able to see sequences of numbers, how they ascend and descend, what the maximum values they get to are, and so on. If a major error occurs, you can see at what value it is occurring.

You can reset the application title bar afterward by setting it to an empty string in code:

```
Application.Caption = ""
```

Avoiding Bugs

Careful design and planning of the application is important and will help reduce bugs. Often it is best to break the application down into smaller component parts that are easier to code and test. It is easier to think of a small portion of code than to try to tackle an entire project in one thought. Make sure you document and comment your code using the single quote (') character. The comments will turn green within your code. If the application is complicated, it is often difficult to go back even after just a few days to determine what the code is doing. Even professional programmers find if they go back to code they wrote a few months ago, they have difficulty understanding what the code was doing. Comments may provide the help needed. Also, if a programmer leaves an organization, it can be difficult for a new or different programmer to pick up where the former employee left off without any documentation about the intent of the code.

It is important to know what all your variables represent and what each function does. Once your application starts growing and begins to get complicated, its documentation becomes more important. Without such documentation, you will need a good memory to keep track of what every variable means!

Errors and the Error Function

Runtime errors can creep into code very easily, through no fault of the programmer. The user does something outside the scope of the code and causes an error message to occur that stops all execution of code. This may occur where you are accessing an external data source such as a database. The user may also take an action that the programmer never envisioned.

No matter how carefully you try to provide for all conditions, there is always a user who does something that you never thought of and effectively breaks the set of rules that you have written. It may be as simple as including a name with an apostrophe in such as O'Brien. If you use this name in a SQL query string, it will cause problems in the way it is handled.

Another example is reading a file in from a disk device. The programmer may allow the user to select the drive letter for the file to be read. You assume that the files will mainly come from network drives, and a D: CD/DVD option is just nice to have, but it will probably never be used. However, if the user selects D: (CD/DVD drive), then there is a possibility that there will not be a disk in the drive. This will create an error that will stop execution of your program. The user will be very unhappy and will lose a great deal of faith in your application. The error needs to be trapped, and an appropriate action needs to be taken from within the VBA code.

Error handling is also used on common dialog forms (see Chapter 10) to show that the Cancel button has been clicked. In order to test whether the user clicked the Cancel button, you had to have set the **CancelError** property to True and then put in an **On Error** statement to direct the code where to go for an error.

Try this simple example *without* a disk in drive D. Place the code into a code module and then run it by pressing F5:

```
Sub Test_Error()

    temp = Dir("d:\*.*")

End Sub
```

This will produce an error message saying that the D drive is not ready. In normal terms, your program has crashed and will not work any further until this error is resolved. Not very good from the user's point of view!

You can place a simple error-trapping routine as follows:

```
Sub Test_Error()
    On Error GoTo err_handler
        temp = Dir("d:\*.*")
    Exit Sub
    err_handler:
    MsgBox "The D drive is not ready" & "    " & Err.Description
End Sub
```

The first line sets up a routine to jump to when an error occurs using the **On Error** statement. It points to **err_handler**, which is a label just below the **Exit Sub** line further down that will deal with any error condition. The purpose of a label is to define a section of your code you can jump to by using a **GoTo** statement.

The line to read the D: drive is the same as before, and then there is an **Exit Sub** line, because if all is well you do not want the code continuing into the **err_handler** routine.

If an error happens at any point after the **On Error** line, the code execution jumps to **err_handler** and displays a message box that says drive D is not ready. However, you may have noticed that the code execution jumps to **err_handler** when *any* error occurs, not just the drive not ready error. An error could occur because you made a mistake in typing this code in. This could have unfortunate consequences in your code.

Fortunately, you can interrogate the error to find out what went wrong. You can also use the **Err** object to give the description of the error and to concatenate it into your message so that it also says "Drive not ready." You do this using the **Err** function. This will return the number associated with the runtime error that happened. You can add this into the previous example as follows:

```
Sub Test_Error()
    On Error GoTo err_handler
    temp = Dir("d:\*.*")
    Exit Sub
    err_handler:
    If Err.Number = 71 Then
        MsgBox "The D drive is not ready"
```

```
    Else
        MsgBox "An error occurred"

    End If
End Sub
```

You saw from the first example that the number for "Drive not ready" came up in the error message box as 71. The program looks at **Err** (a system variable that holds the last error number) and checks to see if it is 71. If it is, it displays the message box, "The D drive is not ready"; if it is not, it displays the message box, "An error occurred."

The Resume Statement

The **Resume** statement can be added to make the code execution branch back to the statement where the error occurred. This gives the opportunity for the user to intervene—for example, to put a CD into drive D and for the code to then reinterrogate drive D. You can include this in your error-handling routine so that the line that created the error will be tried again following user intervention:

```
Sub Test_Error()
    On Error GoTo err_handler
    temp = Dir("d:\*.*")
    Exit Sub
    err_handler:
    If Err.Number = 71 Then
        MsgBox "The D drive is not ready"
    Else
        MsgBox "An error occurred"

    End If
    Resume
End Sub
```

You can also add the statement **Next** to **Resume**. This will skip over the statement that created the error and therefore ignore the error.

```
Sub Test_Error()

    On Error Resume Next

    temp = Dir("d:\*.*")

End Sub
```

If there is no disk in drive D, the code will still run perfectly because of **On Error Resume Next**—it skips over the line of code creating the error.

Resume Next can be useful for dealing with errors as they occur, but it can make debugging code very difficult. In a later stage of your program, you may have incorrect or nonexistent data being produced due to the fact that an error condition earlier was ignored. You can end up with a program that appears to run okay, but in fact does nothing because it has some hidden bugs or incomplete data. This is because every time an error is encountered, the execution just skips over it. This can give a false impression of what is actually happening, so if you do use **On Error Resume Next**, make sure that you check all inputs and outputs to the code to ensure that everything is working as it should be. Make sure that your **On Error Resume Next** statement cannot cover up an error in a read from a spreadsheet cell or from a file. This could cause disaster in your program because the **On Error Resume Next** statement would make it appear to work perfectly.

Implications of Error Trapping

When you use an **On Error** statement in your code, that error trap remains throughout the procedure unless it is disabled. As you just saw, you can set up a routine to check whether the D: drive has a disk in it and take action accordingly. However, it is important to turn this off once the possibility of the error has taken place. If you do not do this, then all subsequent errors within that procedure will use the same error-handling routine. This gives extremely confusing results to the user, as the error message is likely to be totally meaningless in relation to the error generated. A subsequent error could relate to division by zero, but the error message will come up saying "Drive D not ready."

If **On Error Resume Next** has been used and not switched off, all sorts of errors could be taking place without the user being aware of them. You disable the error-trapping routine as follows:

```
On Error Resume Next
On Error GoTo 0
```

The **On Error Resume Next** statement that you saw previously ignores all errors. The **On Error GoTo 0** cancels any error handling and allows all errors to be displayed as they normally would. This cancels out the **On Error Resume Next** and puts everything back to normal error handling.

Generating Your Own Errors

Why would you want to generate your own errors? After all, you want to achieve error-free code. Sometimes it is useful when you are testing your own applications or when you want to treat a particular condition as being equivalent to a runtime error.

You can generate an error in your code with the **Error** statement:

```
Sub Test_Error()

    Error 71

End Sub
```

This simulates the "Drive not ready" error. You could also use **Err.Raise(71)** to do this. In addition, you can regenerate the current error by using the following:

```
Error Err
```

The purpose of this is to raise the "Drive not ready" error message as if the drive really was not ready because this is the current error found. If another error message is then created, this becomes the current error.

CHAPTER
9

Dialogs

I n Chapter 5, we discussed how to use the message box, which is in effect a simple
dialog box. These are easy to use from within your code and offer a simple way to
communicate to the user. They can halt execution of your code while something is
drawn to the user's attention, and allow the user to make choices where necessary.

However, what if you want to do something more complicated, such as request that the
user supply parameters or select a worksheet? This is done with a UserForm, which allows
you to design your own custom user interface, using standard windows controls, so that you
end up with a form that has the look and feel of a standard Windows form.

To use a UserForm, you must first insert one into your project. Select Insert | UserForm
from the code window menu to insert a blank UserForm into your project. Your screen
should look like Figure 9-1.

The form is a blank canvas on which you can place controls. Notice that a Toolbox
window has also been opened; this allows you to select controls to place on the form such as
text boxes, check boxes, and so on.

You can also see that the Properties window reflects the properties for the form, of which
there are many. (If the Properties window is not open, select View | Properties Window from
the VBE menu or press F4.) The UserForm is similar to a Visual Basic form and has similar
properties, events, and methods. The UserForm is an object and has a place in the VBA
Project tree.

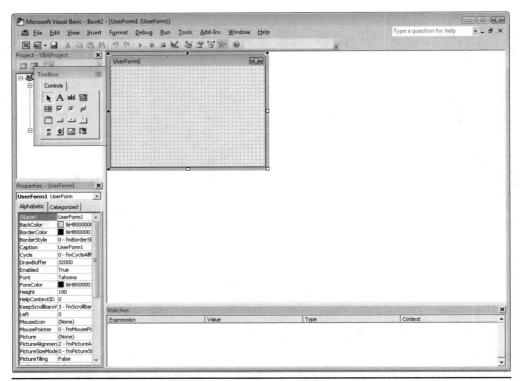

Figure 9-1 *Preparing a UserForm*

These are the main properties for the form that you need to consider:

Property	Description
Name	References the form in your code. You should change it to something more meaningful than UserForm1.
BackColor	Dictates the background color of your form. Standard gray is quite useful because it follows the general scheme of things, but you may wish to use a different color scheme for certain forms. Click the gray box and hexadecimal number, and a drop-down arrow appears. Click the drop-down and then click the palette in the window that appears underneath, as shown in Figure 9-2.
BorderColor	Same as for **BackColor**, but sets the color for the border.

Property	Description
BorderStyle	Sets whether you have a border for your form or not.
Caption	Sets the title of the form as it appears in the title bar at the top of the form.
Enabled	Normally set to True so that users can interact with the form controls. If you set it to False, everything is grayed out (disabled) and the form cannot be used. This may be useful when a procedure takes time to process and you don't want the user doing other things on your form while this is happening.
Font	Changes the Font characteristics on the **form** object, as shown in Figure 9-3. Bear in mind that this only sets the font on text printed on the **form** object itself—it does not affect objects placed on the form such as text boxes and list boxes, although they have similar properties that can be set separately.
ForeColor	Operates in the same way as the **BackColor** property and sets the color of any text that you print on the form—it does not affect objects placed on the form such as text boxes and list boxes, although they have similar properties that can be set separately.
Height	Can be set by clicking and holding the sizing handles on the edge of the form and dragging them to the size that you want.
Left	Indicates the distance from the left-hand side of the screen container (Excel) where the form will appear.
Picture	You can add a picture to the form as a background. Click the word (None) and a box with an ellipsis (...) will appear to the right. Click that box and you will be taken to a file selection dialog. Select your graphic file and click OK. To remove a picture, delete the contents of the property and it will be replaced with (None).
PictureAlignment	Gives you a drop-down that allows you to set where the picture will be aligned in relation to the form, for example, top left, bottom right, and so on.
PictureSizeMode	Gives you a drop-down with options for how the picture is to be displayed. **0 – Mode Clip** The default. The picture is displayed as normal size and cropped to fit onto the form. **1 – Mode Stretch** The picture is stretched both horizontally and vertically to fit onto the form. This can lead to a distorted image. **3 – Mode Zoom** The picture is enlarged to fit the form without distorting the image.
Picture Tiling	If you are using a small picture, you can opt to tile it across the form by setting this property to True. This can be used for a company logo.
Width	This can be set by clicking and holding the sizing handles on the edges of the form and then dragging them to the size that you want.

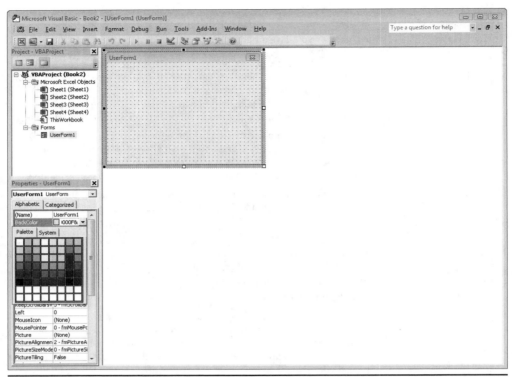

Figure 9-2   The color palette for the BackColor property

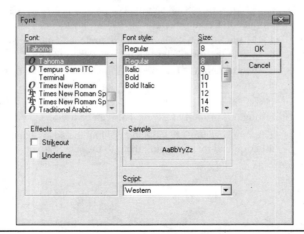

Figure 9-3   The font property

Viewing Your Form

As you design your form, you may want to see what it looks like when it is running. You can do this in design mode on the form by selecting Run | Sub/UserForm or pressing F5.

As usual with Visual Basic objects, each form has its own module to deal with events on the form, as shown in Figure 9-4. To access the module, double-click the design form, select View | Code from the menu, or press F7.

You can see a drop-down list on the right-hand side of the module that lists events for the form that you can attach code to. For example, one of the events is **Initialize**, which is fired off when the form is called. Click Initialize, and header and footer code will automatically appear for that event. Add a message box as follows:

```
Private Sub UserForm_Initialize()
      MsgBox "This is my form"
End Sub
```

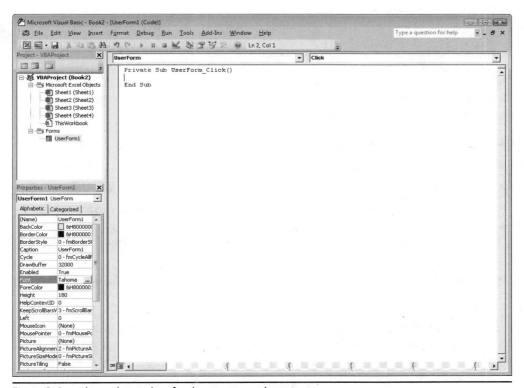

Figure 9-4   *The code window for the UserForm showing events*

Now press F5 to run the form. Your message box appears first, and then the form appears after you click OK. By examining the list of events, you will see that there are a number that you could put code into. Try the **MouseMove** event. Click MouseMove to get the code header and footer and then insert the following code:

```
Private Sub UserForm_MouseMove(ByVal Button As Integer, ByVal Shift _
 As Integer, ByVal X As Single, ByVal Y As Single)

If UserForm1.Caption = "UserForm1" Then

    UserForm1.Caption = "You moved the mouse"

Else

    UserForm1.Caption = "UserForm1"

End If
End Sub
```

You will find that when you move the mouse over the form, the caption in the title bar of the form keeps changing.

Note that the **MouseMove** event also passes you parameters for the X and Y position of the mouse on your form and for any mouse buttons or SHIFT key being pressed. You will see events for **KeyDown**, **KeyUp**, **MouseDown**, and **MouseUp**:

► **KeyDown** Fired off when a key is being pressed down by the user.

► **KeyUp** Fired off when the key is released from being pressed down by the user.

► **MouseDown** Fired off when a button on the mouse is pressed down by the user.

► **MouseUp** Fired off when the user releases a mouse button from being pressed down.

► **KeyPress** Fired off when a key on the keyboard is pressed and then released. The parameter in this event will give you the value of the key pressed. This is a combination of both **KeyDown** and **KeyUp**.

► **Click** Fired off when the mouse is clicked on a control such as a command button or a list box.

All the events procedures pass different parameters, depending on what event they are dealing with. Try placing a message box on each event to display these parameters and show what event is being called. This way you will see very clearly when an event is called and what parameters are passed to it.

Displaying Your Form in Code

You can view the results of your form by pressing F5, but you need to be able to link it into your code. You can use the **Show** method to do this:

```
UserForm1.Show
```

When this statement is executed, command is transferred to the UserForm1 window. Any code in the **Initialize** event is executed and then awaits user intervention. This could be the user closing the window or clicking an OK button on the form.

You can also hide a form once it has done its work. Although the form is hidden and not visible to the user, the application is still running. You use the **Hide** method:

```
UserForm1.Hide
```

The only other decision is from where you fire the form off. You need to connect it to a user event, such as when a new sheet is added to the workbook. Remember how in Chapter 1 you added a "Hello World" message box to the **NewSheet** event? You can do the same thing to display a form. Double-click ThisWorkBook in the Project tree to open up the Workbook module. On the drop-down on the left-hand side of the module window, select Workbook and then NewSheet from the right-hand drop-down. Enter the code as follows:

```
Private Sub Workbook_NewSheet(ByVal Sh As Object)
      UserForm1.Show
End Sub
```

Now go to the Excel worksheet and insert a new sheet. Your form will appear.

Populating Your Form

Your form now works well, but it does not do anything. You need to put some controls on it to interact with the user. These can be combo boxes, text boxes, or command buttons. First, the mouse event code that you inserted in the last section needs to be removed, or you will still get the form caption changing when you move the mouse over the running form.

You can view the Toolbox window by selecting View | Toolbox on the VBE menu. The Toolbox window normally appears to the left of your form and contains the most popular controls. If it is not visible, click the UserForm, and the Toolbox window will appear, as shown in Figure 9-5. The toolbox displays icons for the controls that are available to you.

To place a control onto your form, simply click it in the toolbox and drag it to the required position on your form. You can subsequently drag it to a new position on the form or resize it by dragging on the handles around the edge of the control. To see what a control is (if it is not apparent from the icon), place your cursor on the icon and view the tooltip text.

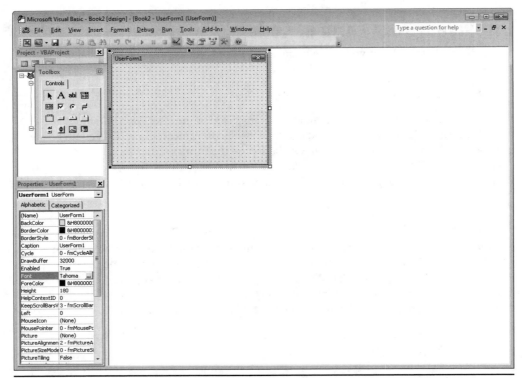

Figure 9-5   *The Toolbox window*

Default Toolbox Controls

The following sections discuss the controls that initially appear in the toolbox.

Label

The Label control displays text on the form. You can enter text by entering it in the **Caption** property in the Properties window at the bottom left-hand corner of screen.

Other properties that can be set for the label include **BackColor**, **ForeColor**, **Font**, **TextAlign**, and **WordWrap**. This is not a complete list of properties; many more can be set. You can see other properties available within the Properties window for that control.

TextBox

The TextBox control is similar to the label control, but it allows the user to input text at runtime. You can also reference it to a control source (via properties), such as a spreadsheet cell, like sheet1!a1. If you do this, not only does the text box take the value of that cell, but anything typed into the text box is written back to that cell—the cell effectively acts as a variable in storing the data.

Properties that can be set include **BackColor**, **Enabled**, **ForeColor**, **Font**, **Locked**, **TextAlign**, **MaxLength**, **Mulitiline**, **PasswordCharacter**, and **WordWrap**.

NOTE

Enabled means it is ready for use. If it is disabled, the control is grayed out. **Locked** *means it can normally be seen (not grayed out), but the user cannot enter text.*

ComboBox

The ComboBox control is the familiar horizontal box in which a list of values appears when you click the downward pointing arrow. It shares the same properties we discussed for the text box, apart from the password character. There are also some new properties:

Property	Description
ControlSource	This can reference a cell, such as Sheet!a1. This works the same as the control source for a text box in that the cell acts as a variable to hold the selected result. For example, if the control source cell holds "Richard," then when the combo box appears, it will have the value "Richard" in it. If the user changes this value on the combo box to "Shepherd," then the control source cell will have the value "Shepherd" written into it. The control source can only refer to one cell.
MatchRequired	This means that the value the user types in has to match a value in the list, which is a way of making sure that only values in the list are used.
RowSource	This can be referenced to the cells in your spreadsheet that are the source of the rows in the drop-down list. It can refer to multiple cells, such as sheet1!a1.a10.

ListBox

The ListBox control shows a permanently displayed list of optional values. It has similar properties as the combo box but there is an extra MultiSelect property:

Property	Description
BoundColumn	A list box allows you to have more than one column of data from the row source. The **BoundColumn** property dictates which column will put data back into the control source if data is selected.
ColumnCount	Dictates how many columns will be used. This is linked to the **BoundColumn** and **RowSource** properties. If the column count is more than one, then **RowSource** can go across more than one column in the spreadsheet.

Property	Description
ColumnHeads	If set to True, the cells directly above **RowSource** are used.
ColumnWidths	You can set the column widths in points by using a semicolon (;) to separate the numbers, such as 20;30.
MultiSelect	You can specify whether the user can select more than one item from the list. If you allow multiselecting, you cannot read this by using the **ControlSource** property. You must use code instead, and it must be placed on the form module itself. The values can be **fmMultiSelectSingle**, **fmMultiSelectMulti**, and **fmMultiSelectExtended**.

In the example in Figure 9-6, the **RowSource** property is set to sheet1!a2..b4, the **ColumnCount** property is set to 2 (to give two columns of data), and the **ColumnHeads** property is set to True (meaning that the first row above the row source data will provide the column headings).

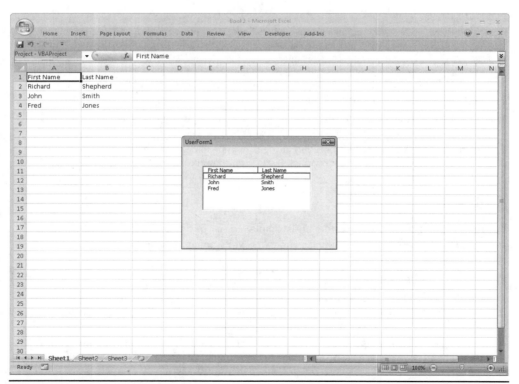

Figure 9-6 *A list box on a UserForm*

To read multiple selections, double-click the list box to get to the module and then click the **Exit** event on the drop-down on the right-hand side. Enter the following code:

```
Private Sub ListBox1_Exit(ByVal Cancel As MSForms.ReturnBoolean)
    For n = 0 To UserForm1.ListBox1.ListCount - 1
      If UserForm1.ListBox1.Selected(n) = True Then
        MsgBox UserForm1.ListBox1.List(n, 0)

      End If
    Next n
End Sub
```

When the form is closed, this fires off the **Exit** event on the list box that then looks through each value in the list to see if it was selected. Note that it starts at index 0, so you need to subtract 1 from the **ListCount** property for the For..Next loop (see Chapter 4 on looping). This will then display all rows selected. The second parameter (0) is optional—this denotes the column. Note that it starts at 0, not 1. You know what has been selected because the **Selected** property is set to True.

Refer back to Figure 9-5 for an example screen of a multicolumn list box using data from a spreadsheet.

CheckBox

The CheckBox control allows the user to check or uncheck a check box. The text can be set by double-clicking the control or by setting the **Caption** property. It can be linked to a cell by setting the **ControlSource** property to point to a cell such as sheet1!a1. If the cell contains no value, the check box will contain a check and therefore a True value by default. Note that the control source cell will display the value True or False to reflect the state of the check box.

NOTE

The **Enabled** and **Locked** properties work the same way for check boxes as they do for text boxes.

The code to interpret the check box would be the same as for the **ListBox** control but with the check box **Change** event:

```
Private Sub CheckBox1_Change()
    MsgBox UserForm1.CheckBox1.Value
End Sub
```

Every time the check box is checked or unchecked, you will get a message box showing its value.

OptionButton

Option buttons are sometimes known as radio buttons when there is a group of them because they behave like the pushbuttons on an old car radio. You need to have at least two of these on your form for them to work properly because as you switch one on, the others are automatically turned off. If you have only one, you can never turn it off (although you could turn it off using VBA code)!

Option buttons can be linked to a cell using the **ControlSource** property, such as sheet1!c1. The cell holds a True or False value dependent on whether the option button has been clicked.

NOTE

*The **Enabled** and **Locked** properties work the same way for option buttons as they do for text boxes.*

You can use code to interpret the value of each radio button. Try the following code on the option button **Change** event:

```
Private Sub OptionButton1_Change()

    MsgBox UserForm1.OptionButton1.Value

End Sub
```

ToggleButton

A toggle button changes from raised to sunken and back each time it is clicked. Its operation is similar to a check box: you change the caption on it by setting the **Caption** property in the properties box. It can be linked to a cell by setting the **ControlSource** property, such as sheet1!d1.

NOTE

*The **Enabled** and **Locked** properties work the same way for toggle buttons as they do for text boxes.*

You can use code to interpret the value of the toggle button. Try the following code on the toggle button **Change** event:

```
Private Sub ToggleButton1_Change()

    MsgBox UserForm1.ToggleButton1.Value

End Sub
```

Frame

Frames allow you to put a frame around a set of related controls to describe what they do. You can only set the caption of the frame by setting the **Caption** property—you cannot double-click it as with the check box and the option button. One of the problems with a Frame control is that it overlays previous controls, even at runtime. When using a Frame control, you should define the Frame control first and then make the other controls sit inside the frame on top of it. If you do it the other way around, the controls will not be visible.

CommandButton

The CommandButton control is a powerful control that frequently is used on forms. You can alter a command button's caption by double-clicking it or by setting the **Caption** property. You can also make a button the default button on the form by setting the **Default** property to True. This means that when the form is loaded, this button has the focus—if the user presses ENTER, then the code for that button will run.

 NOTE

Enabled and *Locked* properties work the same way for command buttons as they do on text boxes.

To make the button do something, you need to put code in an event. Double-click the form to enter the module and then select your button control from the drop-down on the top left-hand side. Select the **Click** event and enter the following code:

```
Private Sub CommandButton1_Click()
     MsgBox "You pressed the button"
End Sub
```

TabStrip

The TabStrip control allows you to put a tab strip onto your form. You can use a TabStrip control to view different sets of information for related controls. The client region of a TabStrip control is not a separate form. Instead, the region is a portion of the form that contains the TabStrip control.

You can select the tabs at design time by clicking the tab while holding down SHIFT. You can add pages, rename pages, and delete pages by right-clicking a tab. You need to use code to interpret the user's actions on the tab strip. Double-click the form to view the module and select TabStrip from the top-left drop-down. Select the **Change** event from the top-right drop-down and enter the following code:

```
Private Sub TabStrip1_Change()

    MsgBox TabStrip1.SelectedItem.Index
```

```
      MsgBox TabStrip1.SelectedItem.Caption

End Sub
```

When you run the form and click the tabs, you will see the index of the selected tab (first tab is 0) and the caption on it.

You can further see the effect of the TabStrip control by putting the following code under the **Change** event:

```
Private Sub TabStrip1_Change()

      Select Case TabStrip1.SelectedItem.Index
      Case 0
          TabStrip1.ForeColor = QBColor(12)
      Case 1
          TabStrip1.ForeColor = QBColor(15)
      End Select
End Sub
```

Each time you click a tab, the text color on the tabs will change. Note that both tabs change to the same color; they are not separate forms.

MultiPage

The TabStrip control is still only one form. The MultiPage control is different forms selected by tabs and is more useful in a lot of ways. You can select each tab at design time by clicking it and right-clicking the tab to insert, delete, or rename pages. You can drag controls onto each individual tab page. Try putting a text box onto the first page and then putting a command button onto the second page.

When you run the form, each page behaves like a separate form, displaying the controls that you set up on it. They all behave as if they were on a separate form. Notice that when you click each page at design time, there are separate Properties windows for each page, which was not the case for the TabStrip control.

You can use code to interpret the user's actions much as you did with the TabStrip. Double-click the tab page, and it will enter the module at the **Change** event for the MultiPage control. Enter the following code:

```
Private Sub MultiPage1_Change()
      MsgBox MultiPage1.SelectedItem.Caption
End Sub
```

ScrollBar

The ScrollBar control places a vertical scroll bar onto your form, similar to the ones that you see in many Microsoft applications. There are properties for maximum and minimum values and for small and big changes, called **SmallChange** and **BigChange**. A small change is

when you click one of the arrows on the scroll bar; a big change is when you click the area
between the arrow and the cursor on the scroll bar.

   BigChange and **SmallChange** are set by default to 1, the maximum value is set to 32767,
and the minimum to 0. This means that clicking the arrows or the space between arrow and
cursor does not really move anything very far: **BigChange** needs to be about 1000 and
SmallChange needs to be about 100 if the maximum is set to 32767.

   You can link this control to a spreadsheet cell using the **ControlSource** property, such as
sheet1!a1. The value of the scroll bar will appear in the cell, but it is only updated when the
scroll bar has lost focus (when you click another control).

   You can also use code to read the value of the scroll bar. Double-click the scroll bar, and
this will take you into the scroll bar **Change** event. Enter the following code:

```
Private Sub ScrollBar1_Change()
     MsgBox ScrollBar1.Value
End Sub
```

   Every time the scroll bar is moved, a message box appears with the new value. You can
see how it changes according to what value you set **BigChange** and **LittleChange** to.

SpinButton

The SpinButton is a control that can be used on a form. It is a box which accepts a number
and has an up and down arrow key to increase or decrease the value. A familiar example of
it is on the Excel print dialog Print Pages From and To. This control is normally linked to
another control, such as a text box, in order to display a value.

NOTE

Enabled and *Locked* properties work the same way for spin buttons as they do for text boxes.

   You can link the control to a spreadsheet cell by using the **ControlSource** property, such
as sheet1!a1. The value of the spin button will appear in the cell, but it is only updated when
the spin button has lost focus (when you click another control).

   The **SmallChange** property sets the increment of the change. The **Orientation** property
sets whether the control is split vertically or horizontally.

   You can also use code to read the value of the spin button. Double-clicking the spin button
will take you into the spin button **Change** event. Enter the following code:

```
Private Sub SpinButton1_Change()
     MsgBox SpinButton1.Value
End Sub
```

Image

The Image control is one that can hold a picture or an image. To insert a picture, click the
Picture property and then click the ellipsis (...) box that appears. This will take you into a

screen where you can select an image file. Click OK and the picture will be inserted into your control.

To delete the picture, delete the value in the **Picture** property box. This will be replaced with (None).

NOTE

The **AutoSize** property automatically sizes your control to the size of the picture you inserted into it.

RefEdit

The RefEdit control collects details about a range of cells selected by the user. It also allows the user to manually type their range in, which means they can edit a cell reference. When you place this control on a form, it is best to size it like a text box using small height and large width.

When the form runs, the user can either type in the cell references manually or click the button on the right-hand side of the control. The form will then collapse and a range selection window will appear. Drag the cursor over a selection with the mouse, and the selection details will appear in the window. Click the button on the right-hand side with red in it, and the form will be redisplayed with the selection in the control box.

You can also use code to read the value of the RefEdit box. Double-clicking the RefEdit box will take you into the RefEdit **Change** event. Enter the following code:

```
Private Sub RefEdit1_Change()
     UserForm1.Caption = RefEdit1.Value
End Sub
```

When you close the selection box and the UserForm reappears, you will see that the title bar of the form now has your selection details in it.

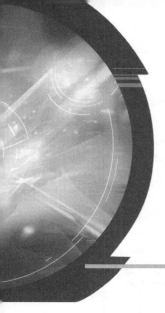

Common Dialog Control

The Visual Basic language includes a Common Dialog control that allows you access to standard Microsoft dialogs for opening files, saving files, printing, selecting color, and selecting fonts. All the dialogs for these purposes that you see in standard Microsoft applications are yours for the taking to use within your own programs.

There is a complete interface to allow you to choose what dialog to display and to be able to set various parameters to alter the appearance of the dialog to suit the purpose of your program. Even better, you can then retrieve the parameters that the user has selected and have your code act on them accordingly. For example, if the user selects a file to open, you can easily find out the file and pathname, and write the code accordingly.

An important point is that these are only dialogs to provide a common interface to the user. You must still write the code to handle the selections or events that the user chooses; it does not happen automatically. For example, if you display the Save dialog, and the user types a filename and presses OK, nothing will happen unless you have written the code to collect the filename chosen and the code to save the data to that filename.

Microsoft provides an important helping hand here so that you do not have to reinvent the wheel to provide components for common user interfaces. However, you still have to do some of the work in selecting the options that will be available on the dialogs and interpreting what to do with the user's selection.

These Common User Interface dialogs work exactly the same as in any Microsoft application, but by manipulating the properties, you can use the values they produce in your code.

Using the Common Dialog Control

By default, the Common Dialog control is not in the Forms toolbox, so you need to add it. To do this, you need to be in a form window with the toolbox window visible. If you do not have a user form added, select Insert | User Form from the VBE menu. You should then see the form and a toolbox window. If the toolbox window is not visible, click the form area to bring focus to the window.

Select Tools | Additional Controls from the VBE menu. This will take a short time while VBA searches your computer for all available controls. Your screen should now look similar to Figure 10-1. If you do not have this control available, then you will need to manually register it. You can do this by running **Regsvr32 [/u] [/s] <OCX File Name>** at the command (DOS) prompt (accessed through All Programs | Accessories on Windows).

This screen provides a list of additional controls available and is very comprehensive. The list of available controls will depend on what applications are loaded onto your computer.

Scroll down the list until you come to Microsoft Common Dialog control. Check the box and click OK. A Common Dialog control will now be visible in the toolbox. If you cannot see which icon it is, hover your mouse over each icon in turn and read the tooltip text box that appears when you do this. You will eventually come to Common Dialog.

Click the control and drag it onto a user form. The form it goes onto and its position do not matter, because it is invisible at runtime. The control is used from VBA code and the form is only a container for it. The form does not even have to be running for the code to work, so it can be referenced from anywhere in your application.

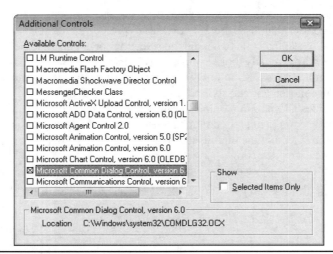

Figure 10-1   *Adding the Common Dialog control*

The Open Dialog

The Open dialog allows the user to select a drive, a directory, a filename extension, and a filename, as shown in Figure 10-2.

To display the dialog, set the properties for filters and then set the action property. Type the following code into a module and then run it:

```
Sub Show_Open()
     UserForm1.CommonDialog1.CancelError = True
On Error GoTo errhandler
UserForm1.CommonDialog1.Filter = _
"All files (*.*)|*.*|Text files (*.txt)"
UserForm1.CommonDialog1.Action = 1
MsgBox UserForm1.CommonDialog1.FileName
errhandler:
Exit Sub
End Sub
```

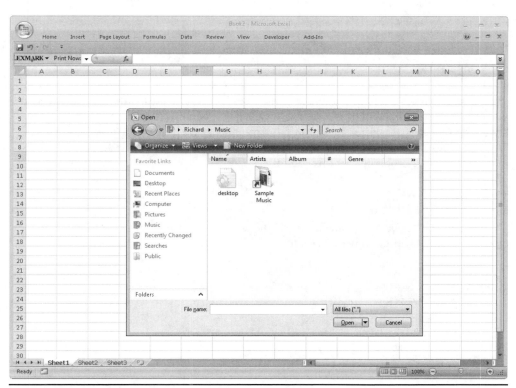

Figure 10-2   *The Open dialog*

The **CancelError** property is first set to True. On a File Open dialog, you get an OK button and a Cancel button. Setting the **CancelError** property to True produces an error when the Cancel button is pressed. Unfortunately, this is the only way of testing whether the user pressed the Cancel button or the OK button; it is not an elegant way to do this.

This brings you to the next line of code that sets up what to do if there is an error. Code execution jumps to a code label called errhandler later on in the code. A code label is inserted by using a unique name and inserting after it. This sets up a reference point in your code that you can branch to using **GoTo**.

The next line sets up the filter for file type. In this example, there is a filter for all files and for text files only. This dictates what appears in the File Type combo box. The vertical bar used to separate the filter information is obtained by using SHIFT and \. The example gives two filters—one for all files (*.*) and one for text files (*.txt). If you wanted only Word or Excel files, you could use the filters *.docx or *.xlsx, respectively.

Finally, the **Action** property is set to 1, which means display the Open File dialog. The user then makes a selection and clicks OK. The message box then displays the filename selected. If the user clicks Cancel, an error is created and the code execution jumps to errhandler and exits.

You can alter the caption in the title bar by setting the DialogTitle property:

```
UserForm1.CommonDialog1.DialogTitle = "Open"
```

If you do not want the Read-Only check box, then you can set the Flags property:

```
UserForm1.CommonDialog1.Flags = 4
```

You can set more than one parameter in the **Flags** property by using the **Or** statement, as you saw earlier in Chapter 6 (for example, **8 Or 4**). All the properties you wish to apply to the dialog must be set before the **Action** property is set or they will have no effect.

You can also use the Object Browser (press F2 and search on CommonDialog) to investigate further properties for this control.

The Save As Dialog

The Save As dialog works in almost exactly the same way as the preceding Open dialog example, but the **Action** property is set to 2:

```
Sub Show_Save()
  UserForm1.CommonDialog1.CancelError = True
  On Error GoTo errhandler
  UserForm1.CommonDialog1.Filter = _
  "All files (*.*)|*.*|Text files (*.txt)"
  UserForm1.CommonDialog1.Action = 2
  MsgBox UserForm1.CommonDialog1.FileName
  errhandler:
  Exit Sub
End Sub
```

The Color Dialog

The Color dialog allows the user to select a color from a palette or create and select a custom color, as shown in Figure 10-3.

The code works in the same way as for the Open dialog except that the **Action** property has a value of 3 and the action returns a color value that has been selected by the user:

```
Sub Show_Color()

  UserForm1.CommonDialog1.CancelError = True

  On Error GoTo errhandler
  UserForm1.CommonDialog1.Action = 3
  MsgBox UserForm1.CommonDialog1.Color
  errhandler:
  Exit Sub
End Sub
```

The message box displays the number of the color selected by the user.

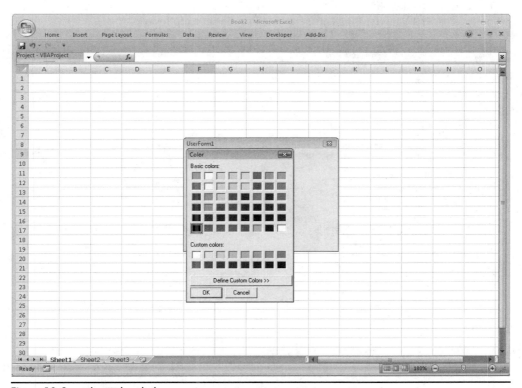

Figure 10-3   *The Color dialog*

The Font Dialog

The Font dialog allows the user to select a font by specifying a typeface, point size, color, and style, as shown in Figure 10-4. Once the user makes selections in this dialog, the following properties contain information about the user's selection:

Property	Determines
Color	The selected color
FontBold	Whether bold was selected
FontItalic	Whether italic was selected
FontStrikeThru	Whether strikethrough was selected
FontUnderline	Whether underline was selected
FontName	The selected font name
FontSize	The selected font size

To select Color, Strikethrough, or Underline, you must set the **Flags** property to &H100& (hexadecimal). You can combine this with other flag values by using the **Or** operator.

The code to display this works in the same way as the Open dialog, but the **Action** property is set to 4, and the **Flags** property needs to be set as follows:

Display	Property Value
Screen Fonts	1
Printer Fonts	2
Both	3

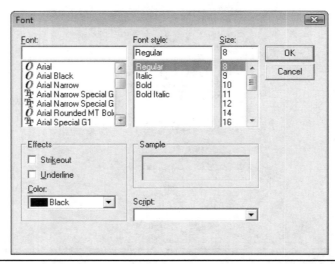

Figure 10-4   *The Font dialog*

Note you must set the **Flags** property before displaying the Font dialog or you will get the error message "No Fonts Exist."

```
Sub Show_Fonts()
  UserForm1.CommonDialog1.CancelError = True
  On Error GoTo errhandler
  UserForm1.CommonDialog1.Flags = 3 or &H100&
  UserForm1.CommonDialog1.Action = 4
  MsgBox "FontBold is " & UserForm1.CommonDialog1.FontBold
  MsgBox "FontItalic is " & UserForm1.CommonDialog1.FontItalic
  MsgBox "FontName is " & UserForm1.CommonDialog1.FontName
  MsgBox "Font Size is " & UserForm1.CommonDialog1.FontSize
  MsgBox "Font Color is " & UserForm1.CommonDialog1.Color
  MsgBox "Font StrikeThru is " & UserForm1.CommonDialog1.FontStrikethru
  MsgBox "Font Underline is " & UserForm1.CommonDialog1.FontUnderline
  errhandler:
  Exit Sub
End Sub
```

Note that the **Color** property returns the number of the color much as the Color dialog does; **FontName** and **FontSize** return actual values. The rest return True or False based on the selection in the dialog.

The Print Dialog

The Print dialog allows the user to specify how output should be printed. The user can specify a range to be printed and the number of copies, as shown in Figure 10-5. This dialog also allows the user to select a printer and allows the user to configure that printer. Bear in mind any changes made to a printer configuration apply to all applications.

This dialog does not print to a printer—you have to write your own code to do that. An easier method might be to use the dialogs built into Excel for printing; see the next section for more information on how to do that.

When the user makes a selection at runtime, the following properties hold information about that selection:

Property	Determines
Copies	The number of copies to print
Orientation	The printer orientation: 1=portrait, 2=landscape

In Excel, the Pages option is unavailable.

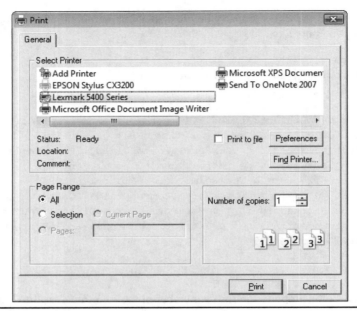

Figure 10-5 *The Print dialog*

The code to display this works in the same way as for the Open dialog, but the **Action** property is set to 5:

```
Sub Show_PrintDialog()
  UserForm1.CommonDialog1.CancelError = True
  On Error GoTo errhandler
  UserForm1.CommonDialog1.Action = 5
  MsgBox "Orientation = " & UserForm1.CommonDialog1.Orientation
  errhandler:
  Exit Sub
End Sub
```

Default Dialogs

A further helping hand that Microsoft built into Excel is default dialogs. Each time you use an Excel spreadsheet, you are calling up dialogs to enter parameters; this might be to format a cell or to apply an advanced filter. When you take one of these actions, a dialog appears to allow you to make choices. If you take the action Format | Cells from the Excel menu, a dialog will appear. This is one of many built-in dialogs within Excel that your code can access.

Within Excel VBA, there is a Dialogs collection you can use to display any one of the Excel dialogs from within your code. The downside to this is that you cannot manipulate the appearance of the dialog in the same way you can with the Common Dialog control, and you cannot access the return parameters directly.

However, these dialogs can still play an important part in your code where it is not necessary to interpret the user's action. All the code in these default dialogs is already written to take care of the user's actions, and all you need to do is to show the dialog. It then runs as if the user had selected it from the menu themselves.

In the preceding section, we discussed using the Common Dialog control to show a printer dialog, but you still have to write your own code to do the printing. A shortcut is to use the Excel dialog to do your printing using the **Application** object and **Show** method:

```
Sub Printer_Dialog()
  Application.Dialogs(xlDialogPrint).Show
End Sub
```

When you run this macro, your screen will look like Figure 10-6.

This is far more suited to Excel because Excel does all the work, whatever selection the user makes—it even offers a Print Preview button! As previously mentioned, you cannot capture the selection the user is making, but in the case of printing, this is not absolutely necessary.

To get an extensive list of available dialogs, you can type **Application.Dialogs** in the code windows. Almost any dialog you can get in Excel from the normal Excel menu is available to use in your program in this way. Experiment with the constants to see all the dialogs that can be displayed.

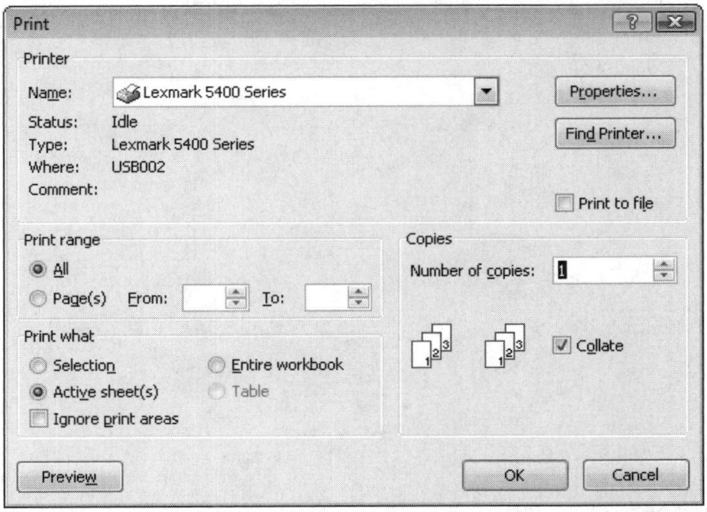

Figure 10-6   *Using the Excel default Print dialog*

Command Bars and Buttons

In previous chapters, you saw how to write code in VBA and how to run it by pressing F5 or clicking the Run icon on the toolbar. However, at some point, you will want the user to be able to run your code as a professional application, and it's unlikely they'll want to go to the code window and press F5. Many users will not even know how to do this, and if they are busy people or not technically savvy, they may just give up on your application.

When writing professional applications, it's important to remember that the less the user has to do to interact with the application, the better. Users tend to want everything as easy as possible and do not want longwinded instructions on how to run your macro. You may not even want them to be able to access the code—they could easily alter it and render it useless, or it could be a security issue that no one should be allowed to see a particular formula easily.

To address these issues, you could call your code from an event such as **Workbook_Open**, but then it will only run when the workbook opens up and will not allow the user to make use of all the wonderful procedures you have written.

You could also make use of the ribbon feature, which is new to Excel 2007. This is described in Chapter 21. This allows you to customize the ribbon with your own controls and to link them to your custom procedures. It is fairly complicated and requires a good knowledge of XML. The ribbon can only be modified when the file is loaded, and cannot be programmatically changed to suit circumstances while the user is in the worksheet.

For maximum flexibility, you can use the **CommandBars** object to set up a menu, or you can place a command button on the spreadsheet itself. By using the **CommandBars** object, you can create new menus as part of the Microsoft Excel structure of menus; this effectively bypasses the ribbon, although it is still part of it.

In previous versions of Excel you had free rein to extend the menu structure and customize it how you wanted to. You could add extra menus and pop-ups to any of the Excel menus to give a very professional look to your program.

In Excel 2007, all custom menus are applied to a new item on the menu bar called Add-Ins. This has one ribbon control called Menu Items, which is where all custom menu items are displayed. Unfortunately, this takes away a great deal of the flexibility that was available before, but it is all that is now available.

Command Bars

The **CommandBars** object represents the Classic Excel spreadsheet menus and allows you to add your own menu commands into the Excel Add-Ins menu item.

For example, you can add a new menu group under the Add-Ins ribbon called My Code with a submenu item to call your procedure. This adds a very professional look to your application and, provided you include the means to remove the entry from the Add-Ins ribbon, the user will be impressed that your custom menu item forms part of the standard Excel menu system.

Here is a simple example that adds a new menu item under Tools and attaches some code to it. Insert a module and then add the following subroutine:

```
Sub MyProc()
     MsgBox "You pressed my menu item"
End Sub
```

When this is run, it will display a message box with the message "You pressed my menu item."

Now add the following code:

```
Sub AddMyMenu()
      Dim Cbar As CommandBar
      Dim CBarCtl As CommandBarControl
      Set Cbar = Application.CommandBars("Worksheet Menu Bar")
      Set CBarCtl = Cbar.Controls.Add(Type:=msoControlPopup)
      With CBarCtl
          .Caption = "My Code"
          With .Controls.Add(Type:=msoControlButton)
              .Caption = "My Proc"
              .OnAction = "MyProc"
          End With
      End With
   End Sub
```

Run the code only once and then go to the spreadsheet. (If you run this code again, a second menu item called My Code will appear, which could be confusing.)

You will now see that there is an additional menu item on the menu bar called Add-Ins. Click this item and a single ribbon control called Menu Items will appear containing your new menu group called My Code.

Click My Code and you will see your submenu item called My Proc. Click My Proc and your message box will appear as defined in the subroutine "MyProc."

The first line of the code adds the menu bar MyMenu to the Excel menu Add-Ins item. The second line of code describes what action to take when the user does this. The **OnAction** property is set to point to the subroutine **Test_Menu**, which you just created.

If you exit Excel and load the application again, even without your file present (this is the file containing the code that you used to generate the new menu items), your menu item will still be there. It appears to be permanent, and a new innovation in Excel 2007 is that even if you click your new menu item without your original file loaded, Excel will load the file with the VBA on-action code in it so that your menu item still works.

How can you remove the menu entry? By using this **Delete** method:

```
Sub RemoveMyMenu()
        Dim Cbar As CommandBar
        On Error Resume Next
        Set Cbar = CommandBars("Worksheet Menu Bar")
        Cbar.Controls("My Code").Delete
End Sub
```

Run this code, and the Add-Ins item on the menu bar will vanish. In Excel 2007 you can run this code again without it producing an error. In Excel 2003 you had to include an On Error Resume Next statement to get around this.

NOTE

You cannot delete the existing Excel menus. After all, how would you recreate the menu?

In Excel 2003, before the ribbon came along, menus were split into sections using a horizontal bar to split menu items into groups. You can add this line to command bars by using the **BeginGroup** method. The following code is an extension of the earlier creation code, but it now creates three menu items; you create the last item as a new group by setting the BeginGroup property for it to True.

```
Sub AddMyMenu()
        Dim Cbar As CommandBar
        Dim CBarCtl As CommandBarControl
        Set Cbar = Application.CommandBars("Worksheet Menu Bar")
        Set CBarCtl = Cbar.Controls.Add(Type:=msoControlPopup)
```

```
        With CBarCtl
            .Caption = "My Code"

            With .Controls.Add(Type:=msoControlButton)
                .Caption = "My Proc"
                .OnAction = "MyProc"
            End With

            With .Controls.Add(Type:=msoControlButton)
                .Caption = "My Proc Again"
                .OnAction = "MyProc"
            End With

            With .Controls.Add(Type:=msoControlButton)
                .Caption = "A new group"
                .BeginGroup = True
                .OnAction = "MyProc"
            End With
        End With

End Sub
```

Run this code, and the item "A new group" appears in a group of its own within the My Code menu. You can also specify where on the menu list you want the item to appear.

The default is to always appear at the bottom, but the **before** parameter allows you to specify where the item will be placed within the menu:

```
Sub AddMyMenu()
        Dim Cbar As CommandBar
        Dim CBarCtl As CommandBarControl

        Set Cbar = Application.CommandBars("Worksheet Menu Bar")
        Set CBarCtl = Cbar.Controls.Add(Type:=msoControlPopup)

        With CBarCtl
            .Caption = "My Code"

            With .Controls.Add(Type:=msoControlButton)
                .Caption = "My Proc"
                .OnAction = "MyProc"
            End With
```

```
        With .Controls.Add(Type:=msoControlButton)
            .Caption = "My Proc Again"
            .OnAction = "MyProc"
        End With

        With .Controls.Add(Type:=msoControlButton, before:=2)
            .Caption = "A new group"
            .BeginGroup = True
            .OnAction = "MyProc"
        End With
    End With

End Sub
```

The **before** parameter is set to 2, which makes it the second item. Subsequent items in the menu bar will be moved down so that the existing menu item 2 will not be lost—it now becomes menu item 3.

You can also enable and disable your menu items by setting the **Enabled** property:

```
CommandBars("Worksheet Menu Bar").Controls("My Code").Enabled = False
```

This will show your menu item grayed out, or disabled within the ribbon control. Setting it to True will enable it.

You can also enable and disable the individual menu items within your main control "My Code" as follows:

```
CommandBars("Worksheet Menu Bar").Controls("My Code"). _
Controls("My Proc").Enabled = False
```

You can make your menu item invisible by setting the **Visible** property:

```
CommandBars("Worksheet Menu Bar").Controls("My Code"). _
Controls("My Proc").Visible = False
```

Your menu item will no longer be in the list, but it can be made visible again by setting the **Visible** property to True.

Excel 2007 is more restrictive than previous versions in how it allows you to develop custom menu structures. The Add-Ins menu item is the root of all your custom menus, and everything goes into the ribbon control of menu items, whereas with Excel 2003 there was far more flexibility about where you could locate your menus (see Figure 11-1).

However, the good news is that it does still give you the same programmatic flexibility that you had before in terms of positioning menus and enabling/disabling them. In a lot of ways this is a better option than using RibbonX (see Chapter 21), as you do not need to use XML and you have control over the menus at runtime in your code.

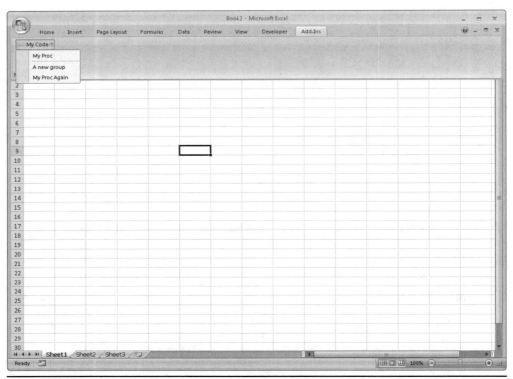

Figure 11-1 *An additional menu structure created in Excel*

RibbonX produces very spectacular results, but because it is governed by XML it is embedded in the file and cannot be changed dynamically by means of VBA code.

Command Buttons

You can insert controls directly onto the spreadsheet itself using the Control toolbox. Any control can be used, such as a drop-down list or a command button. Click the Developer item in the menu bar and then click the Insert icon in the Controls window of the ribbon. The Control toolbox will appear, just as it does on a UserForm within the VBA editor. Select the button (top left-hand control) from the **Active X** controls, not the **User Form** controls (this can be confusing, since these two groups appear on the same dialog).

If you use the button in the User Form controls, you will not be able to switch it out of design mode and there is a danger that users will be able to modify it how they wish. You will also get a dialog asking you to assign a macro to the button, and this will show you that you have clicked the wrong control.

If you do not have the Developer item in your menu, click the Office button in the top left-hand corner of the Worksheet screen and then click Excel Options at the bottom of the form that appears. Check the box in the top group for Show Developer Tab in the Ribbon.

Select the Command Button icon by clicking it (look at the tooltip text on each icon if you're unsure which one it is) and drag it onto the spreadsheet, as shown in Figure 11-2.

Select the new button, right-click it, and then click the Developer item in the menu. Click View Code within the Controls window on the ribbon. This will take you into the code window, and the subroutine **Button1_Click()**. You can then place your code here or call another subroutine. You could, for example, place a message box on the code.

You can change the text on the button by right-clicking the button and selecting Properties. Edit the **Caption** property to your requirements. The button caption will read CommandButton1 by default. You can change this to read MyButton or whatever title you wish to give it.

When you complete your button, exit design mode by clicking the Developer item in the menu and the Design Mode icon in the Controls window of the ribbon. This toggles design mode on and off on the worksheet. When you click the button now, it is no longer in design

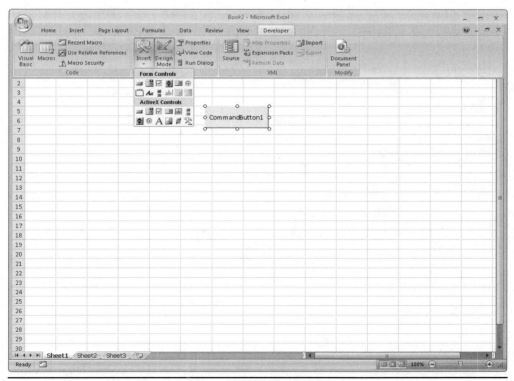

Figure 11-2   *Placing controls directly onto a worksheet*

mode and will run instead of having handles around it. Your button is now ready to run. Click it to see it run your code.

You may wish to make further amendments to the button or even delete it completely if you are not happy with it. The only problem now is that every time you click it, it runs the code, and right-clicking does nothing because Excel VBA does not interpret the right mouse click on a command button! What you need to do is to put the Control toolbox back on screen by again clicking the Developer item in the menu and then clicking the Design Mode icon in the Controls window of the ribbon. You can now select the button, resize it, delete it, and so on.

You can change the code behind the button without having to go into design mode. The code is completely separate from the spreadsheet itself. The code appears on the sheet object module for that particular sheet and can be easily edited.

Object Models

In this part, you will learn all about the Excel object model and how to use it within your code. The Excel object model is at the heart of VBA programming for Excel. It empowers you to do anything in code that you can do from the Excel menu and—as you will find in the practical examples later on in the book—plenty more that cannot be done from the Excel menu!

You will also learn how to use Excel object models to interact with other Microsoft applications. For example, you will learn how to send custom e-mails through Microsoft Outlook and create a custom Word document.

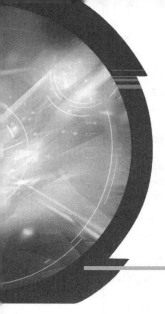

The Excel Object Model

The Excel object model is at the heart of using VBA in Excel. It distinguishes programming in Excel from programming in other VBA applications by providing additional commands to access the worksheets and workbooks and by providing all the functionality that the user would normally obtain from the menu structure of Excel. The object model in Microsoft Access, for example, contains commands and objects specifically relating to the database, giving the means to manipulate tables, queries, forms, and reports. In Excel, the whole application is oriented toward a structure of workbooks and spreadsheets, so the object model is written around this. Excel is a three-tier application: the client services tier, the object model, and the data services layer. The usual spreadsheet interface that you view is the client services tier and is the layer that normally communicates with the user.

Underneath this sits the Excel object model. Each time you do something on your spreadsheet, you are issuing commands through the Excel object model. For example, if you open a workbook, the underlying code behind File | Open uses the same functionality as the command **Workbooks.Open** to open your workbook and add it to the workbooks collection object. Similarly, if you have Calculation set to manual in the Options dialog and are using F9 to recalculate, the same functionality as the command **Application.Calculate** is used each time you do this. Using the Excel object model and a programming language such as Visual Basic, it's not difficult to develop your own Excel front end with exactly the same functionality as the Microsoft Excel front end. Every menu command and function key on the Microsoft Excel front end is represented within the Excel object model. This is not to say that these are the exact objects that Excel uses itself, but Microsoft has empowered you with all the objects and methods for you to do anything in code that can be done from the Excel menu, and as you will find out in the practical examples later on in this book, a whole lot more besides.

Strangely enough, if you decided to write your own front end, there would be relatively little code to write because all the functionality is contained in the object model. Below the

Excel object model sits the data services layer, which holds the data in the spreadsheets and is modified by commands from the Excel object model.

The Excel object model contains a large number of objects—for example, **Workbooks**, **Worksheets**, **Ranges**, **Charts**, **Pivot Tables**, and **Comments**. These Excel objects are discrete entities that offer various pieces of data analysis functionality. Most important, they can be controlled from your code.

When programming in Excel using VBA, you use standard VBA commands and functions such as For..Next, If..Then..Else, and MsgBox, but you use the object model to communicate with the Excel application by manipulating the properties and methods of the various objects at your disposal, such as the **Workbook** object or the **Worksheet** object.

An object is a programming structure encapsulating both data and functionality that is defined and allocated as a single unit, and for which the only public access is through the programming structure's interfaces.

An object is a part of the Excel program. The objects are arranged in a hierarchy. For example, at the top of the object model is the **Application** object, which is Excel itself. Under the **Application** object is the **Workbook** object, and within the **Workbook** object are **Worksheet** objects. Within each **Worksheet** object are **Range** objects, and so on. Each object can contain settings, called properties, and actions that can be performed on the object, called methods. For example, if you want to enter data into a cell reference using code, you refer to the range property of the worksheet. You specify a cell or a range of cells in the range property and then use the text or value property to place your data in the cells. An example might be

```
Worksheets("sheet1").Range("a1").Value="MyData"
```

This enters the text "MyData" into cell A1 on sheet1.

Properties and Methods Explained

All objects in the Excel object model have properties or methods or both. Some have very few; others have many, depending on the complexity of the object. A *property* is a scalar attribute that defines various parameters of an object. An example is the **Visible** property of a worksheet, which can be **xlSheetVisible (–1)**, **xlSheetHidden (0)**, or **xlSheetVeryHidden (2)** and dictates whether the worksheet is visible to the user or is hidden. This is done here using built-in constants (numeric values are in parentheses). The **Workbooks** object has a **Count** property that defines how many workbooks are loaded into the Excel application. The properties hold the parameters that define the object. Properties are very much dependent on the objects that they are part of, and their values can be text or numeric.

Methods are ways of executing actions based on a particular object. They provide a shortcut to doing something on a particular object. For example, you may want to delete a worksheet from a workbook. To do this, use the **Delete** method on the worksheets collection, specifying the worksheet you wish to delete. Similarly, the **Open** method opens an existing workbook. The hard work has been done for you, and all you have to do is to call these methods from your code.

Take your computer, for example. It is an object and you can define properties and methods for it. A property is a measurable aspect of an object, so for your computer you could have the following properties:

Property	Value
Make	Compaq
Year	2008
RAM	4GB
Hard Disk	160GB
Processor	Intel

Note that these are not all numeric. It is easy to get the idea that a property is always something directly measurable, such as the height of an object, and is therefore always numeric. However, properties may also be text, Boolean (True or False), graphic (in the case of pictures or icons), or enumerated from a specific list relating to that property. They can be any data type.

Methods are words that represent actions that can be performed by the object. For your computer these could be

▶ Cold boot

▶ Warm boot

▶ Shut down

▶ Set up

Transferring this theory to Excel and using a workbook object as the example, you have properties such as

Property	Description
Author	The person who built the workbook
FullName	The full name of the workbook
HasPassword	True or False, depending on whether the workbook has a password
Path	The path the workbook was loaded from

Of course, there are many other properties for a workbook, but this gives you an idea of what some properties look like. Examples of **Workbook** object methods are

Method	Description
Activate	Makes this workbook the current workbook
Close	Closes the workbook
NewWindow	Creates a new window for the active workbook
PrintOut	Prints the workbook

Properties can be either read-only or read/write. Read-only means you can access the property's value (setting) but not change it. Read/write means you can both access and change a property's value. This can have an important effect on your program because you may find your code writing to properties that can only be read. For example, a workbook has a property called **HasPassword** that shows True or False according to whether the workbook is protected by a password. You might think if you change this to False, you will remove password protection from the workbook without knowing the password. However, Microsoft thought of this and made the property read-only to prevent this. To preserve the integrity of the workbook and the object model, it is important to keep them read-only. For example, the **Count** property of any collection of objects is always read-only. Altering the **Count** of worksheets within a workbook could lead to very unpredictable results. For instance, the workbook might have four worksheets within it. If you could change it to two worksheets, you would lose two worksheets because they would be deleted!

Methods are effectively like subroutines or shortcuts to actions that you can call from your code to perform certain actions, such as opening a workbook or adding a new worksheet. To try writing the code to open a workbook would be impossible because you do not know the finer points of the file format and what each byte represents; nor do you know how to incorporate that file into the Excel front end structure. Without VBA, you'd need to know the intricacies of C and have the source code to get the workbook open. However, Microsoft did all the hard work for us. They know the answers to all these questions, so all you need is one line of code calling the **Open** method. With methods, you usually pass parameters as well; for example, the **PrintOut** method can be given parameters for **From**, **To**, **Preview**, **Printer**, and so on.

Manipulating Properties

If a property is read/write, it can be manipulated. This means that you can substitute other values into it to provide different effects, depending on the object and the property. For example, you may want to use code to alter the text in a cell on a workbook. You can do this by writing your new text to the **Value** property for that particular cell, referencing it from the **Worksheet** object.

Properties are generally manipulated by using code at runtime, when your program is executing. However, some properties are available at design time and can be changed using the Properties window within VBE. Design time is when you are viewing the code window and designing and making changes to your code. To see an example of this, click the object **This Workbook** in the VBA window. Open the Properties window by pressing F4 and then click the **Saved** property, and it will allow you to change it to True or False. However, you normally change these properties using code, in response to user actions.

Two examples of the syntax for reading properties are shown here:

```
MsgBox Workbooks("book1").Saved
MsgBox ActiveWorkbook.Saved
```

All collections have indexes that define individual objects within the collection. The title **"book1"** shown in parentheses defines that it is book1 within the **Workbooks** collection that the code is referring to. There could be several workbooks loaded at once, and this is how VBA distinguishes between them.

Some objects are grouped together into other objects, or collections. For example, Excel can have many workbooks open. Each individual workbook is an object. All currently open workbooks in the Excel application are grouped together into the **Workbooks** object or collection. Accessing an individual item or member in a collection involves either specifying its numeric position in the collection or accessing its name (if it has one). The preceding code example accesses the workbook named **book1** in the **Workbooks** collection.

The first of the preceding syntax examples provides the Saved status of workbook **book1**, True or False, displaying it in a message box. The second syntax example gives the Saved status of the active workbook in a message box. If **book1** is the only workbook loaded into Excel, these examples will represent the same information because the active workbook has to be **book1**. If there is more than one workbook loaded, the second example will give the Saved status of the workbook that the user is currently working on. The workbook (as defined) is the object, and **Saved** is the property. The message box will display True if the workbook has been saved and has no new changes. The message box will return False if the workbook has been changed and has not yet been saved.

Note that a dot is used as a separator between the object and the property. This is a bit like using a back-slash (\) when defining pathnames for files. You can have more than one dot separator because objects can have subobjects and properties can have subproperties. For example, a workbook is a collection of worksheets, so one of the properties of the workbook object is a worksheets collection. If you want to refer to one worksheet out of the collection, it would look like this:

```
MsgBox Workbooks("book1").Worksheets("sheet1").ProtectContents
```

This will display True or False depending on whether **sheet1** in **book1** has its contents protected. The **ProtectContents** property holds a True or False value according to whether the worksheet is protected or not. This demonstrates how the property is part of the overall picture of the object that is the worksheet. If the worksheet is protected, the property will display True; if it is not protected, it will display False.

You can change properties if they are not read-only. For example, to set the workbook property **Saved** to True, regardless of whether it has been saved or not, you could use the following code:

```
Workbooks("book1").Saved = True
```

The result is that if you close the workbook, you will not get prompted for saving. This is an example of needing to know what you are doing when writing to properties so that you can preserve the integrity of your application. For example, if you place this code in a workbook's **SheetChange** event, every time the user makes changes to the data in the worksheet, the **Saved** property will be set back to True. When the user finally closes down the workbook, there will not be any prompt to save because the program will check the **Saved** property, find it set to True, and assume that it is already saved. The spreadsheet will not be saved, which could easily lead to the loss of work, with the user none the wiser on why it happened. This is certainly not the way to write professional VBA code.

Calling Methods

As explained earlier, methods are effectively subroutines based on objects that take certain actions, sometimes dependent on parameters passed to them. The method is effectively a shortcut to an action, but you may need to specify parameters to define to VBA exactly what it is that you want to do.

An example is opening a workbook from a file. You use the **Open** method on the **Workbooks** collection to do this, but you also have to pass parameters, such as the filename and pathname, so that VBA knows what it is required to open. For example, in the following code,

```
Workbooks.Open ("c:\MyFile.xlsx")
```

C:\MyFile.xlsr defines the location of the file to be opened; this is a mandatory parameter for this method. There are other optional parameters that can be passed, such as a password if required, and read-only. Optional parameters are shown in the tip text for the method with square brackets around them, such as [Title]. The tip text appears as you type in the VBA statement. You will see a tip text box with a yellow background appear, which shows all available parameters.

Sometimes it is unnecessary for a method to have arguments, such as when you save the workbook to its original location with the **Save** method. This assumes that you already have a workbook loaded called **book1** and that it has already been saved under that name.

```
Workbooks("book1").Save
```

This will perform a save on **book1**, assuming that it has already been saved previously, similar to the File | Save command on the menu. However, if the file has not been already saved, you will not be prompted for a filename. Instead, it will be saved as book1.xls and placed in the default path set by Excel or the last folder chosen from the last Open or Save operation.

You can also use the **SaveAs** method, which does have a parameter for saving a workbook with a different filename and/or to a different location. This example assumes that you already have a workbook loaded called **book2** and that it has already been saved as **book2**.

```
Workbooks("book2").SaveAs "newfile", , "apple"
```

This passes the parameter **"newfile"** as the filename. In Excel 2007 it is a good idea not to put the suffix in the filename parameter but to let Excel work it out for itself. This is because there is now a large variety of options for the type of Excel file that can be created.

This is called passing by order because the parameters are being passed in the order in which they are defined in the function, separated by commas. In this case, you are passing a filename called newfile.xls and ignoring the file format parameter (which is optional) and providing a **password** parameter of **"apple"**.

When you enter the opening parenthesis, you will see a list of parameters appear, highlighted in bold as you enter each one. You have to stick to the order shown. If this is a function that assigns the result to a variable, you do not need to include the parentheses. You will get an error in some cases if you include them.

Some methods, such as **SaveAs**, have a large number of parameters, and many of them are optional. Optional parameters are shown with square brackets [ ]. Passing by order becomes more complicated with optional parameters because you may be using a function that has ten possible parameters even if you want to use only two of them. Consider the following example for opening a workbook. This example assumes that you already have a workbook file called "newfile" on the root directory of the C: drive.

```
Workbooks.Open "C:\newfile", , True, , "apple"
```

You can see that three parameters are being passed to open the file, although at least two parameters are not being used, as shown by the Null values between the commas. This is because these are optional parameters and do not have to be given a value. For example, not all files have a password, so when a workbook is opened in this way the password is purely optional. The split between mandatory and optional parameters depends on what the method is doing and how the code in the Excel Object Library has been written. Optional parameters are always shown with square brackets ([ ]) around them in the tip text box.

The filename is mandatory, the read-only parameter is set to True, and the password is "apple." It looks confusing, and anyone reading the code will not be able to immediately interpret what is going on and what the parameters mean. If you are looking at a VBA application that has been written by someone else, it may take more time to interpret what is going on than if the passing by name method was used. Code should always be easy for another person to understand in case they have to perform maintenance of it. If you have written a professional application for commercial use and you are suddenly unavailable to maintain it, someone else needs to be able to look at your work and quickly understand your code.

Passing by name is another way of passing parameters that makes it less confusing and shows the names of the parameters being passed. Passing by name enables you to selectively pass arguments without having to specify Null values for arguments you don't want to use. It also makes it easier to understand what is being passed to the method. If you pass by name, the preceding example can be rewritten as follows. As before, this example assumes that you already have a workbook file called "newfile" on the root directory of the C: drive.

```
Workbooks.Open FileName:="C:\newfile", ReadOnly:=True, _
Password:="apple"
```

You can define each parameter by naming the parameter and following it with a colon and an equals sign (:=). When passing by name, you can pass the parameters in any order, unlike passing by order, which strictly defines the order passed.

You can also save this file under another name, as follows (this example assumes that you have a workbook loaded called "book1"):

```
Workbooks("book1").SaveAs FileName:="NewFileAgain.xlsx"
```

If you run this code and save the file as NewFileAgain, you must then refer to that workbook by its new name in subsequent code; otherwise, you will get the error "Subscript out of range," meaning the previous filename, book1, can no longer be found. The following example correctly refers to the newly saved file. This example assumes that there is a worksheet called Sheet1 within the workbook NewFileAgain:

```
Workbooks("NewFileAgain").Worksheets("sheet1")
```

Collections Explained

In object-oriented programs, it is important to understand the concept of collections. *Collections* are objects that contain a group of the same objects. An example is the **Worksheets** collection, which contains all the worksheet objects for a given workbook. All the worksheets are like objects because they have the same properties and methods. An object such as a **Chart** has different properties and methods and so cannot be part of the **Worksheets** collection, but it would fit into the **Charts** collection.

In Excel, all objects are either singular objects referenced by name or objects in a collection referenced by index or name. Collections also have their own properties and methods apart from the objects that they hold. For example, collections always hold a **Count** property that represents the number of objects within the collection, and they always have an **Add** method to add a new object into the collection.

Collections have their own properties and methods that are entirely separate from the objects that they contain. These objects also have their own properties and methods and can also contain further collections of objects. An example is the **Workbooks** collection, which contains a collection of **Workbook** objects, representing all workbooks currently loaded into Excel. As you have already learned, it has a **Count** property to index the number of workbooks, and it has an **Open** method to load another workbook. Each workbook has properties such as **HasPassword** and methods such as **Save** or **SaveAs**. However, there is also a collection of worksheets within each workbook that then has its own properties, methods, and collections.

In Excel, you can have a collection of worksheets inside a workbook called the **Worksheets** collection, and each worksheet inside this collection will have an index number and a name to identify it. The index number is a reference for an object within that collection, commencing at 1.

The same thing is true of workbooks: several workbooks can be loaded at once within the Excel application. There is a collection of workbooks called the **Workbooks** collection, and each workbook inside will be enumerated with an index number and a name to identify it. There are other collection objects such as **Windows**, **ChartObjects**, and **Borders**, but the **Workbooks** and **Worksheets** collections are the main ones for referring to cells and so are the focus of this section.

Collections can be cycled through. *Cycling* is the best term to describe what happens in a For Each..Next loop. For Each..Next loops are covered in Chapter 4. You use the following syntax: For Each Object within Collection, Next. This cycles through each object within the collection, giving you the chance to examine or manipulate the properties of it or to use a method by calling it (for example, **Workbooks("book1").Save**).

Try putting the code shown in the following listing in a VBA module. If you do not already have a module displayed, use Insert | Module from the VBE menu. Press F5 to run it, and you will see each sheet's name displayed.

```
Sub ShowName()
Dim w As Worksheet
For Each w In Worksheets
      MsgBox w.Name
Next w
End Sub
```

Initially, this code sets up a variable **w** to represent a worksheet object. This represents the current worksheet being cycled through. The code then cycles through the **Worksheets** collection using a For Each..Next loop. The code takes each worksheet in turn, gets the name property, and displays it in a message box onscreen, as shown in Figure 12-2. Your code sheet should look like Figure 12-1.

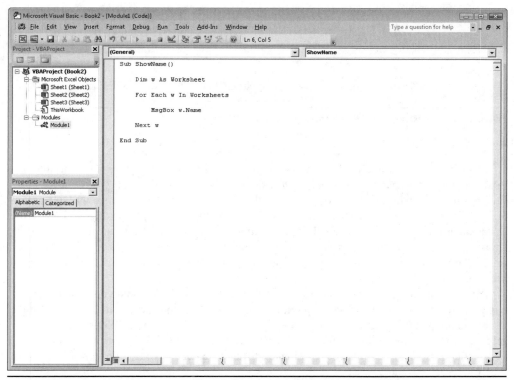

Figure 12-1   *Displaying names of all worksheets within the Worksheets collection*

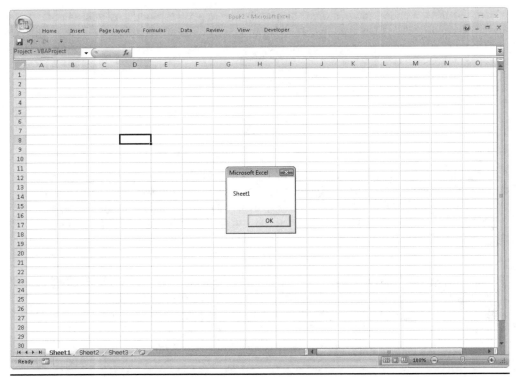

Figure 12-2   *Message box displaying names of worksheets*

The **Dim** statement is short for *Dimension*; it creates a space in memory for a variable. In this case, it creates space for a standard worksheet. You can run this routine without the **Dim** line, but it does have advantages because it will give you automatic assistance with properties and methods. When you type the **Dim w As** statement, a list box appears when you get to the **Worksheet** part. When you type in **MsgBox w.name**, a list box will appear after you type **w** showing all the properties and methods that you can use. This is extremely helpful when programming because it allows you to immediately see what your options are for the next piece of code.

The structure of the Excel object model is extremely complicated, and you should not expect to remember every object, collection, property, and method within it. If you do not use the automatic list boxes that appear as you type object code in, you will be constantly referring to the Object Browser for this information because it can be difficult to know what command to use next. It is also easy to make mistakes that cause your code to produce errors when you run it.

Using the Object Browser

The Object Browser is a useful tool for looking at the properties, methods, and constants of an object—in this case, the Excel **Application** object. To access the Object Browser, select View | Object Browser from the VBE menu or press F2. Use the pull-down that says <All Libraries> to find the Object Library, and click it. This will show all the classes of the Excel object and the properties and methods. It will also show the relationships and hierarchy of the objects themselves. Figure 12-3 shows how it looks onscreen.

You can search on specific strings by entering your search string into the box underneath the pull-down showing Excel and then clicking the binoculars symbol or pressing ENTER. For example, you may want to know which parts of the Excel object model deal with charts. Simply type **Chart** into the Search box, click the binoculars symbol, and you will see all references containing the word *Chart*. This is far easier than investigating each hierarchical structure, which could take some time.

You can click a class (which is an object) to see all the properties, methods, and collections underneath it. If you have searched on the word *Chart,* click Class Charts (which is the actual

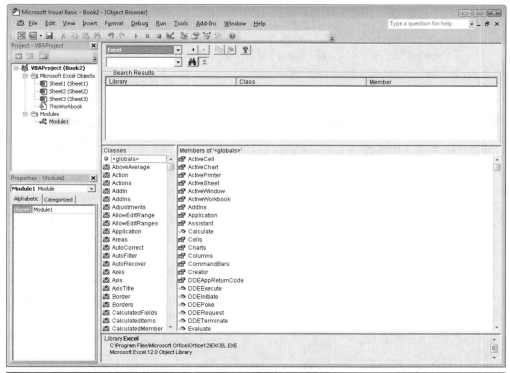

Figure 12-3   *The Excel object model in the Object Browser*

collection of all charts) and examine the methods and properties available in the Members box to the right of the class. Methods have a green icon, and properties have a gray icon with a hand holding it.

Clicking a property will show whether a property is read-only or if you can write to it. The window at the bottom of the Object Browser will show the property type and if it is read-only. Clicking a method displays the syntax for parameters and which ones are optional and which are mandatory. The window at the bottom of the Object Browser displays the full syntax of the method, with optional properties shown in square brackets ([ ]).

Communicating with the Spreadsheet

One of the main uses of VBA in Excel is to communicate with spreadsheets and to manipulate values within cells. To do this you must use the **Range** object. The **Range** object is something of a hybrid between a singular object and a collection in that it can be used to reference one cell or a collection of cells. For example, to reference a single cell, your code would look something like this. This example assumes that you have a loaded workbook called book1 and it has a worksheet in it called sheet1.

```
Workbooks("book1").Worksheets("sheet1").Range("a1").Value = 10
```

Place this code into a module and then run it by clicking the cursor on the procedure. Press F5 and check the value of cell A1 on sheet1 in book1. This will show the value of 10.

You can also reference a range (or collection) of cells:

```
Workbooks("book1").Worksheets("sheet1").Range("a1.a10").Value = 5
```

This fills the cells from A1 to A10 with the value 5. Notice that the dot is used between **a1** and **a10** to separate the cell references.

This is not the only way of doing this, as Microsoft very kindly gave us a number of choices. You can also use a colon (:), a comma (,), or a double dot (..). You can also go the full way and give individual cell references for start and finish:

```
Workbooks("book1").Worksheets("sheet1").Range("a1","a10").Value = 5
```

Personally, I do not make life hard for myself, and I use the dot because it is the least number of keypresses. (Also, because you use it in other parts of the programming language, it falls to hand quite easily.)

Conversely, you can also read the value of A1 back into your code. You may be writing an application that takes values out of a worksheet, processes them in some way, and then puts them back onto the same worksheet, or even into another workbook.

```
MsgBox Workbooks("book1").Worksheets("sheet1").Range("a1").Value
```

This will show the value 5. However, if you try reading the value of a range of cells, you will get a Type Mismatch error. A Type Mismatch error occurs when you are trying to put data into a variable that does not accept this type of data. For example, this might occur if you try to put a string of text into a variable that has already been dimensioned as an integer (numeric). It is a bit like trying to bang a square peg into a round hole, and VBA does not like it.

When reading a range of cells, the **Value** property of the **Range** object can return only one cell at a time. If you force it to read a range of cells, it will try to bring too much information back. When reading the **Value** property, a mismatch error occurs because it is not designed to hold an array of information.

You have probably noticed by now how much code references the "tree" of objects. For example, you can start off with the **Application** object, reference a workbook in the **Workbooks** collection underneath it, then reference a worksheet within the **Worksheets** collection for that workbook, and finally reference a range and a value. The **Application** object is the root, the **Workbook** and **Worksheet** objects are the branches, and the **Range** object is the leaves. This can become somewhat laborious if you're working with many lines of code and you have to keep writing out this enormous reference to identify a particular cell. As a shortcut, you can refer to the worksheet name, for example:

```
MsgBox Worksheets("sheet1").Range("a1").Value
```

This will work, but suppose you have more than one workbook loaded and they both have a sheet1 in the workbook? Excel will choose the sheet in the active workbook. Confusion reigns supreme. Fortunately, there is a way to cut down the amount of referencing and keep the integrity of the code by using the **Dim** statement to create a **Workbook** object in memory.

Creating a Workbook Object in Memory

When you create a **Workbook** object in memory, you define a variable to represent that workbook by dimensioning a variable with the **Dim** statement. You can call your variable anything you want as long as it has not already been used in your code and is not a reserved word (see Chapter 2).

The advantage of creating a **Workbook** object is that it can be set to represent a particular workbook with a **Set** statement. After that, you can use that variable to reference that workbook, and the automatic list boxes showing the underlying properties, methods, and collections will still work with it. You can work without the **Set** statement, but it means working without the automatic list boxes and providing a full hierarchy in every line of code. This example assumes that you have a loaded workbook called **book1** and it has a worksheet in it called **sheet1**.

```
Dim w As Workbook, s As Worksheet

Set w = Workbooks("book1")

Set s = w.Worksheets("sheet1")

MsgBox s.Range("a1").Value
```

The **Dim** statement creates two variables: **w** as a workbook and **s** as a worksheet. The first **Set** statement sets **w** to point at **book1** in the **Workbooks** collection. The second **Set** statement sets **s** to point at **sheet1** within the **Worksheet** collection of **w** that is already set to **book1**.

Now you can use **s** as the worksheet object for **sheet1**. This has the added advantage that, as you write your code, all the list boxes of properties and methods will automatically appear to show the options available for that particular object. Type **s** and then a dot in the procedure, and the list box will appear next to your code. You need only click the item required in the list box to complete your code.

Hierarchy

Within the Excel object model there is a hierarchy of objects. It is important to understand how this hierarchy works because of the implications in referring to objects. In most organizations, there is a hierarchy of jobs, for example. In the armed forces, you have generals of varying grades at the top of the hierarchy, with four-star generals at the very top. The structure then cascades down to colonels, majors, captains, and lieutenants. Orders are sent down from the top via the command structure. The Excel object model works in a very similar way.

Consider the **Application** object as the four-star general in charge; a structure that radiates out from the general. The **Workbooks** collection object could be considered a colonel, with the **Worksheets** collection object below it a major. Cell range objects would be the captain level.

The hierarchy is very important for issuing commands, and the order in which they are issued must go down the hierarchy. For example, a major cannot give an order to a general or a colonel. The major has to accept orders from generals and colonels, but the major can give orders to captains and lieutenants. In the same way, in the Excel object model, a **Worksheet** object does not have properties and methods (commands) that apply to the **Workbook** object or the **Application** object. You cannot use a **Worksheet** object and then issue a command to save the workbook. This will create an error message because the **Worksheet** sits within the **Workbook** object, not the other way around.

```
Worksheets("sheet1").Workbooks("book1").Save
```

Just as a major cannot give a general an order to advance and attack, the given syntax will not work because the **Workbooks** object is at a higher level than the **Worksheets** object in the hierarchy. It breaks all the rules of the hierarchy.

There is one way around it: if the general happens to be the major's father! The general would listen to his son and then give the order, even though the suggestion comes from lower down the tree. VBA can work the same way by using the **Parent** property. This gives access to the methods of the **Parent** object:

```
Worksheets("sheet1").Parent.Save
```

If you type this example without using the Parent property, the code will produce an error because individual worksheets cannot use the Save method.

The highest object in the hierarchy is called **Application**; this represents Excel itself. The most commonly used object collections below this are as follows:

Object Collection	Description
Dialogs	Collection of built-in dialogs in Excel
Windows	Used to access different windows in Excel
Workbooks	Collection of all current workbooks loaded into Excel
CommandBars	Collection of menu items in Excel
Worksheets	Collection of all worksheets within current workbooks in Excel

The third, fourth, and fifth tiers of the hierarchy of the Excel Object Model contain further objects to access functionality on the second-tier objects. The Excel object structure has a tree-like structure. The **Application** object is the root, the **Workbook** objects are the trunk, the **Worksheet** objects are the branches, and the cells become the leaves. For example, if you go down from the **Workbook** object, you come to worksheets, windows, and charts.

The structure of the object model is discussed in more detail in Chapter 13. To understand the structure of the object model well, you need to examine the Object Browser for Excel (press F2 on the code sheet to access it) and experiment on a module with the various objects.

Recording Macros

An Excel *macro* is a set of instructions that will perform an operation on an Excel worksheet. It is a great way of seeing how specific actions on the spreadsheet are interpreted in code and how the Excel object model is used to do this. If you ever get stuck as to what object or what collection you should be using, try recording a macro and see how the recorder uses the object model. It is very useful to see what parameters are being passed for specific methods and what properties and methods belong to various objects. You can then use this as the basis for building your own code. Unfortunately it is not totally infallible in Excel 2007, and you may not always see what you expected in the generated code.

When you record a macro, a module is created (if it is not already available) and the code is written into it. You can view this code and see exactly how Excel has tackled the problem in VBA. You can modify this code or use it in other procedures.

To record a macro, click the Developer menu item and then click the Record Macro icon in the Code control of the ribbon. Your screen will look like Figure 12-4.

You can give the macro another name and a shortcut key if needed. The naming conventions are that there must be no spaces or illegal characters such as a slash. The rules are the same as for names of functions or subroutines in VBA, because all you are doing is using the macro recorder to create the subroutine.

From now until you click the Stop Recording button, everything that you do on the spreadsheet is translated into VBA code using the Excel object model. For example, select a range of cells C8 to F16 on Sheet1 (it does not matter if these are empty). Right-click the selected range and choose Copy. Go to Sheet2 and click cell D10. Right click the cell and

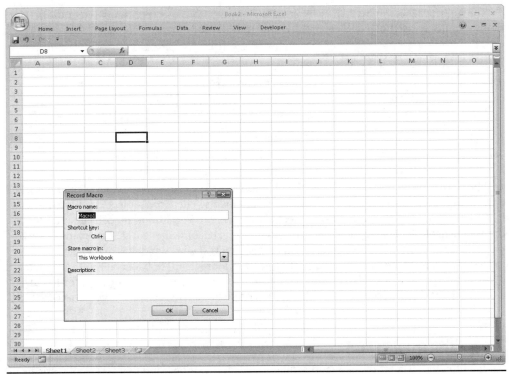

Figure 12-4   *Recording a macro*

choose Paste. Now select the Developer menu item and click on the Stop Recording icon in the Code control of the ribbon, and your macro is complete.

Look in the code window by pressing ALT-F11, and you will find that a new module has been inserted that contains the code for the macro you recorded:

```
Sub Macro1()
'
' Macro1 Macro
' Macro recorded 17-11-08 by Richard Shepherd
'


    Range("C8:F16").Select
    Selection.Copy
    Sheets("Sheet2").Select
    Range("D10").Select
    ActiveSheet.Paste
End Sub
```

Comments are automatically added to show who recorded it and on what date. The first statement selects the range C8 to F16. The **Selection** object's copy method is then used. The **Selection** object represents the currently selected range. Next, Sheet2 is selected, followed by the range on that sheet, D10, being selected. Finally, the **ActiveSheet** object's **Paste** method is used.

You can see how Excel uses the Excel object model to carry out your commands. However, Excel does make some assumptions because when this particular macro was recorded, only one workbook was loaded. If more than one workbook is loaded, the macro will be run against whichever is the active workbook, which will be the one visible in Excel. This is not always the result that you want to achieve.

Excel assumes that this is the only workbook loaded. If there are several workbooks loaded and the macro runs while in one of them, it will produce different results and even possible errors if there is not a "Sheet2" in that workbook.

If it was run in the wrong workbook, it could also run the risk of overwriting valid data in the spreadsheet, with terrible results. This is because the macro does not explicitly refer to a specific workbook. It assumes you want the macro run on the currently active workbook.

The **Workbook** tier is ignored, and the workbook to use is not defined, nor is the sheet the macro should start off in.

The lesson is that you should not assume that a recorded macro will work under every circumstance. You may find that you need to modify it to make it totally secure—by including a reference to the workbook being used, for example.

Recording macros is a great way to see your way around problems. After all, if you can do it manually on the spreadsheet, then Excel can record a macro to do it. However these macros do have limitations and should only be used as a guide in professional Excel development. After all, the whole purpose of this book is to get you to the stage where you can just sit down and write the code right off the top of your head.

The Excel Object Model — Main Objects

I n the preceding chapter, we looked at the Excel object model in terms of how it works, its hierarchy, and passing parameters. In this chapter, we'll look in more detail at the main collections and objects that you will be using within your code to communicate with the Excel spreadsheet.

The objects discussed are **Application, Workbook, Windows, Worksheet**, and **Range**.

Application Object

The **Application** object is at the highest point in the hierarchy of the object model and represents the whole Excel application. It contains the collections of workbooks and worksheets that make up spreadsheets in Excel, and it will give high-level information about the application itself, such as the active cell (the cell where the cursor currently is) and the active worksheet (the worksheet that has the focus of the cursor). It also has methods for functions such as calculating the spreadsheet (in the same way as pressing F9 on your Excel spreadsheet) or retrieving the Open filename or the Save As filename of the Excel application. You can also quit the Excel application and close it completely. Note that the **Application** object has no print options, as it is only an **Application** object and not a worksheet or workbook.

The **Application** object is the default object and does not have to be specified within the syntax of the statement for some properties. For example, the statement ActivePrinter returns the details of the active printer.

Main Properties, Methods, and Collections

This section details the main properties, methods, and collections that you will use within the **Application** object.

ActiveCell

The **ActiveCell** property represents the active cell the cursor is currently on within your Excel spreadsheet. You can use it to obtain the cell address of the active cell by going to the next tier down represented by the **ActiveCell** and using the **Address** property:

```
Msgbox Application.ActiveCell.Address
```

This will return the address of the active cell in absolute format, for example, $C$4. Note that it will only give the address of the cell and not the full address including the worksheet and workbook references.

ActivePrinter

This property returns the name of the active printer and the connection it is using, such as LPT1 or EPUSB1 if you are using a USB port. This gives the same information as selecting the File Print option from the VBE (Visual Basic Editor window) or Excel spreadsheet menu.

```
MsgBox  Application.ActivePrinter
```

In my case, this displays the string "Lexmark 5400 Series on Ne03:" This is useful if your code is going to print information out and you want to know where the print job will be sent on the network.

ActiveSheet

This property represents the active worksheet being displayed in Excel. One use of **ActiveSheet** is to select a cell on that worksheet:

```
Application.ActiveSheet.Cells (10,10).Select
```

This moves the cursor to the cell 10 rows down and 10 columns across on the active worksheet.

ActiveWindow

This property represents the active window in Excel. Selecting Window from the Excel menu displays a list of all open windows. One of these will have a tick against it to show that it is the active one. You can use **ActiveWindow** to get the caption (title bar text) of the active window:

```
MsgBox Application.ActiveWindow.Caption
```

ActiveWorkbook

You can use this property to find out the name of the active workbook in Excel:

```
MsgBox Application.ActiveWorkbook.Name
```

This will display "Book1" or whatever your current workbook is called.

It is easy to confuse **ActiveWorkbook** with **ActiveWindow** from the preceding section. On the face of it, it may look as if one workbook is the same as one window, but this is not the case. You can select View from the Excel menu and then click the New Window icon on the Window control of the ribbon to insert another instance of the current workbook. This has exactly the same information as the other window, but you can make completely different selections on it. If you select Windows from the Excel menu, there will be two windows, both based on one workbook, and either window could be the active one.

AddIns

This collection represents all the add-ins currently loaded into Excel. You can list the names of these, including the pathname they were loaded from, by using the following subroutine:

```
Sub test()
Dim MyAddin As AddIn
For Each MyAddin In AddIns
    MsgBox MyAddin.FullName
Next
End Sub
```

This is very useful if your code depends on a certain add-in being available to Excel. If it has not been loaded, your code will crash. Checking in the **Addins** collection for it allows you to display your own message that it is not present.

Calculate

This method forces recalculation of the entire spreadsheet, just as when you press F9.

```
Application.Calculate
```

Calculation

This property sets the method of calculation used in the Excel application. It can be set to **xlCalculationAutomatic, xlCalculationManual**, or **xlCalculationSemiautomatic**.

```
Application.Calculation = xlCalculationManual
```

This is the same as selecting Tools | Options from the Excel menu and then selecting the Calculation tab and clicking the Manual Calculation button.

Caption

This property holds the caption for the Excel application that is found in the window bar for Excel. For example,

```
MsgBox Application.Caption
```

will display "Microsoft Excel - Book1," assuming it is done on a fresh workbook.

You can also change the caption with the following code:

```
Application.Caption = "MyApplication"
```

You can reset the application title by writing an empty string:

```
Application.Caption = ""
```

This changes only the caption, not the current workbook.

Columns and Rows

These collections represent the rows and columns of the current spreadsheet; you can use them to select individual rows or columns:

```
Application.Columns(3).Select
```

This selects column C, just as when you click the column border.

```
Application.Rows(10).Select
```

This selects row 10, just as when you click the row border.

Dialogs

This collection gives access to the built-in **Dialogs** collection. See Chapter 10 for details on how to use this to display the Excel dialogs.

Help

This method will call up the standard Excel help file; or, if you have access to the Microsoft Help Compiler, you can create your own customized help system:

```
Application.Help
```

OperatingSystem

You can use this property to check out the operating system that Excel is currently being run on.

```
MsgBox Application.OperatingSystem
```

You may want a minimum version level of the operating system being used. If you are running your code as an add-in that is not part of any particular spreadsheet, and you are using API calls (Chapter 17) within your code, the effect could be critical, depending on what operating system is used.

OrganizationName

This property returns the name of the organization entered into Windows:

```
Msgbox Application.OrganizationName
```

There is an interesting way to safeguard your application and make sure another employee in the workplace does not take your work to a new employer when they leave. When your worksheet or add-in loads up, check the **OrganizationName** property. If it is not what it should be, abort the load using **Quit**, discussed next. This can be bypassed, but it is enough to deter the casual observer.

Quit

This method closes down the Excel application completely, just as if you selected File | Exit from the Excel menu. You will still be prompted to save any unsaved files.

```
Application.Quit
```

RecentFiles

This is a collection of the most recent files loaded into Excel.

```
Sub Recent_files()
For Each file In Application.RecentFiles
    MsgBox file.Name
Next
End Sub
```

This displays the recent files loaded just as when you select File from the Excel menu and look at the list at the bottom of the menu bar.

Selection

This property holds the current selection object within the Excel application. You can get the cell address through the **Address** property:

```
Msgbox Application.Selection.Address
```

This returns the address in absolute format—for example, $B$1—but will not tell you which sheet it is on. You can find this out by using the **Worksheet** property of the selection:

```
MsgBox Application.Selection.Worksheet.Name
```

Sheets

This collection represents all the worksheets within the current workbook. This sounds similar to the **Worksheets** collection that we will be looking at later, but it does have different properties and methods. Also, there is no individual **Sheet** object, as there is within the **Worksheets** collection.

Another important difference is that you can use **Sheets** to print or print-preview individual sheets; a **Worksheet** object does not have a method to do this.

You may have a need to print out only one worksheet. This is how you do it (assuming that you have a worksheet called sheet1 with some data on it):

```
Application.Sheets("sheet1").PrintOut
```

You can also preview from within your code with the **PrintPreview** method (this will display a print preview window, but its appearance is different from what you may be used to in previous versions of Excel):

```
Application.Sheets("sheet1").PrintPreview
```

ThisWorkbook

This property represents where the current macro code is running:

```
MsgBox Application.ThisWorkbook.Name
```

Undo

This method undoes the last action on the Excel application. It is the same as selecting Edit | Undo from the Excel menu. This code will generate an error if there is nothing to be undone. This situation would occur when the workbook is first opened and no changes have been made to it.

```
Application.Undo
```

UserName

This property returns the name of the user logged on to the Windows system.

```
MsgBox Application.UserName
```

You may want your application to check that the user accessing your spreadsheet is someone whom you wish to have access. Although Excel has its own security through password protection, you may wish to be able to give different users different access to parts of your workbook. You can do this by comparing to a list of valid names:

```
If Application.UserName = "Richard Shepherd" Then
```

Version

This property returns the version number of Excel / VBA being used:

```
MsgBox Application.Version
```

If you have written an add-in, you may want it to check for the version of VBA before it starts running so that it does not crash if an older version is being used.

Workbook Object

The **Workbook** object represents an entire workbook loaded into Excel. The default workbook is **Book1**. It is one level down from the **Application** object.

The **Workbook** object forms a part of a **Workbooks** collection, which represents all the workbooks currently loaded into Excel. You cannot reference the **Workbook** object directly; you must access it through the **Workbooks** collection. See the example in the next section for how to do this.

Main Properties, Methods, and Collections

These are the main properties, methods, and collections you will use within the **Workbook** object.

Activate

This method activates the workbook specified in the **Collection** object. It will automatically go to the active sheet within that workbook. This is the same as selecting Window from the Excel menu and clicking a workbook. However, a window does not necessarily equal a workbook. See the section "Windows Object," later in this chapter, for more details.

```
Workbooks("book1").Activate
```

ActiveSheet

This property references the active sheet within a particular workbook. You may remember that **ActiveSheet** was also mentioned in relation to the **Application** object, but in that case it refers to the active sheet anywhere within the application. If several workbooks are loaded, it refers to the last sheet that was given the focus.

The **Workbook** object allows you to fine tune your selection and to specify which workbook you want to see the active sheet in:

```
MsgBox Workbooks("book1").ActiveSheet.Name
```

This returns "Sheet1" if this is the active sheet.

Close

This method closes the workbook just as when you select File | Close from the Excel menu. There are optional parameters to save the file, give it a different filename, and route the workbook:

```
Workbooks("book1").Close (True,"Myfile")
```

HasPassword

This property returns True or False, depending on whether the workbook is protected by a password. For obvious reasons, it is read-only!

```
MsgBox Workbooks("book1").HasPassword
```

PrintOut

This method prints out the active sheet of the referenced workbook to the current printer. You need to ensure that there is data on your active sheet; otherwise, nothing will be printed.

```
Workbooks("book1").PrintOut
```

PrintPreview

This method provides a print preview on the active sheet of the referenced workbook:

```
Workbooks("book1").PrintPreview
```

ReadOnly

This property returns True or False, depending on whether the workbook is read-only. This could be quite important if your code changes spreadsheet cells, because the workbook would then need to be saved under a different name.

```
MsgBox Workbooks("book1").ReadOnly
```

Save and SaveAs

These methods save your workbook, normally before it is closed. You can save to the same name, or you can use the **SaveAs** method to save to a different filename. **Save** will overwrite the previous version; **SaveAs** will create a new version. This example assumes that you already have a workbook called **book1** loaded that has already been saved off:

```
Workbooks("book1").Save
```

Saved

This property returns True or False, depending on whether the workbook has been saved pending any changes the user has entered. If the workbook has been saved and no further changes have been made, this will display True. If changes are then made, it will display False. This example assumes that you already have a workbook called **book1** loaded.

```
MsgBox Workbooks("book1").Saved
```

Sheets

Sheets work exactly the same way as the **Sheets** collection described in the section "Application Object" in this chapter.

Windows

This collection represents all the windows within the **Workbook** object. See the section "Windows Object" later in this chapter.

Worksheets

This collection represents all the worksheets within the **Workbook** object. See the section "Worksheet Object" later in this chapter.

Windows Object

This object represents all the windows within the Excel application. It is easy to confuse this with the **Workbooks** collection, but they are not always the same thing. You can open a new window by selecting Window | New Window from the Excel menu. This produces another window with a copy of the existing workbook within it. If you select Window from the Excel menu again, you will see that at the bottom of the menu bar there are now two windows, Book1:1 and Book1:2, but both are based on one workbook.

The **Windows** collection represents what you see when you select the Window option on the Excel menu, and many of this object's methods relate to the options on the Window menu, such as Split or Freeze Panes.

Main Properties, Methods, and Collections

These are the main properties, methods, and collections you will use within the **Windows** object.

Activate, ActivateNext, and ActivatePrevious

These methods allow you to activate a particular window from within your code by specifying the window within the **Windows** collection. Index with the name or number of that window and then use the **Activate** method. For this example to work correctly, you need to have a workbook already loaded called **book1**.

```
Windows("Book1").Activate
```

You can also refer to the window by its index number:

```
Windows(1).Activate
```

You can use **ActivateNext** and **ActivatePrevious** to move to windows relative to the active one:

```
ActiveWindow.ActivateNext
ActiveWindow.ActivatePrevious
```

ActiveCell

This property gives the active cell details for a particular window. The active cell is the cell that the cursor is on. The following example shows how to get the address of the active cell. You need to have a workbook called **book1** loaded; otherwise, you will get an error.

```
MsgBox Windows("Book1").ActiveCell.Address
```

ActivePane

This property is unique to the **Windows** collection because it works in terms of the window itself and not the worksheet. It allows you to get the details of the pane itself, such as the visible area—that is, the cell addresses that the user can see onscreen.

Select Windows | Split from the Excel menu so that your worksheet window splits into four panes. One pane will have the active cell on it and will also be the active pane. You can find the visible area of this pane by using the following:

```
MsgBox Windows(1).ActivePane.VisibleRange.Address
```

This assumes that you are in window number 1. This will return a range address of the visible cells within the worksheet, such as $C$1:$L$7.

ActiveSheet

You can use the **ActiveSheet** property to find out the name of the worksheet that is active within that particular window:

```
MsgBox Windows(1).ActiveSheet.Name
```

This displays **Sheet1** or whatever the active sheet is.

Caption

This property alters the caption in the window:

```
ActiveWindow.Caption = "MyWindow"
```

Interestingly, sending an empty string does not return it back to default but blanks the caption completely:

```
ActiveWindow.Caption = ""
```

If you need to change it back to its original setting, you need to save the original caption in a variable.

Close

This method closes the window just as if you clicked the X symbol in the top right-hand corner of the window. You can include optional parameters for **SaveChanges**, **FileName**, and **RouteWorkBook**.

Display Properties

The **Windows** object has a rich variety of display options that allow the following settings:

> DisplayFormulas
> DisplayGridlines
> DisplayHeadings
> DisplayHorizontalScrollBar
> DisplayOutline
> DisplayRightToLeft
> DisplayVerticalScrollBar
> DisplayWorkbookTabs
> DisplayZeros

These properties are all Boolean, which means they hold a True or False value. They reflect the settings when you select Tools | Options from the Excel menu. Click the View tab and you will see check boxes for all of these.

You can alter your display considerably by manipulating these properties, for example,

```
ActiveWindow.DisplayWorkbookTabs = False
```

This will remove the tabs from the bottom of the active window.

FreezePanes

This property works the same way as locating the cursor on a cell in the worksheet and then selecting Window | Freeze Panes from the Excel menu. It holds a Boolean value (True or False). The panes are frozen on the current cursor position.

```
ActiveWindow.FreezePanes = True
```

GridLineColor

This property alters the color of gridlines in the window display:

```
ActiveWindow.GridLineColor = QBColor(14)
```

You can also use RGB (Red Green Blue) colors.

NewWindow

This creates a new window based on the active window, just as if you selected Window | New Window from the Excel menu:

```
ActiveWindow.NewWindow
```

Panes

This is a collection of all the panes within the window that you can use to find out how many panes are in a particular window. Panes on a worksheet are a means of splitting the current worksheet window into different areas. You can do this by selecting View on the ribbon menu and then clicking Split.

```
MsgBox ActiveWindow.Panes.Count
```

The **Pane** object within the **Panes** collection allows you to access further properties and methods.

RangeSelection

This very useful property tells you what range the user selected:

```
MsgBox ActiveWindow.RangeSelection.Address
```

It displays a single cell, such as $C$10, or a range of cells if the user selects several cells, such as $B$10:$E$12.

SelectedSheets

This is another very useful collection that determines what selection the user made. You may have noticed in the previously covered **RangeSelection** property that, although the information returned was extremely useful in obtaining the cells that the user selected, there was no mention of which sheets they selected.

If you want to write professional code for Excel, you must take into account that the user can not only select cells on a particular worksheet, but can also select the same cells on other worksheets and these worksheets may be noncontiguous. For example, the user may select **Sheet1, Sheet4**, and **Sheet5**.

This method is very useful for add-ins where the user can be working across several worksheets and possibly workbooks.

By cycling through the **SelectedSheets** collection, you can find out which sheets have been selected:

```
Dim MySheet As Worksheet
For Each MySheet In ActiveWindow.SelectedSheets
    MsgBox MySheet.Name
Next MySheet
```

This displays in turn all the sheets that have been selected. Concatenate this with the **RangeSelection** to address all cells that are selected.

You will see this being used in some of the practical examples presented in Chapters 20–41.

Split

This property splits the current window into panes or sets it back to one pane. It will split at the current cursor position.

```
ActiveWindow.Split = True
```

This is the same as selecting Windows | Split from the Excel menu.

TabRatio

This property sets the size of the tab display area. Its values go from 0 to 1. It dictates how much of the bottom of the screen will be designated for the worksheet tabs and how much for the horizontal scroll bar. A value of zero means no tabs showing, only the horizontal scroll bar. A value of 1 means tabs showing, no horizontal scroll bar. A value of 0.5 means 50 percent of the area is for tabs and 50 percent is for the horizontal scroll bar.

```
ActiveWindow.TabRatio = 0.5
```

WindowState

This property will allow you to find out the state of a window or to set it to one of three states:

Window State	Property Value
Window Maximized	xlMaximized
Window Minimized	xlMinimized
Window Normal	xlNormal

```
ActiveWindow.WindowState = xlMinimized
```

This will set the Active Window to a minimized state, just as when you click the Minimize button in the top right-hand corner of the window. You can also use it to check the state of the window, as this property it is read/write.

Zoom

This sets the **Zoom** property of the window, just as if you selected View | Zoom from the Excel menu.

```
ActiveWindow.Zoom = 80
```

This will give a zoom of 80 percent.

Worksheet Object

This object represents the actual worksheet that you work on. In the hierarchy of the Excel object model, it sits below the **Workbook** object because all **Worksheets** are part of a **Workbook**.

Main Properties, Methods, and Collections

These are the properties, methods, and collections you will use within the **Worksheet** object.

Calculate

This method calculates one particular worksheet, assuming that the calculation method has been set to manual.

```
Worksheets(1).Calculate
```

This is useful if your workbook has many complex calculations and you want only a particular sheet to be calculated.

CheckSpelling

This method checks the spelling within a worksheet, just as if you selected Tools | Spelling from the Excel menu.

```
Worksheets("Sheet1").CheckSpelling
```

You can add optional parameters for **Custom Dictionary, Ignore Uppercase, Always Suggest**, and so on.

Comments

This is a collection of all the comments added to the selected worksheet. **Comments** are the additional text that can be tagged onto a cell. They show up as a red triangle in the top right-hand corner of the cell and appear in full when you hover the cursor over that cell. You can insert, delete, or edit a comment by right-clicking the cell and following the menu options on the pop-up.

You can use this to find out how many comments there are in a worksheet:

```
MsgBox Worksheets("sheet2").Comments.Count
```

Delete

This method deletes a worksheet, just as if you selected Edit | Delete Sheet from the Excel menu.

```
Worksheets("sheet1").Delete
```

PrintOut and PrintPreview

These methods allow you to print out a particular worksheet or to preview the printing of it. You must have a worksheet called "sheet2" and some data on it for this example to work.

```
Worksheets("sheet2").PrintOut
Worksheets("sheet2").PrintPreview
```

Protect

This method enables you to protect a worksheet just as if you selected Tools | Protection | Protect Sheet from the Excel menu. You can supply an optional password as a parameter—just make sure that a record is kept of it!

```
Worksheets("sheet2").Protect
Worksheets("sheet2").Protect ("apple")
```

In the first sample, no password is given, so you will not be prompted for a password to unprotect. In the second example, the password is "apple."

Range

This is a very important object within the worksheet and is described in the section "Range Object," later in this chapter.

SaveAs

This method saves the workbook under a different filename. Although it is part of the **Worksheet** object, it saves the entire workbook.

```
Worksheets("sheet2").SaveAs ("MyFile")
```

Select

This method selects a particular **Worksheet** within a **Workbook**; it is the same as clicking the tab buttons at the bottom of the window.

```
Worksheets("sheet2").Select
```

This selects Sheet2.

SetBackGroundPicture

This method places a picture, such as a BMP file, in the background of the spreadsheet:

```
Worksheets("sheet2").SetBackgroundPicture ("c:\MyPic.bmp")
```

With a little bit of imagination, you can display some hilarious sequences on your spreadsheet!

Unprotect

This method allows you to unprotect a sheet in code and works in partnership with the **Protect** method discussed earlier in this section.

```
Worksheets("Sheet2").Unprotect ("apple")
```

You can provide a password, although this is optional. If a password is required but not provided, the password dialog will appear.

Protect and **Unprotect** can be useful if you have a protected sheet that you want to make some changes to using code. You unprotect the sheet giving the password, make your changes, and then protect the sheet again giving the same password.

Visible

Setting this property to True or False dictates whether a worksheet can be seen. This is the same as hiding a worksheet using Format | Sheet | Hide from the Excel menu, for example,

```
Worksheets("sheet2").Visible = False
```

This hides Sheet2. To make the sheet visible again, set the property to True.

Range Object

This object communicates with a range of cells or individual cells and makes changes in them. Without this object, you cannot change multiple cells on a worksheet at one time.

Main Properties, Methods, and Collections

These are the main properties, methods, and collections you will use within the **Range** object.

Activate

This method activates a particular cell or range of cells to make them into the active cell or cells. For this sample to work, Sheet1 has to be the active worksheet:

```
Worksheets("sheet1").Range("a1").Activate
```

This only activates one cell, even if you enter a range such as a1.b10.

AddComment

This method allows you to add a comment into the cell defined by the range:

```
Worksheets("sheet1").Range("a1").AddComment ("MyComment")
```

If you try to add the comment to a cell that already has a comment, you will get an error message. If you enter a range of cells instead of a single cell reference, you will get an error.

To edit the comment, you need to reference the comment within the **Comments** collection. See Chapter 22 to learn how this is done.

Address

This very important property gives you the address of a range—for example, the range the user selected. You can use this property with the earlier examples.

```
MsgBox Worksheets("sheet2").Range("a3").Address
```

This will return $A$3.

BorderAround

This method draws a border around a group of cells or a single cell.

```
Worksheets("sheet2").Range("a3.b10").BorderAround (1)
```

This will put a single-line border around the range a3.b10 on sheet2 of the workbook. By changing the parameter number, you can draw other border types.

Calculate

This method calculates a specified range, assuming that autocalculation is not set to On for the workbook.

```
Worksheets("sheet2").Range("a3.d12").Calculate
```

You will see this being used as part of an application in Chapter 23.

Cells

This is a collection of cells within the range specified. You can find out how many cells are within the range, for example,

```
MsgBox Worksheets("sheet2").Range("a3.d12").Cells.Count
```

This will display 40.

CheckSpelling

This method checks the spelling in an individual range just as you can within a worksheet.

```
Worksheets("sheet2").Range("a3.d12").CheckSpelling
```

You can add optional parameters for **Custom Dictionary, Ignore Uppercase, Always Suggest**, and so on.

Clear

This method clears the contents of the range of cells. Bear in mind that it clears everything, including comments and formats.

```
Worksheets("sheet2").Range("a3.d12").Clear
```

ClearComments

This method clears comments only from the range of cells specified.

```
Worksheets("sheet2").Range("a3.d12").ClearComments
```

ClearContents

This method clears the contents of a cell or range of cells only—that is, the actual data that was typed in. It does not clear the format or the borders.

```
Worksheets("sheet2").Range("a3.d12").ClearContents
```

ClearFormats

This method clears the format of a range of cells.

```
Worksheets("sheet2").Range("a3.d12").ClearFormats
```

Column and Row

These properties return the first column number or the first column row within the range defined.

```
MsgBox Worksheets("sheet2").Range("b3.d12").Column
```

This will return 2 because B, which is the first column of the range, is column 2.

```
MsgBox Worksheets("sheet2").Range("b3.d12").Row
```

This returns 3 because the first reference of the range is B3, which is row 3.

Columns and Rows

These collections work in a similar way to the **Column** and **Row** properties just discussed, but return the actual number of columns and rows within the specified range. This is useful if you want to use a For..Next loop to work through each cell within the range:

```
MsgBox Worksheets("sheet2").Range("b3.d12").Columns.Count
```

This displays 3, which is the number of columns within the range.

```
MsgBox Worksheets("sheet2").Range("b3.d12").Rows.Count
```

This displays 10, which is the number of rows within the selected range.

ColumnWidth and RowWidth

These properties return or set the width of columns or the height of rows within the range specified:

```
Worksheets("sheet2").Range("b3.d12").ColumnWidth = 4
Worksheets("sheet2").Range("b3.d12").RowHeight = 10
```

Copy and PasteSpecial

These useful methods copy and paste a range of cells. You will see how they work in Chapter 21.

```
Worksheets("sheet2").Range("f19.g20").Copy
Worksheets("sheet2").Range("h19").PasteSpecial
```

This takes the cells at range F19.G20 on Sheet2 and pastes them to range H19 on Sheet2.

PasteSpecial allows the use of optional parameters that define whether you want to paste only values or formats. Note that you need to have something on the clipboard first!

```
Worksheets("sheet2").Range("h19").PasteSpecial Paste:=xlPasteValues
```

PrintOut and PrintPreview

When used with the **Range** object, these methods will allow print preview and printout of the specified range only.

```
Worksheets("sheet2").Range("f19.g20").PrintPreview
Worksheets("sheet2").Range("f19.g20").PrintOut
```

Replace

A useful method that does exactly what it says and replaces a specified character found within the range with another one:

```
Worksheets("sheet2").Range("f19.g20").Replace "a", "b"
```

This replaces all the lowercase *a*'s with lowercase *b*'s.

Select

This important method allows you to select a range of cells in code:

```
Worksheets("sheet2").Range("f19.g20").Select
```

This selects the range F19 to G20 just as if you had dragged the cursor across the range yourself.

Text

This property returns the text in the cell of the range. The range can only be a single cell; otherwise, you will get an error. The name **Text** is not strictly true because it can also return a number as a text string. You cannot write back to this property in order to put a value into a cell—you need to use the **Value** property to do this.

```
MsgBox Worksheets("sheet2").Range("f26").Text
```

Value

This property is similar to **Text**, but it is read/write, so you can write data into a spreadsheet with it:

```
MsgBox Worksheets("sheet2").Range("f26").Value
Worksheets("sheet2").Range("f26").Value = 10
```

When reading you can only use a single cell value or you will get a Type Mismatch error, but when writing you can set a range of cells to one value:

```
Worksheets("sheet2").Range("f26.g40").Value = 10
```

The value of the **Text** property is also 10, but you cannot write to it.

WrapText

This property sets the **WrapText** flag for a range of cells. You can also read the value of the property. This sets whether the text will wrap within a cell or stay on one line and spill into the adjacent cells:

```
Worksheets("sheet2").Range("f26.g40").WrapText = True
```

Using Excel to Interact with Other Office Programs

A ll Microsoft Office applications use VBA as their underlying macro language, and they all have their own object model in the same way that Excel has. Because of this, Excel VBA provides an enormous advantage over non-Microsoft programming languages when it comes to driving other Office programs. For example, you can create a Word document from within Excel without Word ever appearing onscreen. This may sound farfetched, but it is very easy to do. For example, you may design some code to manipulate data on a spreadsheet. Your user may require the output to end up in a Word document or as part of that document. Excel gives you the facility to open an external Word document, enter your data into it, and then save it, without even having any knowledge of how the file structure works in Word.

This can be done by using the CreateObject method in VBA. In order to use CreateObject, you must first add a reference in your application to the appropriate Microsoft Office Object Library file—in this case, the Word Object Library. If you have Office installed, this file will already be available and will automatically appear in the References list without your having to browse for its location. If you do not have all of Microsoft Office installed, then you may not have this library file available unless it has been installed previously as part of another application.

When you add a reference to an Object Library, it then allows you to create objects for that application and to use the object model of that application, just as if you were programming in VBA inside that application.

You can add a reference by selecting Tools | References from the menus. All available reference files will appear in a dialog. You need to select the Microsoft Word Object Library and check the check box next to it, as shown in Figure 14-1.

Note that the location shown at the bottom of the References window points to an OLB file that is basically the Object Library for Word. The location points to the OLB file in the directory where Microsoft Office was originally installed. Click OK and you will be ready to use Word in VBA.

Here is a sample of code to create a new Word document and to save it to the local hard drive. This code will produce the same results whether Word is loaded or not, but it always looks more spectacular if Word is not running onscreen—it will look as if you have done something very clever!

```
Sub Test_Word()
Dim oWd As Word.Application, oWdoc As Word.Document
Set oWd = CreateObject("Word.Application")
Set oWdoc = oWd.Documents.Add
oWdoc.Sections(1).Range.Text = "My new Word Document"
oWdoc.SaveAs ("MyTest")
oWdoc.Close
oWd.Quit
Set oWdoc = Nothing
Set oWd = Nothing
End Sub
```

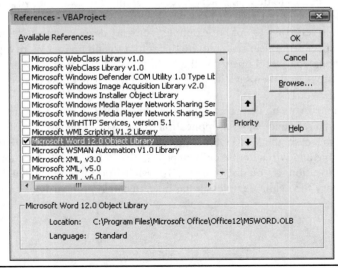

Figure 14-1 *Selecting the Microsoft Word Object Library*

The first line declares the variables for the application and the document objects. Because you have a reference to the Object Library included, you will see the Word objects, methods, and properties appearing in the drop-down lists as you type the code in. If you did not have the reference to the Object Library, VBA would not recognize these object types and the application would fail.

You then use the application variable (**oWd**) to hold the created object for the Word application. Note that in the **CreateObject** parameter, the description goes inside quotation marks. This description uses the class name for the object and does not appear automatically because it is being entered as a string. You are not offered a list of choices for it. The string "Word.Application" is the class name for the application object within Word, which is why it is used here.

The **oWdoc** variable is now set to hold a new document based on the application variable (**oWd**). This is exactly the same as if you had loaded Word and then clicked the Office Start button and created a new Word document.

The text "My new Word Document" is then added to the first section of the document. This appears on the first section because you loaded the Word document, effectively in the same way as if you had opened Word and then opened the file in Word. The cursor automatically defaults to the top of the document when this happens, and exactly the same thing happens in your code, because you are emulating the document being opened.

The document is saved as MyTest to the Documents folder on the local hard drive, and the Word document is then closed. Leaving it open causes reservation problems, which means that your application has exclusive write access to it. If anyone loads this document into Word, they can only load it as read-only because your application has the reservation on it. This can also cause problems when exiting Excel. Because this is a virtual application, the document stays in memory if it is not closed (even if Excel is shut down) properly, even though Excel only had a reference to it. However, this particular instance of Word does not appear on the Windows taskbar because it was created virtually in code. The only way to detect its presence is to look in Task Manager.

If you do not close the virtual object down properly, when Windows shuts down, the virtual Word application will ask if the document needs saving because it still considers that there is an open document. This can be extremely confusing to the user, since they may have no idea that a Word application was open. To avoid this situation, the variables **oWd** and **oWdoc** are set to Nothing, and all memory held by them is released.

Try loading your newly created file into Word and you will see that it works as a perfectly normal Word document, just as if you created it using Microsoft Word.

This is a very simple example of manipulating Word from within Excel using VBA. This can be very useful—for example, you could have a standard document with tables that the macro populated from the spreadsheet data. You can run your macro and the data will be transferred into the document tables.

Recently, I had the task of writing a program to populate an SLA (Service Level Agreement) Report. The SLA Report was a Word document with many tables of data and charts, but the input came from nine spreadsheets. Using the methods just detailed, I was able to write VBA code that worked through the individual spreadsheets, extracted the relevant data, and placed the figures in the correct tables or charts in the Word document. Previously, it had taken someone half a day to do this manually, but the code accomplished it in under five minutes.

```
Sub Test_Word()
Dim oWd As Word.Application, oWdoc As Word.Document
Dim orx As Word.Range, ot As Word.Table
Set oWd = CreateObject("Word.Application")
Set oWdoc = oWd.Documents.Add
Set orx = oWdoc.Range
Set ot = oWdoc.Tables.Add(r, 4, 5)
ot.Cell(1, 1).Range.Text = "test"
oWdoc.SaveAs ("MyTest")
oWdoc.Close
oWd.Quit
Set oWdoc = Nothing
Set oWd = Nothing
End Sub
```

This example cannot be done from within Excel unless you manually copy and paste, which could get laborious if there is a lot of data. This is a good example of the macro language giving the user enormous power to automate tasks within Microsoft Office and enabling you to work outside the menu structure that Microsoft has put in place.

Driving Microsoft Outlook

You can use exactly the same technology to drive Microsoft Outlook and make it send e-mails from your spreadsheet or capture address book entries. Of course, there are e-mail features within Excel for e-mailing an entire spreadsheet, but this method lets you supply just a part of the sheet.

In order to use this code, you must have Microsoft Outlook installed on your computer (not Outlook Express or Windows Mail), although Outlook does not need to be actively running for this to work.

Start off by adding a reference to the Object Library file for Outlook. You do this by selecting Tools | References from the Visual Basic Editor menu. You select the Microsoft Outlook Object Library and then click the check box next to it, as shown in Figure 14-2. Next enter the following code into a module:

```
Sub Test_Outlook()
Dim oFolder As Outlook.MAPIFolder
Dim oItem As Outlook.MailItem
Dim oOutlook As New Outlook.Application
Dim MoOutlook As Outlook.NameSpace
Set MoOutlook = oOutlook.GetNamespace("MAPI")
Set oFolder = MoOutlook.GetDefaultFolder(olFolderOutbox)
Set oItem = oFolder.Items.Add(olMailItem)
```

```
With oItem
      .Recipients.Add ("richard.shepherd@anywhere.com")
      .Subject = "Test Excel Email"
      .Body = "This is a test of an email from Excel VBA"
      .Importance = olImportanceHigh
      .Send
End With
Set oItem = Nothing
Set oFolder = Nothing
End Sub
```

When this code is run, you will get a pop-up dialog warning that e-mail address information is being accessed in Outlook. This is to prevent e-mail viruses, which use exactly the same code as this.

The first four lines set up variables based on the Microsoft Outlook types. These are for the Outlook application, the NameSpace, the Outlook folder, and the Mail item. The variable **MoOutlook** is set to point to the namespace MAPI. This represents one of the messaging service provider layers that Outlook depends on for data storage. MAPI is the only type of namespace that Outlook supports.

The variable **oFolder** is then set to the default folder for the Outbox for the namespace. This sets up an object that represents the Outbox, and into which you can then place your mail item. You do this by setting the variable **oItem** to a new mail item within that folder. This is exactly the same as when you open a new mail item in Microsoft Outlook itself. The code then goes through all the stages it normally does from the front end of Microsoft Outlook to create your e-mail.

The address of the recipient is added. At this point, you can add in your own address as a string to try out the example. If the recipient is internal to your network and is on the Outlook address

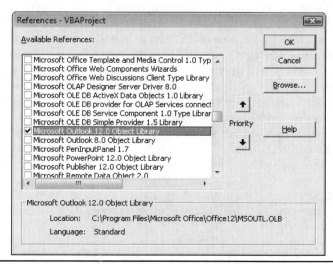

Figure 14-2   *Selecting the Object Library file for Microsoft Outlook*

list, you can simply use the name. The subject is what you would see in the title for the message. The body is the e-mail text itself. Don't forget you can use Chr(13), Chr(10), or vbCrLf to provide carriage returns in a string so that you can insert a "Regards" statement at the end.

Importance allows you to set what priority you want the e-mail to have. The Importance constants are shown in a list box as you type this statement in and are as follows:

```
olImportanceHigh
olImportanceNormal
olImportanceLow
```

Send is the actual sending of the e-mail. Once the e-mail has been sent, the variables **oItem** and **oFolder** are set to Nothing, and the memory is released.

Note that this uses the same technology as many e-mail viruses do, most notably the infamous Love Bug virus. You need to be careful with this code because if you're not, it can end up sending a lot of automated e-mails, which can clog up the mail system and make for angry recipients.

Microsoft has added security to later versions of Outlook, so, although this code will still work very well, the user will get a message box advising that e-mail is about to be sent. In any instructions to users you provide, you need to point out that this will happen when they use your e-mail macro, and they need to okay the e-mail being sent to them.

Driving Excel from Other Office Programs

In the previous sections, you saw how Excel can be used to drive other Microsoft applications such as Word or Outlook.

By the same token, these other applications can also be used to control Excel. For example, you can write a macro in Word or Access that populates an Excel spreadsheet and then saves it. Excel does not actually have to be running, and the spreadsheet itself does not have to be seen on screen. If Excel is running, then a new workbook will be created, but you do have the option to set the **Visible** property for your virtual application to False so that the spreadsheet never appears. When running this type of application, it is quite entertaining to set the **Visible** property to True and watch the numbers appearing in the spreadsheet as if some ghostly operator were adding them. I have seen it impress a number of senior managers, but the problem is that if someone touches the keyboard or even closes your spreadsheet, it can cause unpredictable results. If you set the **Visible** property to False, there is nothing the user can do to upset the procedure, and they need not even be aware that it is running.

The example I am going to use creates an Excel spreadsheet from within a Word document. VBA works exactly the same in all Microsoft Office applications, except that the object model is obviously too different from application to application to take the functionality of the application into account.

Once you load Word, you need to enter the VBA code window. This works exactly the same as in Excel: press ALT-F11. The code window has exactly the same functionality as the one that you are used to in Excel.

When you used a different application from Excel, you had to put in a reference to the Object Library file first. We have to do the same thing in Word by putting in a reference to the Excel Object Library in order to tell Word how to find the Excel object model.

You use Tools | References from the Visual Basic Editor menu as before, but this time you select the Excel Object Library and check the box next to it, as shown in Figure 14-3.

This now gives your code all it needs to manipulate Excel. Insert a module by selecting Insert | Module from the Code menu, and then enter the following code:

```
Sub Test_Excel()
Dim oEapp As Excel.Application
Set oEapp = CreateObject("Excel.Application")
Dim oWBook As Workbook, oWSheet As Worksheet
Set oWBook = oEapp.Workbooks.Add
Set oWSheet = oWBook.Worksheets(1)
oWSheet.Range("a1").Value = "My test Excel spreadsheet"
oWBook.SaveAs ("TestExcel")
oWBook.Close
oEapp.Quit
Set oWSheet = Nothing
Set oWBook = Nothing
End Sub
```

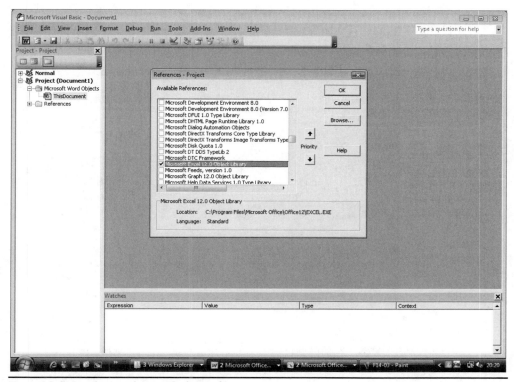

Figure 14-3   *Selecting the Excel Library file*

When this is run, it will create a spreadsheet called TestExcel and cell A1 on sheet1 will have the value "My test Excel spreadsheet." The code creates a variable **oEApp** to hold the Excel application object. It then sets that variable as an Excel object. Variables **oWBook** and **oWSheet** are then created to represent a workbook and a worksheet, and the workbook is set to a new workbook, which is added into the **Workbooks** collection. The **Worksheet** object is set to the first worksheet in the **Worksheets** collection (there must always be at least one worksheet in a workbook).

Cell A1 on the first sheet is set to read "My test Excel spreadsheet," and the workbook is then set as "TestExcel." The workbook is then closed by calling the **Close** method. This is the same as clicking the Office Start button at the top left-hand corner of the worksheet screen and then clicking Close in the menu in the pop-up window.

Next the Application is closed, which is the same as clicking the Office Start button on the worksheet screen and clicking the Exit Excel button at the bottom of the pop-up window. Finally, the workbook and worksheet variables are set to Nothing in order to release all memory used by the Excel objects.

I hope this has given you a taste of the immense power of the VBA language and how you can manipulate other Microsoft applications from within it.

Advanced Techniques in Excel VBA

In this part, you'll learn how to create charts and graphs in code; work with external databases; and use API (application programming interface) calls to do things such as play a WAV file, use XML files, manipulate RibbonX, and work with pivot tables. I'll also discuss class modules and animation. These are powerful topics that will allow you to do some very unusual things with VBA and Excel.

CHAPTER
15

Charts and Graphs

I n Excel 2007 Microsoft has completely redesigned the charting engine and has made it
part of the Shapes object as well as being an object in its own right. Charts can either be
created on a sheet of their own or embedded into an existing worksheet. They are
manipulated in much the same way, but the chart sheet is a **Chart** object, whereas the
embedded chart is part of the shapes collection for that worksheet.

The charting wizard no longer exists on the front end. You will find it as a method of the
Chart object, but it no longer works as expected in Excel 2007 and is there primarily for
backward compatibility.

Beware if you are updating a spreadsheet for Excel 2007 that uses the Chart Wizard. You
will need to modify your code as shown in the next example.

You can create charts and graphs very simply using VBA. You use it in exactly the same
way that you would from within the Excel application, but all the commands and properties
are set using VBA. Because everything you can do as an Excel user is represented in the
object model, it is quite straightforward to do this. First, set up a range of data suitable for a
pie chart, as shown in Figure 15-1.

Give the range the name **ChartData** by right-clicking the range and then clicking Name a
Range in the pop-up menu. Click OK to close the dialog. Now insert the following code into
a module:

```
Sub test_chart()
ActiveSheet.Shapes.AddChart.Select
    ActiveSheet.Shapes(1).Top = 10
    ActiveSheet.Shapes(1).Left = 10
    ActiveChart.ChartType = xl3DPie
    ActiveChart.PlotArea.Select
    ActiveChart.SetSourceData Source:=Range("ChartData")
```

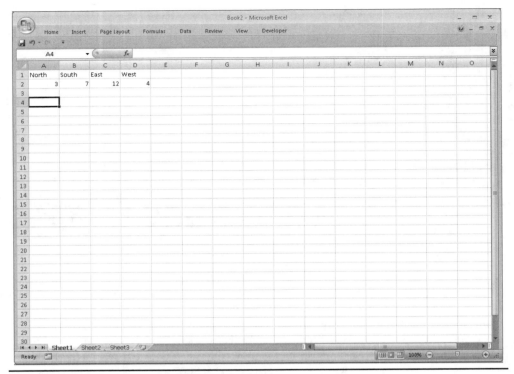

Figure 15-1 *A data range suitable for a pie chart*

```
        ActiveChart.HasTitle = True
        ActiveChart.ChartTitle.Text = "A chart"
End Sub
```

The code uses the Shapes collection for the active sheet to create the chart. This creates the chart as an embedded object in the active worksheet. The shape created by the chart can be given Left and Top coordinates to specify its position on the worksheet (notice that this is not available within the **Chart** object). The chart type is set to a 3D Pie chart, and the source range is set to "ChartData," which was the range that you defined earlier in the example above. Notice that the **HasTitle** property has to be set to True before defining the text for the title of the chart.

Run this code, and your chart should look like Figure 15-2.

You can also modify this code slightly so that the chart is created as a sheet on its own:

```
Sub AddNewChart()
    Charts.Add
    ActiveChart.ChartType = xl3DPie
    ActiveChart.PlotArea.Select
    ActiveChart.SetSourceData Source:=Range("ChartData")
```

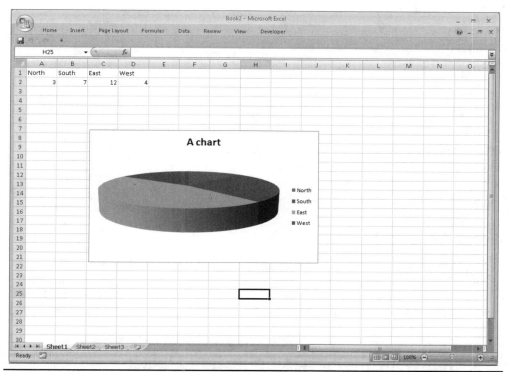

Figure 15-2   *A pie chart created using the VBA example*

```
    ActiveChart.HasTitle = True
    ActiveChart.ChartTitle.Text = "A chart"
End Sub
```

In terms of the Chart Type, Excel versions 97 and onward have built-in parameters to define the various types of charts. These all correspond to the gallery in the Chart Wizard that you see if you insert a chart into a spreadsheet:

Constant	Description	Value
xlArea	Area Chart	1
xlBar	Bar Chart	2
xlColumn	Column Chart	3
xlLine	Line Chart	4
xlPie	Pie Chart	5
xlRadar	Radar Chart	−4151
xlXYScatter	XY Scatter Chart	−4169

Constant	Description	Value
xlCombination	Combination Chart	–4111
xl3DArea	3-D Area Chart	–4098
xl3DBar	3-D Bar Chart	–4099
xl3DColumn	3-D Column Chart	–4100
xl3DLine	3-D Line Chart	–4101
xl3DPie	3-D Pie Chart	–4102
xl3DSurface	3-D Surface Chart	–4103
xlDoughnut	Doughnut Chart	–4120

For the **PlotBy** property, you use the following parameters:

```
xlRows = 1
xlColumns = 2
```

This parameter indicates to the charting engine how the chart data is shown on the spreadsheet, whether the source range goes across the worksheet with headings at the top of each column or down the worksheet with headings on each row. If this is not set, the default is xlColumns, which means that the headings are considered to be at the top of each column.

Working with the Series Collection Object

In Excel 2003 you could use the Chart Wizard method to manipulate your charts using a number of parameters. The Chart Wizard no longer exists in Excel 2007, so it is a more complicated procedure to make changes to a standard chart. You do this using series collections.

You can use VBA to turn the data labels on or off on the Pie Chart by setting the **HasDataLabels** property to True or False:

```
ActiveChart.SeriesCollection(1).HasDataLabels = True
```

You can also explode slices of the Pie Chart:

```
ActiveChart.SeriesCollection(1).Explosion = 8
```

The **Explosion** property is a Long Integer and works on the basis that each bit represents one slice in the Pie Chart. As there are four slices, setting this to 8 explodes all slices. If you set it to 4, this would explode the third slice only of the chart. Setting the property to 0 indicates that no slices are exploded.

You can use VBA to manipulate the appearance of labels on your chart. The example assumes that you have a chart called Chart1 on the active sheet of your workbook.

```
ActiveSheet.ChartObjects("Chart 1").Activate
ActiveChart.SetElement (msoElementDataLabelCenter)
ActiveChart.SeriesCollection(1).DataLabels.ShowValue = True
ActiveChart.SeriesCollection(1).DataLabels.ShowCategoryName = True
```

The code assumes that the chart that you are working with is called Chart 1. If you need to find the name of a chart, click the chart. Chart Tools menu items will appear on the menu bar. Click Layout and the Chart Name will be displayed in the right-hand control of the ribbon.

The preceding code sets the label on each slice to display both the value and the category name, which is the name declared on the Legend of the chart.

Exporting a Chart as a Picture File

A chart can be easily exported as a GIF, JPEG, or PNG file using the following code. This example assumes that you have a chart already defined on the active sheet of your workbook.

```
Sub OutputChart()
  Dim ExportFile As String

  ActiveSheet.ChartObjects(1).Activate
  ExportFile = ThisWorkbook.Path & "\" & ActiveChart.Name & ".gif"

  ActiveChart.Export Filename:=ExportFile, FilterName:="GIF"
End Sub
```

Using Macro Recording

The chart object model is far more complicated than it was for Excel 2003, and it is often quite difficult to see how to specify commands to do particular actions. A very good way to find out is to use the macro recorder on the Developer item on the menu bar.

Once you have worked out how to do a particular action via the front end of Excel, turn on the macro recorder by clicking the Developer item in the menu and then clicking the Record Macro icon in the Code control of the ribbon. Take your actions and, when you have finished, click the Developer item in the menu bar and click the Stop Recording icon in the Code control of the ribbon.

A macro will have been created of the actions taken. This is not absolutely foolproof, but it will give a good idea of how the VBA code is put together for your particular task.

CHAPTER 6

Working with Databases

Y ou can make your code interact with any database as long as the database is ODBC (Open Database Connectivity) compatible and the appropriate driver is available. ODBC allows applications to access a database in a standard way from many different languages, including VBA. This can be extremely useful if you want to bring data from a database into your spreadsheet. For example, you may want to import data from an accounting system into your application, such as when the accounting system doesn't provide a needed functionality, but the database has the data you are interested in. If the database has an ODBC driver available, you can bring the data into your VBA application to use as needed.

Databases such as Microsoft Access, Microsoft SQL Server, and Oracle all support ODBC, and provided you have the relevant permissions to the database, you can read data into your spreadsheet and even write data back if need be. Writing data back should be done with extreme care, however, because you can easily destroy the integrity of a relational database in this way. If you change an ID number in a field that is used for a relationship into another table, then the database may appear to be correct, but its relationship and integrity are totally blown.

The safest way is to only use a read-only ID on the database, and this is probably all that the database owner will grant you.

ODBC Links

You need to first set up an ODBC link to point to the database that you want to work with. You do this by selecting Control Panel in Windows, then Administrative Tools, and then Data Sources (ODBC). You will see the ODBC Data Source Administrator dialog, as shown in Figure 16-1.

If you do not already have a data source name (DSN) set up for the database, click Add. This will give you a list of available database drivers, as shown in Figure 16-2. A DSN is exactly what it says: it is a name of an ODBC link to a database that you can use to refer to that ODBC link. There is a wide variety of these and some have titles in different languages, but I am going to concentrate on Microsoft Access because it is an integral part of Microsoft Office, and if you have Excel, you will most likely have Access.

Double-click the Access driver (Microsoft Access Driver *.mdb) , and you will be taken into the screen in Figure 16-3. Enter the Data Source Name as **NWind** and the Description as **Northwind Database**. These two items are merely for identification purposes. This gives a name (DSN) that you can use in your code and a description that states what it is about. If you prefer, the Description field can be left blank because it only identifies what the DSN is about in the DSN screen; it is not used in your code at all.

Click Select and select the NorthWind database. This is a sample database (.MDB or .ACCDB file) supplied with Microsoft Access and should be among the Access files. If you

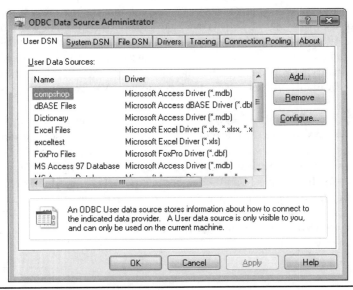

Figure 16-1   *Setting up a data source name*

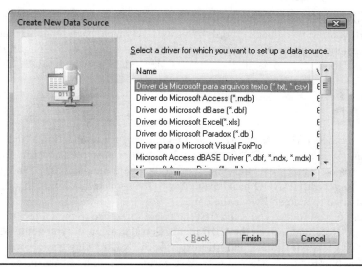

Figure 16-2   *Selecting an ODBC driver for the data source*

cannot find it, locate it by using Search and the Files and Folders option in Windows. Click OK, and you have now created an ODBC link (DSN) to the database with the name of NWind. Click OK again and close the Control Panel.

You can set up ODBC links to other databases on servers such as SQL or Oracle in the same way. However, you need to know the name of the server and the name of the database,

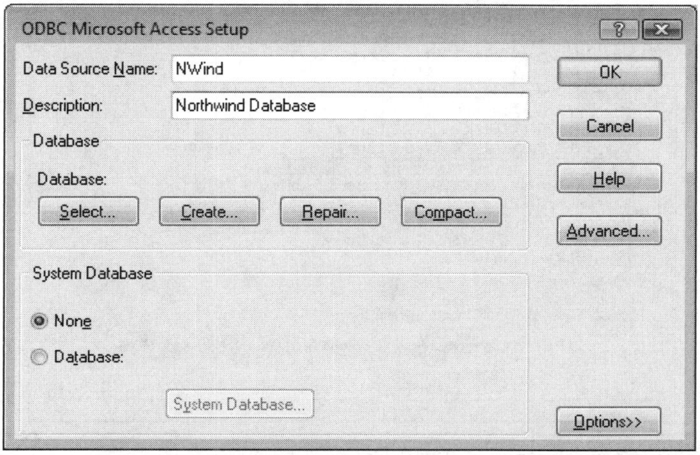

Figure 16-3   *Final steps for setting up a DSN*

and you also need an ID and password that give at least Select permission on the SQL Server (since you will want to bring back records). Settings may have been made so that you do not need this information, but this would give anyone the opportunity of logging in if they knew the connection. You may also need other settings, depending on which ODBC driver is used.

Using ADO

ActiveX Data Objects (ADO) is the Microsoft technology for connecting to databases. ADO is a Component Object Model (COM) that you can direct to use the data from the ODBC link that you just created. The ODBC link tells your code where the database is and gives the ID and password to get into it. ADO provides you with the tools to hook into that database using the ODBC link and to read and write the data.

To use ADO in your code, you must first include a reference to the Object Library by selecting Tools | References from the VBE menu. Scroll down until you get to Microsoft ActiveX Data Objects 6.0 Library and Microsoft ActiveX Data Objects Recordset 6.0 Library, as shown in Figure 16-4. You may have earlier version numbers of these going back to version 2, depending on what version of Windows you are running, but they will still work in the same way. If you do not have Version 6.0, use the latest version that you have. Set both the check boxes on the left and click OK.

It is important to have this reference so that it will give you full functionality to ADO, and it is also good programming practice.

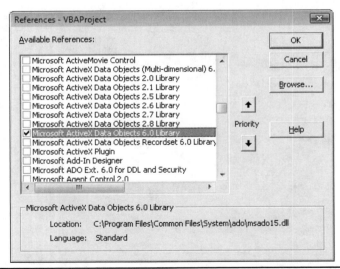

Figure 16-4   *Putting in a reference to Active Data Objects*

Now you can use the following code example:

```
Sub Test_Db()
Dim MyCon As New Connection
Dim co as long
MyCon.Open "NWind"
Set rs = New Recordset
rs.Open "select firstname,lastname,title from employees", MyCon, _
adOpenForwardOnly, adLockReadOnly, adCmdText
co = 1
Do Until rs.EOF
    ActiveSheet.Range("a" & co).Value = rs![first name]

    ActiveSheet.Range("b" & co).Value = rs![last name]

    ActiveSheet.Range("c" & co).Value = rs![job title]

    co = co + 1

    rs.MoveNext
    Loop
rs.Close
MyCon.Close
End Sub
```

The first thing this code does is set up an object called **MyCon** as a **Connection** object. The **Connection** object is then opened using the data source name NWind that you set up earlier and a connection to the database is established based on the information you provided in the DSN.

Next, the code creates a **Recordset** object. A **Recordset** is an object representing a chunk of data that can be a query, a table, or a SQL statement. A query is effectively a named SQL statement. A table is a set of data displayed in table format, and a query and a SQL statement are effectively the same thing, but the detail of it is issued directly to form the recordset.

In this case, the recordset takes data from the Employees table. Parameters are included for cursors and record locking.

A variable called **co** is set to 1, which gives a dynamic reference point to write data into the spreadsheet row by row. As you write each row of data in, this is incremented to point to the next row.

Make sure you include the line **rs.MoveNext**. This is the instruction to move the record pointer to the next record in the recordset. Leaving out this command is a common and easy mistake to make, but if you do not include it, the same record will be read each time, and it will never reach the **EOF** (end of file) marker—the code will never finish and will appear to crash.

The code then loops through, reading a row from the database and writing the row of data into the spreadsheet, until it hits the **EOF** marker on the recordset, meaning all records have been viewed.

Using the **ActiveSheet** object, the code then writes into columns A, B, and C the fields first_name, last_name, and job_title from the recordset. Notice that on the **Recordset** object an exclamation point (!) is used instead of a dot (.). This is to indicate that you are using a field name on the **Recordset** object and not a property or a method, for which you would use a dot.

Finally, the **Recordset** and **Connection** are closed because there can be access problems for other users if these are left open. Your spreadsheet should now look like Figure 16-5.

This VBA code allows you to execute queries on a database and to draw the data onto any position on your workbook. By using an update query, you can also write data back into the database.

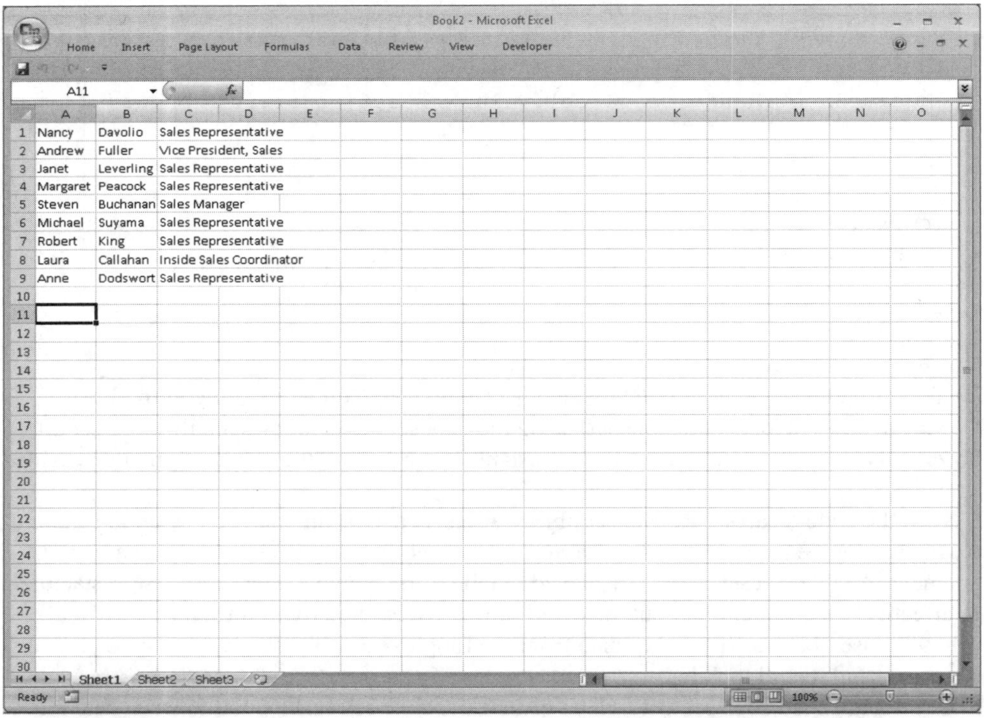

Figure 16-5   *Results of running the example to draw data from a database table*

API Calls

Although the Excel object model and VBA code are very comprehensive in providing you with methods to do various operations on the spreadsheet, you may have noticed that there are a number of functions having to do with Windows that you still cannot do. Even Visual Basic itself does not provide the direct means to do some of these.

For example, you cannot find the amount of available space on a disk device. You cannot read the keyboard directly—you only can read incoming keys on a user form, provided that the form or control has the focus. You cannot determine where the mouse position is. Obviously, there are ways of doing these things, since Windows Explorer can tell you how much space is on your hard disk and Windows knows which key you pressed. VBA does not have the direct commands to deal with these subjects, but it does allow access to the WIN32 application programming interface (API), which in turn allows you to access a treasure chest of information from Windows directly.

API calls are a very advanced subject and can provide an enormous amount of extra functionality to your programs. It is not the purpose of this book to go too deeply into API calls, however, but I will show you some examples of how they can be used to your advantage.

What Is an API Call?

The API (application programming interface) allows you to access the built-in programming functions from DLL and EXE files, particularly the ones that drive Windows. Other third-party applications also use DLL files for libraries of functions, and if you are lucky, you may even be supplied with documentation on how to work the functions.

The purpose of this chapter is to give you an idea of how you can use API calls within your code. The examples given are not comprehensive, and there are large numbers of API calls that you could use for different functions. There are some huge books available on API calls if you wish to investigate this topic further.

API calls are normally functions that return a value of some type, although they often take some action at the same time. There are also subroutines that only take action (remember the distinction made in Chapter 3 between a function and a subroutine). To use them, you must first declare the function or subroutine you wish to use, and this is the hardest part. The **Declare** statement sets up the description of the function or subroutine statement within the dynamic link library (DLL) file. It describes which DLL will be used, what the name of the function or subroutine is, and what the parameters to be passed are. The declarations are quite complicated, and if any mistake is made, the call will not work and may even crash the system. Before making an API call, make sure that your file has been saved, because these calls are not very forgiving when things go wrong. You may find that you have to reboot your computer to get things running again, and this will lose any data that you have not saved. As I mentioned, API calls are not very forgiving if they go wrong, and pressing CTRL-BREAK to stop them will have no effect whatsoever. For example, simply passing the wrong type of value is enough to cause a crash. However, they are an example of the wonderful versatility of VBA, and when used properly, they can provide functionality not normally available in Excel.

Using an API Call

Here are some examples of API calls and how to use them within your VBA code.

Getting Disk Space

For this example, you are going to use an API call that gets the spare disk space from a disk device.

First of all, you must make the declaration. You do this in the declarations section of a module (at the top of the module page). The syntax for this particular declaration is as follows:

```
Private Declare Function GetDiskFreeSpaceEx Lib "kernel32"  _
Alias "GetDiskFreeSpaceExA" (ByVal lpDirectoryName As  _
String, lpFreeBytesAvailableToCaller As Currency,  _
lpTotalNumberOfBytes As Currency, lpTotalNumberOfFreeBytes  _
As Currency) As Long
```

This is quite a long statement, and it has to be completely accurate to work. If you have access to Visual Basic, all the API declarations are contained in a file called API32.TXT and can easily be copied and pasted into your declarations. Further information can be obtained from the Microsoft Developer Network (MSDN) at msdn.microsoft.com, which is the perfect place to find more advanced information on Excel VBA and API calls.

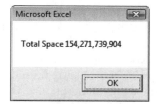

Figure 17-1 *Getting the total space (first message box) from a disk drive using the GetDiskFreeSpaceEx API call*

Basically, this statement sets up a reference to the kernel32.dll that resides in the Windows system directory. It specifies the way parameters must be used and what they are called. Its purpose is to put a function into your code that you can use to call this library function from kernel32.dll.

The next step is to put in code to call this function:

```
Sub Test_Api()
Dim x as Double
Dim FreeBytesAvailableToCaller As Currency, TotalNumberOfBytes As _
Currency,  TotalNumberOfFreeBytes As Currency
x = GetDiskFreeSpaceEx("c:\", FreeBytesAvailableToCaller, _
TotalNumberOfBytes, TotalNumberOfFreeBytes)
MsgBox "Total Space " & Format(TotalNumberOfBytes * 10000, "#,##0")
MsgBox "Free Space " & Format(TotalNumberOfFreeBytes * 10000, "#,##0")
End Sub
```

This code sets up variables to hold the values returned by the API call. The actual value returned through the variable calling it (in this case, **x**) is related to errors. It has a value of 1 for success.

The call is then made passing the root directory "C:\" and the variables already defined. It is then a simple case of multiplying the value by 10,000 (this is because of the way in which the API call returns the values) and formatting to comma format for easy display. A message box (as shown in Figure 17-1) then displays the result.

You can check the values by going into Windows Explorer (right-click the Windows Start button in the bottom left-hand corner of the screen and select Explore), selecting the root of C:, right-clicking this, and selecting Properties. You will see a pie chart showing usage of your C: drive, and the values for total space and free space will agree exactly to numbers displayed by the preceding code.

Reading from and Writing to INI Files

API calls can also be used for reading from and writing to INI files. INI files have now been superseded by the Windows Registry in terms of maintaining program parameters and settings, but they are still useful as a simple way of keeping information.

There are also API calls for the Windows Registry, but you need a very good knowledge of what you are doing if you are going to use API calls to alter the Registry. If you make a mistake, you will end up having to reinstall a particular program related to that setting, and at worst you may damage the integrity of Windows and end up having to reinstall Windows.

One of the useful functions of API calls is creating INI files for your program. INI files are a means of storing settings for your program, such as for control settings that you want to be sticky, or details of user settings for individual applications. Variables and properties in VBA only hold their values while the program is present. Once you close down the program, all is lost, and everything returns to default.

An example might be a text box that holds a directory pathname that is set by the user. The user might put in a different pathname, but when the program is closed, it reverts to the default on reloading. This is irritating for the user, who has to keep putting in the pathname.

The INI file holds this information locally so that it can be retrieved when the program is loaded next time. Of course, you could use a portion of the spreadsheet to store these values, but this could easily be overwritten by other data.

There are two declarations that can be used for your INI file. (There are other declarations for reading and writing to INI files, but you are going to use these in the example.)

```
Private Declare Function GetPrivateProfileString Lib "kernel32" Alias _
"GetPrivateProfileStringA" (ByVal lpApplicationName As String, ByVal _
lpKeyName As Any, ByVal lpDefault As String, ByVal lpReturnedString As _
String, ByVal nSize As Long, ByVal lpFileName As String) As Long

Private Declare Function WritePrivateProfileString Lib "kernel32" Alias _
"WritePrivateProfileStringA" (ByVal lpApplicationName As String, ByVal _
lpKeyName As Any, ByVal lpString As Any, ByVal lpFileName As String) As _
Long
```

These need to be added into the declarations section of a module (top of the module page). They set up references to the kernel32.dll file and describe how the parameters will be passed. You can then use code to pass the parameters and write to the file:

```
Sub Test_INI()
x = WritePrivateProfileString("Parameters", "Path", "C:\temp\", "myini.ini")
s$ = Space$(256)
x = GetPrivateProfileString("Parameters", "Path", "", s$, 256, "myini.ini")
MsgBox s$
MsgBox x
End Sub
```

The first line writes the INI file. If the file is not already there, it is automatically created. The default location is in the Windows directory, although you can change this by adding a pathname onto the filename.

The first parameter (**Parameters**) is the section of the INI file to write the new string. The second parameter is the keyname or the entry to set; if set to Null, it will delete all keys within this section. The third parameter is the value to write for the key. This is "C:\temp\"; if set to Null, it will delete the existing string for that key. The fourth parameter is the name of the INI file. You can use any suffix; you do not have to use an INI suffix. This is quite useful if you want to hide some settings and wish to disguise your INI file—you can give it a DLL or EXE suffix so that it looks like a program file on casual inspection.

This now creates MYINI.INI. If you look in your Windows directory, you will see that the file has been created. If you double-click it, it will be loaded into Notepad because it is a text file, and should look like this:

```
[Parameters]
Path=C:\temp\
```

The next API call reads the path back in. However, before this can happen, you must create a variable for it to be placed in.

The **Space$** command has been used to create a string of 256 spaces. Also, this variable must be specified as a string; otherwise, errors will occur. The return value comes back as a string, so it must be placed into a string variable.

GetPrivateProfileString works in a similar way to **WritePrivateProfileString**, but there are more parameters to pass. The first and second parameters are the same as before and give details of the section and the key to be read. The third parameter has a default value to return if the entry is not found. The fourth parameter contains the variable name for the result to be passed to. The fifth parameter contains the maximum number of characters to load into the variable. The sixth parameter is the filename to search for.

The variable calling the API (**x**) will give the number of characters returned. **S$** will contain the key, terminated by a Null character. If the keyname is left as Null, then all entries in that section will be returned, each terminated with a Null character.

Both these API calls are very forgiving in their operation. If the file is not there, it is created. If the key is not there, it is created. If the file does not exist when you use the read command, then a Null value will be returned.

This method is often used in programs to keep track of user settings so that when the user enters the program subsequently, it is set to that user's personal settings.

Microsoft no longer uses INI files; Windows uses keys in the Registry to record this information.

Read Keyboard Activity

Another useful purpose of API calls is to read the keyboard and find out if a certain key has been pressed. There are events on user forms to manage keyboard events, but these only apply to a particular form or a particular control on the form that has the focus at that time.

For example, suppose you write a macro to do a time-consuming task that involves looping around thousands of times. You may want to give the user a "get out" command to bring it to a halt if it takes too long. You can only do this by checking the keyboard because the only way that you can see a keyboard event is on a UserForm, and this may not have the focus at the time the user presses the "get out" key. You use the API call **GetKeyState** to do this. You must put the following code in the declarations part of a module:

```
Private Declare Function GetKeyState Lib "user32" (ByVal nVirtKey As_
Long) As Integer
```

This will allow you to examine any key while the program is running. You can even differentiate between left and right SHIFT keys or CTRL keys:

```
Sub Test_Key()
x = 0
Do Until x = 1

        If GetKeyState(&H9) < 0 Then x = 1

        DoEvents

Loop
MsgBox "You pressed the TAB key"
End Sub
```

This program effectively runs in an infinite loop and has only been done that way for demonstration purposes. Normally you would place the API call somewhere within a loop within your own code so that the keyboard could be read while other events were happening.

This program sets up a simple Do Until..Loop that keeps running until **x** = 1. This will never happen until the **GetKeyState** line turns up a value for the specified key that is less than 0—that is, it has been pressed. For the purposes of the example, the TAB key is used, which has a value of 09 in hexadecimal. Press any other key on the keyboard when the code is running and nothing happens; but when the TAB key is pressed, **x** changes its value to 1 and exits from the loop. The message box is then displayed. Of course, it helps if you know the values of the virtual key codes if you want to use other key combinations. They are listed in Table 17-1.

The **DoEvents** command is very important here. It literally allows the operating system to catch its breath and finish processing all messages before moving onto the next instruction. If you do not use this, then the message from the keyboard will not be processed before the next loop is started, and the keypress will be missed.

Symbolic Constant Name	Value (Hexadecimal)	Mouse or Keyboard Equivalent
VK_LBUTTON	01	Left mouse button
VK_RBUTTON	02	Right mouse button
VK_CANCEL	03	CTRL-BREAK processing
VK_MBUTTON	04	Middle mouse button (three-button mouse)
—	05–07	Undefined
VK_BACK	08	BACKSPACE
VK_TAB	09	TAB
—	0A–0B	Undefined

Table 17-1   *Key Combinations*

Symbolic Constant Name	Value (Hexadecimal)	Mouse or Keyboard Equivalent
VK_CLEAR	0C	CLEAR
VK_RETURN	0D	ENTER
—	0E–0F	Undefined
VK_SHIFT	10	SHIFT
VK_CONTROL	11	CTRL
VK_MENU	12	ALT
VK_PAUSE	13	PAUSE
VK_CAPITAL	14	CAPS LOCK
—	15–19	Reserved for Kanji systems
—	1A	Undefined
VK_ESCAPE	1B	ESC
—	1C–1F	Reserved for Kanji systems
VK_SPACE	20	SPACEBAR
VK_PRIOR	21	PAGE UP
VK_NEXT	22	PAGE DOWN
VK_END	23	END
VK_HOME	24	HOME
VK_LEFT	25	LEFT ARROW
VK_UP	26	UP ARROW
VK_RIGHT	27	RIGHT ARROW
VK_DOWN	28	DOWN ARROW
VK_SELECT	29	SELECT
—	2A	Original equipment manufacturer (OEM) specific
VK_EXECUTE	2B	EXECUTE
VK_SNAPSHOT	2C	PRINT SCREEN
VK_INSERT	2D	INS
VK_DELETE	2E	DEL
VK_HELP	2F	HELP
VK_0	30	0
VK_1	31	1
VK_2	32	2
VK_3	33	3
VK_4	34	4
VK_5	35	5
VK_6	36	6

Table 17-1 *Key Combinations (continued)*

Symbolic Constant Name	Value (Hexadecimal)	Mouse or Keyboard Equivalent
VK_7	37	7
VK_8	38	8
VK_9	39	9
—	3A–40	Undefined
VK_A	41	A
VK_B	42	B
VK_C	43	C
VK_D	44	D
VK_E	45	E
VK_F	46	F
VK_G	47	G
VK_H	48	H
VK_I	49	I
VK_J	4A	J
VK_K	4B	K
VK_L	4C	L
VK_M	4D	M
VK_N	4E	N
VK_O	4F	O
VK_P	50	P
VK_Q	51	Q
VK_R	52	R
VK_S	53	S
VK_T	54	T
VK_U	55	U
VK_V	56	V
VK_W	57	W
VK_X	58	X
VK_Y	59	Y
VK_Z	5A	Z
VK_LWIN	5B	LEFT WINDOWS (Microsoft Natural Keyboard)
VK_RWIN	5C	RIGHT WINDOWS (Microsoft Natural Keyboard)
VK_APPS	5D	APPLICATIONS (Microsoft Natural Keyboard)
—	5E–5F	Undefined
VK_NUMPAD0	60	Numeric keypad 0

Table 17-1   *Key Combinations (continued)*

Symbolic Constant Name	Value (Hexadecimal)	Mouse or Keyboard Equivalent
VK_NUMPAD1	61	Numeric keypad 1
VK_NUMPAD2	62	Numeric keypad 2
VK_NUMPAD3	63	Numeric keypad 3
VK_NUMPAD4	64	Numeric keypad 4
VK_NUMPAD5	65	Numeric keypad 5
VK_NUMPAD6	66	Numeric keypad 6
VK_NUMPAD7	67	Numeric keypad 7
VK_NUMPAD8	68	Numeric keypad 8
VK_NUMPAD9	69	Numeric keypad 9
VK_MULTIPLY	6A	MULTIPLY
VK_ADD	6B	ADD
VK_SEPARATOR	6C	SEPARATOR
VK_SUBTRACT	6D	SUBTRACT
VK_DECIMAL	6E	DECIMAL
VK_DIVIDE	6F	DIVIDE
VK_F1	70	F1
VK_F2	71	F2
VK_F3	72	F3
VK_F4	73	F4
VK_F5	74	F5
VK_F6	75	F6
VK_F7	76	F7
VK_F8	77	F8
VK_F9	78	F9
VK_F10	79	F10
VK_F11	7A	F11
VK_F12	7B	F12
VK_F13	7C	F13
VK_F14	7D	F14
VK_F15	7E	F15
VK_F16	7F	F16
VK_F17	80	F17
VK_F18	81	F18
VK_F19	82	F19
VK_F20	83	F20

Table 17-1   *Key Combinations (continued)*

Symbolic Constant Name	Value (Hexadecimal)	Mouse or Keyboard Equivalent
VK_F21	84	F21
VK_F22	85	F22
VK_F23	86	F23
VK_F24	87	F24
—	88–8F	Unassigned
VK_NUMLOCK	90	NUM LOCK
VK_SCROLL	91	SCROLL LOCK
VK_LSHIFT	A0	LEFT SHIFT
VK_RSHIFT	A1	RIGHT SHIFT
VK_LCONTROL	A2	LEFT CTRL
VK_RCONTROL	A3	RIGHT CTRL
VK_LMENU	A4	LEFT MENU
VK_RMENU	A5	RIGHT MENU
—	E7–E8	Unassigned
—	E9–F5	OEM specific
VK_ATTN	F6	ATTN
VK_CRSEL	F7	CRSEL
VK_EXSEL	F8	EXSEL
VK_EREOF	F9	ERASE EOF
VK_PLAY	FA	PLAY
VK_ZOOM	FB	ZOOM
VK_NONAME	FC	Reserved for future use
VK_PA1	FD	PA1
VK_OEM_CLEAR	FE	CLEAR

Table 17-1   *Key Combinations (continued)*

Play Multimedia Sounds

You can also use an API call to play a sound within your code from a WAV file. The old macro programming language had a command to do this, but it has not been included in VBA, or for that matter in Visual Basic itself, which makes it a bit restrictive if you want to play sound files. If you want to use Multimedia functions within your code to play sounds or voice files, then the means to play sound files is very crucial. The declaration goes in the declarations section of a module:

```
Public Declare Function PlaySound Lib "winmm.dll" Alias "PlaySoundA" _
(ByVal lpszName As String, ByVal hModule As Long, ByVal dwFlags As _
Long) As Long
```

You can then play the WAV files within your code:

```
Sub test_sound()
x = PlaySound("c:\windows\media\windows exclamation.wav", 0, 0)
x = PlaySound("c:\windows\media\tada.wav", 0, 0)
End Sub
```

This example plays two standard Windows sounds. Notice that the flags parameter is set to 0 in both cases. This indicates that the sound is played synchronously so that the command is not handed back to the VBA code until the sound has finished playing. If you have a microphone on your computer, you can record your own sound effects or speech onto a WAV file and play them back in this way.

These examples give some idea of the power of API calls within a program. There are many books written on this subject if you wish to examine this topic further.

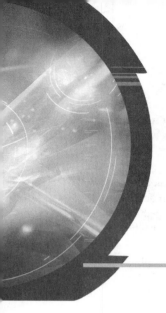

Class Modules

As you program in VBA and insert modules to hold your code, you will notice from the menu that you can also insert what are called class modules. These are different from ordinary modules in that they allow you to create a component object model (COM) of your own by means of creating an add-in.

Class modules cannot be run in the same way as a standard module procedure and must be referenced from your code within a module. This allows you to create your own objects and collections such as the **Workbooks** or the **Worksheets** collection. Unfortunately, you cannot create a DLL (dynamic link library) file, which is what you would do if you were programming in full Visual Basic or C++ / C#. However, a class module can be changed into an add-in, which is a component object, and it effectively adds multitier architecture to your applications. An add-in is a component that can be distributed and used independently of a particular spreadsheet.

Earlier in this book, you learned that Excel is a multitier application because there is a client services layer that has the Excel object model sitting beneath it, and the data services layer sits under that. The class modules allow you to place another layer between the client services layer and the Excel object model or between the client services layer and an external data source, such as Access or SQL Server.

You can turn your application into an add-in, and it can then be used as reference to your object. As soon as the add-in you created is loaded, the public functions and subroutines can be accessed from other modules within a spreadsheet, although if you have password-protected it, other programmers will not see the underlying code. See Chapter 41 for more details on how to create an add-in.

As an example, the workbook is an object. When the workbook is saved, you can provide a password in your code for security; and when the workbook is reopened, your code has to give the password to succeed. There is even a property called **HasPassword** on the **Workbook** object, but the one thing it will not give you is a property containing the password itself. Of course, all the code to encrypt and decrypt passwords is hidden away in the Excel object model, but no methods or properties are provided to access the actual password. Wouldn't life be interesting if you could!

The designers of the Excel object module have written rules saying, "You can save a file with a password, but you cannot view that password." In the same way, you can design your own objects and set the rules accordingly about what can be done with those objects—which properties and methods there will be, and whether a collection can be changed or whether it is read-only.

In the following example, you will create an object of names taken from cells in a spreadsheet. The object collection will be called **PNames**, and it will be a collection of **PName** objects; for example, the names could be the names of people or the names of places.

Inserting a Class Module

Select Insert | Class Module from the VBE menu to create a class module called Class1. You need to change the name immediately, because this will be the name of the object that you create, and Class1 is somewhat meaningless because it does not reflect the functionality of that class. You will use this name within your code to refer to the object and it will become tedious if you keep having to refer to Class1. The name is changed in the properties window; class modules only have one property, the name. To view the properties window, select View | Properties Window on the VBE menu or press F4. Select the name field and overtype it with **PName**. This represents the individual objects within a collection. Double-click the class module within the tree view to display it.

Creating an Object

You need to set up the actual object for items within the collection first because this has to be used in the construction of the **Collections** object. The **PName** object will have one property, the name of the object called **PName**. Remember what a property is: it holds a value for something within that object, in this case, the actual name.

You first need to create a variable to hold the property value, which you do in the declarations section of the module:

```
Private mPname As String
```

This sets up a string variable called **mPname**. Notice that it is private and cannot be seen as part of the object. This is because it is a working variable within the class module and is not there for use by the user. Also, the name must be different from the actual property name the user can see, which is why the *m* is added at the front.

Next, you need to set up code to control access to the property. You need a **Property Let** statement and a **Property Get** statement, and these statements must be public—otherwise, you will not be able to view them within the object. These statements effectively read and write values to the property that you are setting up:

```
Public Property Let Pname(vdata As String)
     mPname = vdata
End Property
```

The parameter **vdata** represents the value being passed to the property within the **Let** statement.

```
Public Property Get Pname() As String
     Pname = mPname
End Property
```

It is very important that the **Let** and **Get** property statements have the same name; otherwise, you will be able to read a property (**Get**) but not write back to it (**Let**), or you will be able to write to it (**Let**) but not read it back (**Get**).

The **Let** property uses a string variable to transfer the data into your **mPname** variable. The **Get** property sets the property value to whatever is held in your **mPname** variable.

You can use Insert | Procedure from the code menu to create a code skeleton for a property, which opens the Add Procedure dialog shown in Figure 18-1. This automatically writes the **Let** and **Get** property statements and ensures that they both have the same name.

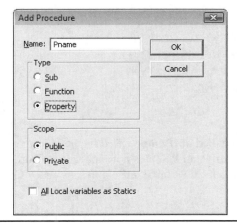

Figure 18-1   *Using the Add Procedure dialog to enter a property*

You have now set up an object called **Pname**. This object sits in a collection called **PNames**, just as the **Worksheet** object sits in a collection called **Worksheets**. The **PNames** collection is created in the next section.

Creating a Collection

The next stage is to create the **Collection** object to hold the individual **PName** objects. Insert another class module using Insert | Class Module from the VBE menu bar. Change the name to **PNames** and double-click the class module to enter it.

The first thing to do is to define a private variable to act as the **Collection** object in the same way you defined a private variable to act as the property for the **PName** object. This needs to be placed in the declarations section of the class module:

```
Private mPnames As Collection
```

This must have a unique name, so an *m* is placed in front of the collection name. The letter *m* distinguishes the variable as a member variable.

Next, select the **Class_Initialize** subroutine. This routine runs when you first use the class and determines what the contents will be. To run it, click the Class section in the top-left drop-down and click Initialize in the top-right drop-down. Enter the following code:

```
Private Sub Class_Initialize()

Dim objPname As Pname

Set mPnames = New Collection
For n = 1 To 3

    Set objPname = New Pname

    objPname.Pname = Worksheets("sheet1").Range("a" & n + 1).Value

    mPnames.Add objPname
Next n
End Sub
```

First, you define an object called **objPname** based on the object you created called **PName**. Notice that the objects **PName** and **PNames** now appear in the drop-down list as you type the code in. You then set the local variable, **mPNames**, as a new **Collection** object. At this point, it is empty.

The For..Next loop adds the objects into the collection from a source of data. This could be an external database, or it could just be a local array holding the information. In this example, a part of the spreadsheet is being used, although at this point there is no data in it.

The variable **objPname**, which was defined as our **PName** object, is set to a new **Pname** for each loop. This creates a new instance of **PName** that can hold data and be added to the **PNames** collection. The data is then taken from Sheet1, column A, and placed in the **Pname** property that was created.

The object **objPname** is then added to the **Pnames** collection. At the end of this For..Next loop, three objects have been added to the **PNames** collection, based on data in Sheet1. Make sure that there is some data in cells A2, A3, and A4. You also need to add a public function called **Item** so that you can refer to individual objects within the collection by their index number. Enter this into the same class module as the rest of the code:

```
Public Function Item(Index As Integer) As Pname

    Set Item = mPnames.Item(Index)


End Function
```

This defines **Item** as a function of the object **Pnames** and sets **Item** to point to the **mPnames** collection based on the index number given. Because **mPnames** was defined as a **Collection** object, it already has the **Item** function built into it. This function provides a "mirror" of what is going on in the **mPnames** collection in the background.

You will need to add a property called **Count** so that your code can establish how many **PName** objects there are in the **PName** collection:

```
Public Property Get Count() As Long
    Count = mPnames.Count
End Property
```

In this case, you only need a property **Get** because this is a read-only property, and it gets updated by the **Class_Initialize** routine adding in the source data. This acts again as "a mirror" against the **mPnames** object, which is defined as a collection and already has the **Count** property built into it.

You have now set up a collection called **PNames** of objects called **PName**, which simply refers to a block of spreadsheet data on Sheet1 in Column A, as shown in Figure 18-2. The collection has a **Count** property and an **Item** method.

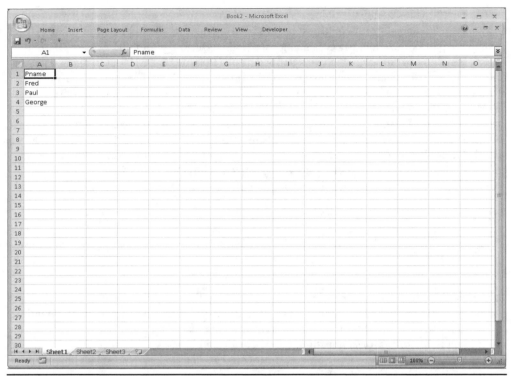

Figure 18-2   *Data used for the Pname collection*

Using the PNames Collection

You can now use your **Collection** object **PNames** within standard code just as you would any other object. You use the code within a standard Excel VBA module:

```
Sub test_class()
Dim pn As New Pnames, n As Integer
MsgBox pn.Count
For n = 1 To pn.Count

    MsgBox pn.Item(n).Pname
Next n
End Sub
```

This creates a new instance of the **Pnames** object. When this procedure is run, the first thing it does is to *initialize* the class module, which means it picks up the data from the spreadsheet and adds the objects to the collection.

The variable **n**, used in the For..Next loop, is defined as an integer because it was defined in the **Item** function in the collection as an integer (index). An integer was used because this is ideal for a For..Next loop variable. If you do not do this, you will get a Type Mismatch error when the code is run.

You then set up a For..Next loop to work through each object in the collection. This is based on the **Count** function of the object. Note that as you type the code in, the function **Item** and the property **Count** will appear in list boxes, just as they do for built-in Excel objects.

Using the **Collection** object, you can now use the **Item** function and the variable **n** to reference each object in the collection. The property **Pname** is used to display each name. This is all wrapped into a message box statement so that each name will be displayed in turn.

Run the code in your module and you will get a message box with the value 3 (three objects in the collection) followed by each name in turn. Next, try changing a cell value on the spreadsheet and rerun the code. The name in the collection will also change because when you create the **Pnames** object (**pn**) in the first line of the code, it reinitializes and takes the new values. If you made the **Collection**'s object **Static**, it would not reinitialize but would keep the old values of the collection:

```
Sub test_class()
Static pn As New Pnames, n As Integer
MsgBox pn.Count
For n = 1 To pn.Count

    MsgBox pn.Item(n).Pname
Next n
End Sub
```

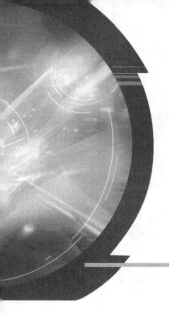

Animation

Believe it or not, it is possible to animate objects in Excel. By taking this possibility to an extreme, you could write a complete arcade game in Excel—all the tools to do this are there. Serious users of Excel would probably not be very impressed to find Space Invaders appearing in their Profit and Loss Account spreadsheet, but it can be done. However, for the purposes of this book, you will simply move an image object about while changing its color randomly.

First of all, you need to draw an image control onto the spreadsheet. You do this by selecting Developer on the menu bar and then clicking the Insert icon on the Controls window of the ribbon to open the Toolbox window. Select the Image control from the ActiveX section (this has an icon of a picture of the sun over a mountain range) by clicking the control in the toolbox; then drag it onto your spreadsheet. It should have the name Image1. If you cannot identify the Image control in the toolbox, hold your mouse pointer over each icon in turn until you see the tooltip box that says Image.

Select a control button in the ActiveX section of the toolbox and drag it onto the spreadsheet. Make sure that you select the button from the Active X section and not the User Form section, as this will not work correctly.

Change the Caption property in the Properties window for the control button to read **My Animation** so that this appears on the button face. Your spreadsheet should look like Figure 19-1.

Double-click the command button to go into the code procedure for the command button Click event. Add the following code:

```
Private Sub CommandButton1_Click()
again:
With VBAProject.Sheet1.Image1
   Randomize
   .BackColor = QBColor(Int((Rnd * 15) + 1))
```

```
    .Top = .Top + 2
    .Left = .Left + 2
     DoEvents
    If .Top > 100 Then .Top = 1
    If .Left > 100 Then .Left = 1
End With
GoTo again
End Sub
```

Bear in mind that when this code runs, it will keep looping continuously forever until you press CTRL-BREAK or you write code within the loop to stop it after a set period of time or some event happens.

Note that the first line sets up a label called **again**. This sets up a loop based on the label so that the routine is continuously executed. A **With** statement is used for the object **VBAProject.Sheet1.Image1** so that it does not have to be coded each time you want to access the image.

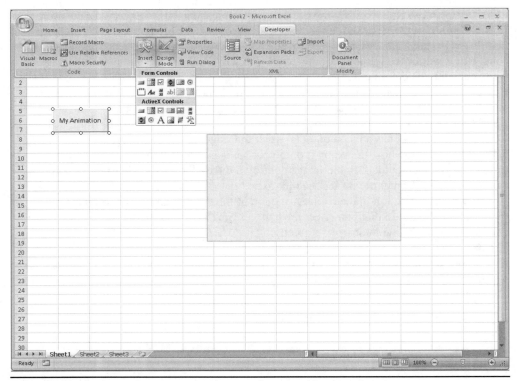

Figure 19-1   *Setting up an animation object and a control button*

The **Randomize** statement sets the seed to create random numbers. A random number is a number chosen without any preset pattern, such as a number coming up in a lottery or on a roulette table. If you do not use **Randomize**, you will keep getting the same sequence of random numbers.

The back color of the image box is then set to a random color using Quick Basic colors—this dates back to the old version of Quick Basic when only 16 colors onscreen were possible. It is still useful when you want to change the color using simple random numbers instead of providing a full 24-bit number for 16.3 million colors. The function **Rnd** creates random numbers between 0 and 1. This is multiplied by 15 to give the full range of colors and set them to integers. Because integer (INT) effectively rounds everything downward by dropping the decimal point, 1 is then added. This command will make the image control display random colors as it moves across the screen.

The **Top** property is then increased by two to make the object move down the screen. The **Left** property is increased by two to make the object move across the screen. If the object reaches a limit of 100 in either direction, it resets back to 1 and the process starts again, moving diagonally to the right. The **With** block ends, and the program loops back around to **again**.

Make sure that you click the Design Mode icon in the top left-hand corner of the Toolbox window to take the command button out of design mode and make it live. Run this code by clicking the My Animation button on the spreadsheet, and you will see the image control move right and downward, randomly changing color at the same time. Press CTRL-BREAK to stop the code.

Simple animation can also be provided by changing the background color of a cell:

```
Sub cell_animation()
again1:
Dim w As Worksheet
Set w = Worksheets("sheet1")
Randomize
For n = 65 To 69
 For m = 1 To 5

    w.Range(Chr(n) & m).Rows.Interior.Color = QBColor(Int((Rnd * 15) + 1))
    DoEvents

 Next m

Next n
GoTo again1
End Sub
```

This code loops around continuously to a label called **again1**. You cannot use the same label as in the previous example if this procedure is placed in the same module.

The first object, **w**, is created as a worksheet and set to point to sheet1. Next, **Randomize** sets the seed for the random number generator as before.

Two nested For..Next loops are created. The **n** For..Next loop goes from 65 to 69—these are the ASCII values of A to E, and they represent columns. Because you want to increment the letter through the VBA code, you need to use the actual numeric value instead of the character itself. The **m** For..Next loop goes from 1 to 5 to represent rows. By changing the **n** value to a character and concatenating it with the changing **m** value, you can get cell addresses for all 25 cells within the loop structure (a five-by-five matrix of cells). A **DoEvents** statement is added to ensure that the previous command takes place before the code moves on to the next line. **DoEvents** was used in Chapter 17 in the example for reading the keyboard.

The cell interior (background) color is set to a random number between 1 and 16—these are the old Quick Basic colors as used in the previous example. Finally, the code loops back to **again1** and resets the background colors again.

If you run this code and click on the spreadsheet, you will see that the cells in the top left of the spreadsheet constantly change color. Press CTRL-BREAK to stop the code.

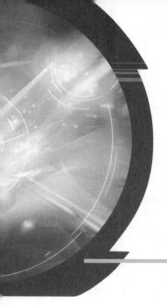

Working with XML Files

XML (the abbreviation stands for Extensible Markup Language) allows files to be created that can interchange data between separate platforms. It is similar in a way to how HTML (the Hypertext Markup Language) works, but you can define your own tags rather than using predefined ones, and this gives you tremendous flexibility.

Excel 2007 actually saves its spreadsheets as a group of XML documents compressed as a ZIP file, which is why the files created by an Excel spreadsheet are much larger than the original XLS files from Excel 2003. The reasoning behind this is that it now allows very easy integration of your spreadsheet into other applications or web pages.

In Excel 2003 spreadsheets were saved in the XLS format. There were options to save in other formats such as text or csv, but the main file format used was XLS. This created the problem that unless you were using Microsoft Office applications, you would have great difficulty in importing that file into another application and maintaining all the formatting. The idea of XML files is to make the spreadsheet file as universally interchangeable as possible.

The XML document is only a text file containing tags, which make it machine readable by a large number of applications. Also, that it is text based it makes it an ideal candidate for data compression, making it easy to store and access data.

The XML Document

If you look at any web page on your Internet browser and then click View | Source on the menu, you will see the HTML code for that page. You will see that there are what are called tags, which are defined by the < . . . > symbols. For example you may see <B>, which means switch the font to bold, or <BR>, which means break and start a new line.

XML documents work in a very similar way, but they can use their own custom tags to mean different things instead of using the predefined set of HTML tags.

An XML document will always start off with a declaration similar to this:

```
<?xml version="1.0" encoding="UTF-8" ?>
```

This contains two attributes: the version, encoding, and standalone. The version is set to version 1 of XML. This has been the standard version since 1998, and changes since then have been relatively small.

The encoding attribute is to fix character encoding issues. It is optional and can be UTF-8, UTF-16, ANSI, or ASCII. It can be omitted in many files.

The standalone attribute tells whether an external data source is being used. If it is set to Yes, then it is standalone and does not reference any external data.

You can enter comments into the file. In VBA you use a single quote mark in front of your comments string. In XML you start with <!— and end with —>. For example, you could include this comment:

```
<!--Created by Richard Shepherd-->
```

This would provide anybody reading the file as raw data with some information on the file and what it was all about.

Let us look at a simple XML file. Here is an example:

```
<?xml version="1.0"?>
  <MyData>
      <Names>
            <FirstName>Richard</FirstName>
            <LastName>Shepherd</LastName>
      </Names>
      <Names>
            <FirstName>Elaine</FirstName>
            <LastName>Shepherd</LastName>
      </Names>
  </MyData>
```

Enter this into a text editor such as Notepad (found by clicking Start | All Programs | Accessories | Notepad) and save it with the program name test.xml. Ensure that it exactly matches this code snippet; otherwise, you will encounter parsing errors when loading it into Excel.

Open Excel and click the Office button on the top left-hand corner. Click Open in the menu and then select the file test.xml. Load this in. A dialog will appear asking how you wish to open the XML file (see Figure 20-1). Stay with the default of As an XML Table and click OK. Click OK on the next dialog so that Excel will then create a schema for the file.

You will see the file loaded into the worksheet as shown in Figure 20-2. This is a demonstration of how a simple XML file is opened in Excel 2007.

There are a number of rules for putting your XML file together:

▶ Every element in the file must have a start tag defined by < . . . > and an end tag defined by </ . . . >. Examples of elements in this file are Names, FirstName, and LastName. MyData is the root element.

▶ You must have a root element within the file. In the case of this file it is MyData. You can only have one root element in an XML document.

▶ Element names are case sensitive. The start and end tags must use the same spelling and cases for all letters; otherwise, errors will occur.

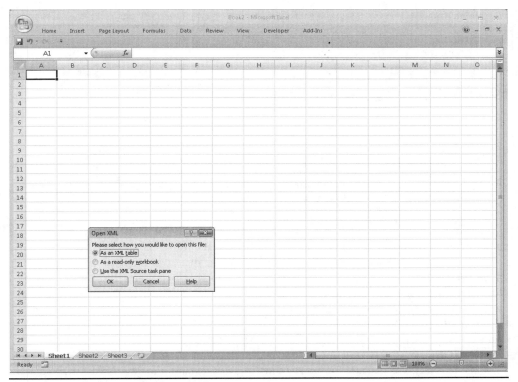

Figure 20-1   *Dialog to open an XML file*

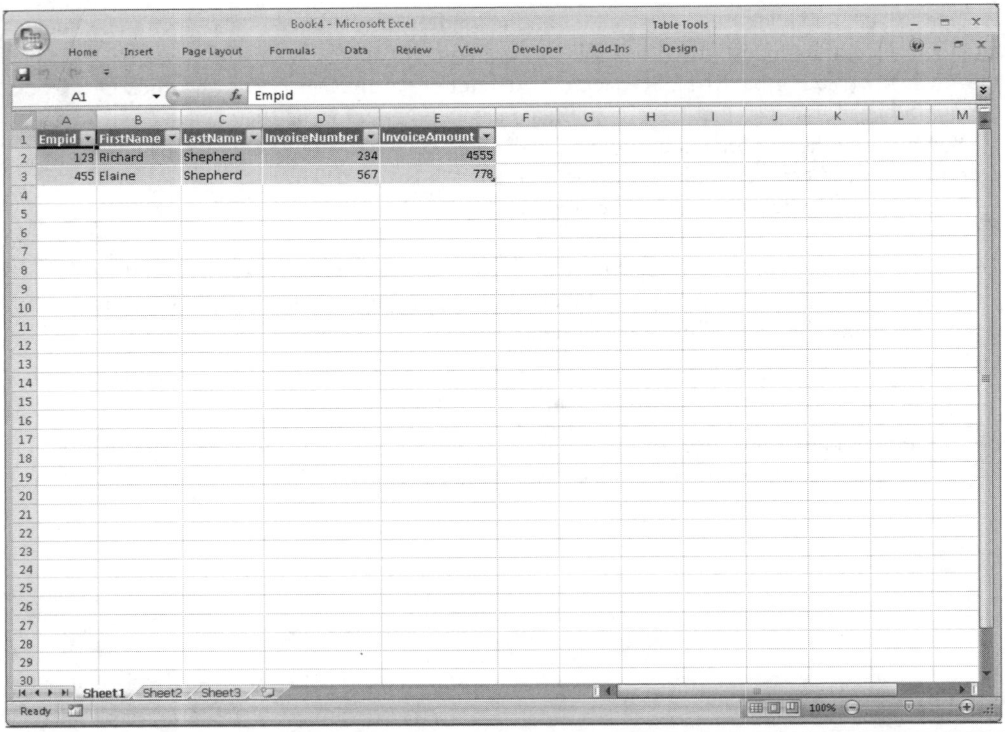

Figure 20-2 *An XML file loaded into an Excel worksheet*

▶ The element name must begin with a letter or an underscore, never a digit. Also, "xml" is reserved and must never be used to start an element name.

▶ The elements can be called anything you want. So long as you adhere to these rules, you can use any terminology that you like.

You can see that the elements are in a parent/child hierarchy. MyData is the root element and has Names as the child. Names then has FirstName and LastName as children.

In the Excel spreadsheet if you click Developer on the menu, you will see an XML group on the ribbon relating to XML. If you click Source in this toolbar, you will see the hierarchy of the file displayed (see Figure 20-3).

If you cannot see the Developer option on the menu toolbar, then click the Start button in the top left-hand corner of the Excel screen and click the Excel Options button at the bottom of the dialog that appears. Check the box titled Show the Developer Tab in the Ribbon and then click OK.

While in Excel, you can add further rows to this data and save it to your XML file. You will need to specify the XML format when you save the data. You can use the XML file almost as a normal spreadsheet, adding, editing, and deleting data and saving it to the XML file.

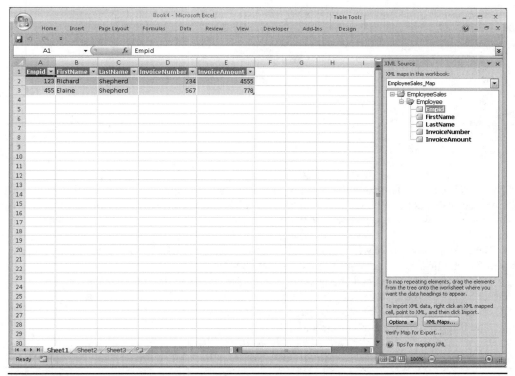

Figure 20-3   *Hierarchy of an XML file displayed in an Excel worksheet*

How Does XML Relate to VBA?

You have so far only seen how to create XML files manually using Notepad or a text editor. One thing that you cannot do is type data directly onto a spreadsheet and then save it as a standalone XML file, as there is no schema or map created for XML.

Excel 2007 now includes an object model to deal specifically with XML files, to manipulate them and create schemas; this allows you to access a large number of functions that are not available from the Excel 2007 user interface.

XML Maps

Creating your own XML map allows you to write data back to an XML document, map elements within the XML document, and integrate data from multiple XML documents. You need to create an XML Schema Description file (XSD), and to do this you need to use VBA.

First, you need to create a simple XML file using a text editor such as Notepad:

```
<?xml version="1.0"?>
    <Data>
        <Citizen>
            <FirstName>Text</FirstName>
            <LastName>Text</LastName>
        </Citizen>

        <Citizen></Citizen>
    </Data>
```

This sets up a root element called Data with a child element called Citizen. Placeholders are effectively set up to hold FirstName and LastName, and Citizen is also shown on the penultimate row as a repeating element. This is so that multiple entries for Citizen can be entered.

Save your file as an XML document; the suffix must be XML. Next load the XML file into Excel, allowing Excel to create its own schema.

Bear in mind that you can change a number of properties in the schema. You can do this either by clicking the Developer option on the menu and then selecting properties on the RibbonX item for XML, or through VBA (more on which later).

The following properties can be addressed:

▶ **Name** This is the name property that specifies the XML map.

▶ **Validate against data schema for import and export** This property ensures that Excel validates any data against the Excel schema when importing or exporting.

▶ **Save data source definition in workbook** This ensures that the XML map is linked to the XML document, enabling data to be refreshed. If it is deselected, then the data becomes static.

▶ **Adjust column width** If this is selected, Excel adjusts the column width to suit the data in the XML file.

▶ **Preserve column filter** Excel preserves the sorting and filtering when refreshing the XML map.

▶ **Preserve number formatting** Excel preserves the number formatting when refreshing the XML map.

▶ **Overwrite existing data with new data** Existing data will be overwritten when the XML map is refreshed.

▶ **Append new data to XML lists** Any new data will be added to the bottom of the existing XML data when the XML map is refreshed.

You will now have created an XML schema in Excel using this XML file. Next you need to extract the schema to an XSD file, but there is no way of doing this from the user interface. This is where you can start using VBA code:

```
Sub GetMapXSD()

    Dim MyXSD As String

    MyXSD = ActiveWorkbook.XmlMaps("Data_Map").Schemas(1).XML

    Open "C:\temp\MyXSD.xsd" For Output As #1
    Print #1, MyXSD
    Close #1

End Sub
```

Running this code creates an XSD file called MyXSD.xsd based on the schema in your original XML file. With this XSD file you can now create an Excel XML-based entry template.

Open a new workbook in Excel and select an XML source by clicking the Developer option on the menu bar and clicking XML Source on the RibbonX control. Click the XML Maps button at the bottom of the dialog, and then click Add in the XML Maps dialog to view the Select XML Source dialog shown in Figure 20-4.

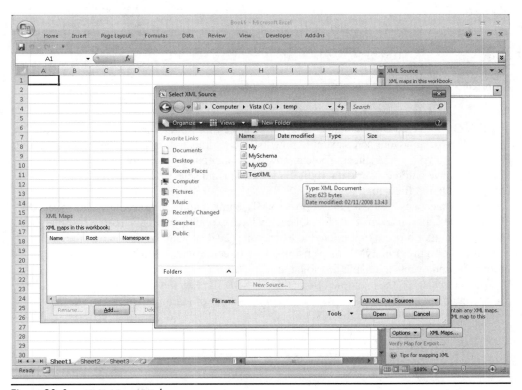

Figure 20-4 *XML Maps Dialog*

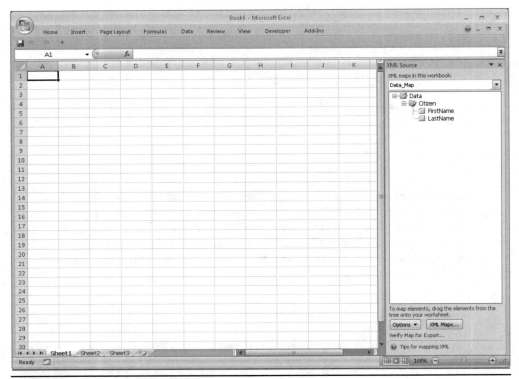

Figure 20-5   *XML Schema elements*

Click Open to create the schema. You will then see the elements available to you. See Figure 20-5 for how your screen should now look. Use drag and drop to transfer the available elements onto your spreadsheet. You can now enter data into your template row by row. When you have entered your data, right-click the data and select XML. Select Export and choose a path and filename.

This demonstrates how you can set up an XML template in Excel to capture data to an XSD template and export it as an XML file. Once you have exported your data as an XML file, then any application or process (not limited to Microsoft) can deal with the data in this file.

You can also program XML maps using VBA. Excel provides a rich set of objects, properties, and events to enable this to happen.

You could also do the example of creating an XSD file like the one just described programmatically without even going through the stages of loading in an XML file. This code sample will create a similar XSD file:

```
Sub CreateXSDFile()
        Dim Temp As String, MyMap As XmlMap
        'Create the XML map as a string based on the structure of an
        'XML file
```

```
        Temp= "<People>"
        Temp = Temp & "<Names>"
        Temp = Temp & "<FirstName>999</FirstName>"
        Temp = Temp & "<LastName>Text</LastName>"
        Temp = Temp & "</Names>"
        Temp = Temp & "<Names></Names>"
        Temp = Temp & "</People>"

'Use your XML string to add an XML map switching the alerts off and
on to 'avoid showing the dialog boxes
        Application.DisplayAlerts = False
        Set MyMap = ThisWorkbook.XmlMaps.Add(Temp)
        Application.DisplayAlerts = True

'Get the schema
        Temp = ThisWorkbook.XmlMaps(1).Schemas(1).XML

'Create and fill an XSD file with your schema
        Open "c:\temp\My.xsd" For Output As #1
        Print #1, Temp
        Close #1

End Sub
```

The code creates the XML Schema as a text string and then adds it into the XML maps for the current workbook. It then gets the XML for that schema and creates the XSD file.

You can load an XML file into a workbook by using VBA as follows:

```
Sub XMLImport()
    'Turn off alerts so that dialog boxes do not appear
    Application.DisplayAlerts = False

    'Use the OpenXML method to open the target file
    Workbooks.OpenXML Filename:="C:\temp\testXML.xml",
LoadOption:=xlXmlLoadImportToList

    'Turn alerts back on so that user will see the alerts under
    'normal use
    Application.DisplayAlerts = True

End Sub
```

This code turns off the alerts so that when the code is run it is not interrupted by dialog boxes, loads in a file in the workbook path called testXML.xml, and then switches the alerts back on. The last step is most important because otherwise users will never see the alerts appearing if they do this process manually. This is in fact the same as if users click the Excel

Start button, click Open, and select the XML file. The only difference is that users will see the alert dialogs that you have disabled in the code.

Once you have loaded the XML file into the workbook and created the map, you can programmatically change the properties of the map. See the earlier list of properties that can be changed. The following code will allow you to change the properties within the XML map (assuming that the map for the XML that was loaded earlier is called "testXML_Map"; otherwise, you will get a "Subscript out of range" error):

```
Sub XMLMap()
        With ActiveWorkbook.XmlMaps("testXML_Map")
            .Name = "MyMap"
            .ShowImportExportValidationErrors = False
            .SaveDataSourceDefinition = True
            .AdjustColumnWidth = False
            .PreserveColumnFilter = True
            .PreserveNumberFormatting = True
            .AppendOnImport = False
        End With
End Sub
```

Note that if you change **SaveDataSourceDefinition** to False, the XML data becomes static and this property cannot be reset back to True. This also means that you cannot use the following line of code to refresh the workbook from any changes that may have happened to the XML file, since the data is now static. An important point here!

```
ActiveWorkbook.XmlMaps("MyMap").DataBinding.Refresh
```

You can also delete the map completely by using

```
ActiveWorkbook.XMLMaps("MyMap").Delete
```

This will turn your XML data into a plain Excel spreadsheet with no XML mapping behind it.

Customizing an XML Map

You can use VBA to customize how the data in your XML schema maps into the Excel spreadsheet. When you load in an XML or XSD file, it maps into the spreadsheet in the way that it is shown on the file schema.

Using the code that follows, you can specify how the columns of data will be mapped into the spreadsheet. This example assumes that you have created an XSD file called C:\temp\Myschema.xsd. The creation of this file is described in the preceding section.

```
Sub MapXMLSchema()
        Dim MyMap As XmlMap
        Dim XPath As String
        Dim MyList As ListObject
```

```
Dim MyNewColumn As ListColumn

'Add an XSD file that has already been created
ThisWorkbook.XmlMaps.Add ("c:\temp\Myschema.xsd")

' Idenfity the target schema map.
Set MyMap = ThisWorkbook.XmlMaps("Data_Map")

' Create a new list in A1.
Range("A1").Select
Set MyList = ActiveSheet.ListObjects.Add

'Find the first element to map.
XPath = "/Data/Citizen/LastName"
' Map the schema element to the first column in the spreadsheet
MyList.ListColumns(1).XPath.SetValue MyMap, XPath

' Add a column to the list
Set MyNewColumn = MyList.ListColumns.Add
' Find the second element to map.
XPath = "/Data/Citizen/FirstName"
' Map the element to the next column in the spreadsheet
MyNewColumn.XPath.SetValue MyMap, XPath
'Give the columns names relating to the new mapping
MyList.ListColumns(1).Name = "LastName"
MyList.ListColumns(2).Name = "FirstName"

End Sub
```

This code needs to be run in a completely blank spreadsheet. If you get bugs and try to rerun it, you will encounter further problems because it will have already loaded in one schema. The way to get around this is to delete existing XML maps by choosing Developer | Source and then clicking XML maps. You will also need to delete any cells populated on the spreadsheet; otherwise, you will get an overlapping table error.

The code assumes that the file Myschema.XSD has a root called Data and a child called Citizen. Citizen then has children called FirstName and LastName. This code reverses their positions on the spreadsheet, so although the XML schema remains the same, LastName is now in column A and FirstName is in column B. See Figure 20-6 for how your screen should look.

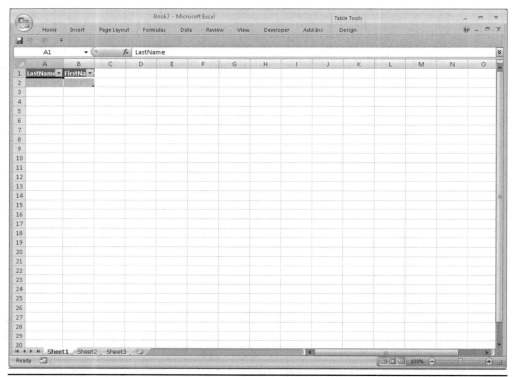

Figure 20-6   *Worksheet screen following amendments to the XML schema*

Importing and Exporting Data

You can use VBA to import data from an existing XML file into an XML map that already
resides in a spreadsheet. This map may have already been created as an XSD file and have
been loaded into the spreadsheet.

```
ActiveWorkbook.XmlMaps("Data_Map").Import URL:=ThisWorkbook.Path &
"\TestXML.xml"
```

Obviously the XML data in the file needs to conform to the structure of the XML schema
within the spreadsheet.

You can use similar code to export the data in a current XML map out to an XML file:

```
ActiveWorkbook.XmlMaps("Data_Map").Export URL:=ThisWorkbook.Path &
"\TestExport.xml"
```

Manipulating XML Files Programmatically

You can use the Document Object Model (DOM) to access and manipulate the data within an XML file. To do this, you need to include a VBA reference to the file MSXML.DLL.

In the VBA Editor window, select Tools | References and select the latest version of Microsoft XML. Select the check box against the program, click it to set it to a tick, and then click OK.

You can use the following code to load the structure of an XML document into a spreadsheet cell:

```
Sub LoadXML()
    Dim MyDoc As DOMDocument
    'Create a new DOMDocument
    Set MyDoc = New DOMDocument
    'Disable asynchronous loading
    MyDoc.async = False

    'Load XML file
    MyDoc.Load ("c:\temp\testxml.xml")

    'Load the XML into cell A1
    ActiveSheet.Range("a1").Value = MyDoc.XML
End Sub
```

The result on the worksheet should look like Figure 20-7.

You can take this further to cycle through and modify the data in an XML file almost as if it were a database. Try the following code (this assumes that you have an XML file called C:\temp\TestXML.xml):

```
Sub FindNode()
    Dim XmlDoc As DOMDocument
    Dim XmlNode As IXMLDOMNode
    Dim XmlNodes As IXMLDOMNodeList
    Dim Coun As Integer
    'Create a new instance of a DOM document and load your XML
    'Document into a DOM Document
        Set XmlDoc = New DOMDocument
        XmlDoc.async = False
        XmlDoc.Load ("c:\temp\TestXML.xml")

    'Find and select the all LastName nodes in the document
        Set XmlNodes =
            XmlDoc.SelectNodes("/Data/Citizen/LastName")
```

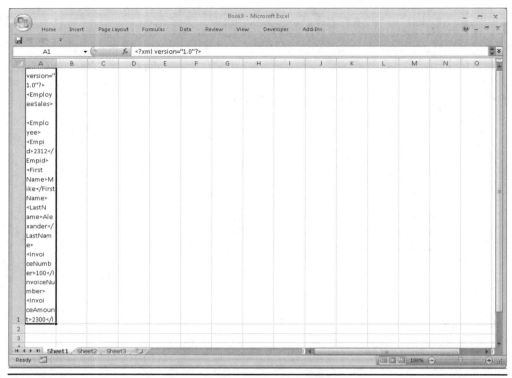

Figure 20-7   *Result of loading the XML structure into a worksheet cell*

```
'Cycle through the nodes and output each LastName into a
'consecutive cell in the active sheet
     Coun = 1
     For Each XmlNode In XmlNodes

          ActiveSheet.Range("a" & Coun).Value = XmlNode.Text
          Coun = Coun + 1
     Next

End Sub
```

The code assumes that the file TestXML.xml has the schema of Data | Citizen | LastName.

By making a small modification to the code (see the bold text) you can then start working with the XML file as if it was a database:

```
Sub FindNode()
    Dim XmlDoc As DOMDocument
    Dim XmlNode As IXMLDOMNode
    Dim Coun As Integer
    'Create a new instance of a DOM document and load your XML
    'Document into a DOM Document

        Set XmlDoc = New DOMDocument
        XmlDoc.async = False
        XmlDoc.Load ("c:\temp\TestXML.xml")

    'Find and select all FirstNames that equal the criteria of
    'Richard
        Set XmlNode =
            XmlDoc.SelectNodes("//Data[FirstName=Richard]")

    'Display the node value at cell A1


            ActiveSheet.Range("a1").Value = XmlNode.Text

End Sub
```

You can use some of the standard database query language when creating your criteria. Not only can you use =, but you can use < (less than) or > (greater than). Unfortunately more powerful operators such as **like** do not work here, which is a great shame. Notice that the highlighted statement refers to a single node and not to the nodes collection as in the earlier code.

Using VBA, you can also change the values of particular nodes (this example assumes that you are using an XML file called C:\temp\TestXML.xml, that it has a node called FirstName, and that the FirstName node has the data value "Richard"):

```
Sub FindNode()
    Dim XmlDoc As DOMDocument
    Dim XmlNode As IXMLDOMNode
    Dim Coun As Integer
    'Create a new instance of a DOM document and load your XML
    'Document into a DOM Document
```

```
        Set XmlDoc = New DOMDocument
        XmlDoc.async = False
        XmlDoc.Load ("c:\temp\TestXML.xml")

    'Find and select all FirstNames that equal the criteria of
    'Richard
        Set XmlNode =
            XmlDoc.SelectNodes("//Data[FirstName=Richard]")
'Edit the value of FirstName  and save the spreadsheet of as an XML
'file
XmlNode.Text="Albert"
Xmldoc.Save "C:\Temp\ModifiedTestXML.XML"

End Sub
```

The Ribbon

The ribbon is a brand new part of Office 2007 and probably has the greatest impact on the user, since it defines how the user navigates through the Office menu structure for each application.

If you use Excel 2007 already, then you will have come across it, since you access all the menu functions in a totally different and sometimes confusing way. Fortunately, the VBA Editor window has maintained the same menu structure that we all know and love, so you can still use your accumulated knowledge here.

A number of Excel VBA developers are producing Excel add-ins that emulate the Excel classical menu and no doubt making a fortune to boot! After having read this book, you may want to try your luck at doing this.

The ribbon opens up a whole new way of programming the user interface. With Excel 2003 and previous editions it was necessary to use the **CommandBars** object (see Chapter 11). This can still be used for backward compatibility, but it does not cover the ribbon.

With the **CommandBars** object it was necessary to write quite a number of lines of code to create a custom menu structure. The result was usually quite impressive to a user who had never seen this done, and I have frequently been asked the question "How did you manage to change the Excel menu structure?" However, it did take a lot of hard work to do this, along with a good memory of how the menu structure operated within the **CommandBar** object.

The ribbon has meant learning a completely new way of creating a custom user interface. Because Excel now uses the XML format for saving files, the ribbon is defined using XML. When the Excel file is opened, Excel reads in the XML code for the ribbon and applies your custom structure. If it is a standard workbook, the custom structure is only available for that workbook, but if you have created an add-in, then the custom structure can be used by all workbooks until the add-in is unloaded.

The custom structure can be manipulated at runtime by use of VBA code, and you can also make use of the predefined structure of the ribbon.

For a first-time user it looks frightening, but fortunately Microsoft has provided a tool to help you and make life easy. There is also an official MSDN web site, which at the time of writing is at http://msdn.microsoft.com/en-gb/office/aa905530.aspx. This contains a download file of all the control IDs in the Office ribbon, and since there are over 1,700 of them, it is very useful for reference purposes. You can also access a number of technical articles on this page.

Creating a Ribbon Customization

To customize the ribbon, you need to first create the XML for your customization and then insert it into the Excel XML file. This is not as easy as it sounds, since the Excel file is saved as a zipped package of several files, including the XML file that you need to edit.

Doing this completely by hand is somewhat laborious, since you would have to unzip the Excel package of files, edit your changes, and then zip them up again, remembering to provide the correct suffix.

Fortunately, there is a tool to help you, called the Microsoft Office 2007 Custom UI Editor, which can be downloaded for free from www.openxmldeveloper.org/articles/CustomUIeditor.aspx.

You only need to download it, agree to Microsoft's terms and conditions, and then run the installer. If you work in a corporate environment, you will need permission from your employer to download this. (I have worked in companies where you can be dismissed for downloading applications from the Internet.)

Using the Custom UI Editor

After you have installed the Custom UI Editor, create a simple Excel file. It does not need any data in it, just to be saved as a file. Close the file in Excel, as you will need read/write access to it from another application.

Click the Windows Start button and click All Programs. You will see a new program called Office 2007 UI Editor. Click this and you will see the opening screen as shown in Figure 21-1.

The interface is very simple and allows you to edit the ribbon on all Office 2007 documents. However, we are only interested in Excel.

Click on File | Open, locate your Excel file, and open it. Nothing appears on screen because there are no customizations for the ribbon in this file yet.

Microsoft has very helpfully provided a sample ribbon customization for Excel in this application, so click Sample | Excel – A Custom Tab. Your screen will now look like Figure 21-2. You can see a whole load of XML code, which will provide a customization for the ribbon. Click File | Save and save your sample Excel file.

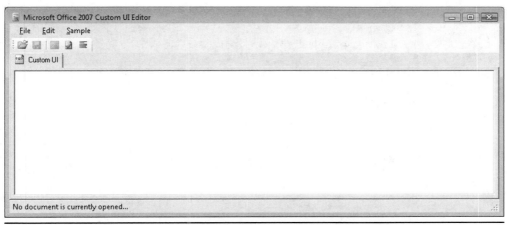

Figure 21-1   *Opening screen of Office 2007 UI Editor*

Go to Excel and load your sample Excel file, which now has ribbon customizations. You will see an extra entry now appears on the menu called Contoso. Your screen should look like Figure 21-3. If you click this, you will see a ribbon with three groups in it.

The first and second groups that you see are exact copies of existing Ribbon groups. The Copy group is exactly the same as if you had clicked Home on the menu and then looked at

```
<customUI xmlns="http://schemas.microsoft.com/office/2006/01/customui">
    <ribbon>
        <tabs>
            <tab id="customTab" label="Contoso" insertAfterMso="TabHome">
                <group idMso="GroupClipboard" />
                <group idMso="GroupFont" />
                <group id="customGroup" label="Contoso Tools">
                    <button id="customButton1" label="ConBold" size="large"
onAction="conBoldSub" imageMso="Bold" />
                    <button id="customButton2" label="ConItalic" size="large"
onAction="conItalicSub" imageMso="Italic" />
                    <button id="customButton3" label="ConUnderline" size="large"
onAction="conUnderlineSub" imageMso="Underline" />
                </group>
                <group idMso="GroupEnterDataAlignment" />
                <group idMso="GroupEnterDataNumber" />
                <group idMso="GroupQuickFormatting" />
            </tab>
        </tabs>
    </ribbon>
</customUI>
```

Figure 21-2   *XML screen for a custom ribbon*

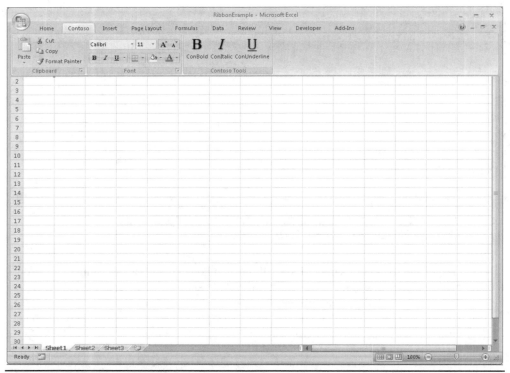

Figure 21-3 *Custom ribbon control Contoso*

the group Copy. Similarly the new Font group is exactly as shown when you click Home on the menu and see the Font group. This part shows how you can leverage existing ribbon functionality to build a custom ribbon.

At this point, load in another Excel file. Notice that on the menu, your new menu item does not appear on the other Excel file. This is because your new customized Excel file is not an add-in and the ribbon customization applies to only that file.

The third group in your new ribbon is a custom group, and this shows the real power of the ribbon. By looking at the XML, you can see that three buttons have been created: **ConBold**, **ConItalic**, and **ConUnderline**. If you try clicking any of these buttons, you will receive an error message stating that it cannot run the macro. This is a piece of code defined by the **onAction** parameter, and at the moment this does not exist. This is very similar to the **OnAction** property in the **CommandBars** object that enabled you to hook a piece of code on to a menu item that you had created (see Chapter 11).

Take some time to look through this sample piece of XML and see how it is constructed. If necessary, refer back to Chapter 20 to see the structure of an XML file. The code is shown here:

```
<customUI xmlns="http://schemas.microsoft.com/office/2006/01/customui">
    <ribbon>
        <tabs>
            <tab id="customTab" label="Contoso" insertAfterMso="TabHome">
                <group idMso="GroupClipboard" />
                <group idMso="GroupFont" />
                <group id="customGroup" label="Contoso Tools">
                    <button id="customButton1" label="ConBold" size="large"
                        onAction="conBoldSub" imageMso="Bold" />
                    <button id="customButton2" label="ConItalic" size="large"
                        onAction="conItalicSub" imageMso="Italic" />
                    <button id="customButton3" label="ConUnderline"
                        size="large" onAction="conUnderlineSub"
                        imageMso="Underline" />
                </group>
                <group idMso="GroupEnterDataAlignment" />
                <group idMso="GroupEnterDataNumber" />
                <group idMso="GroupQuickFormatting" />
            </tab>
        </tabs>
    </ribbon>
</customUI>
```

One of the most important points to bear in mind is that XML is case-sensitive and you need to follow the exact case when putting together your own XML; otherwise, it will not work. Whereas in VBA this all gets taken care of via the editor, it is very important to get it right here.

The XML starts off with a root element:

```
<customUI xmlns="http://schemas.microsoft.com/office/2006/01/customui">
```

Elements are then defined for <ribbon> and <tabs>. The tabs are effectively the menu items on the menu bar in Excel. There is then a tab definition for the new menu item called Contoso. This line provides it with an internal ID, the name as it will appear on the menu bar, and where it will be positioned on the menu bar.

The next lines add in the ribbon groups for **clipboard** and **font**. The third group added in is a custom one with a custom internal ID and a label to define it. Buttons are then added in as child elements providing custom internal IDs, labels, sizes, and images to use. You can see how all these parameters work by comparing what you see in the **ribbon** group on the Excel screen to the actual XML.

The custom group also has a closing element to finish it off: </group>. This defines that the definition of the custom group has finished.

Curiously, three other groups are also defined after this, but their names do not exist in the ribbon model, so they have been ignored.

The XML is then finished off with closing tags for tab, tabs, ribbon, and Custom UI.

Creating Code for Your Custom Buttons

As already mentioned, the buttons in the ribbon custom group only produce an error message because they have no code to run. You need to create code that utilizes the **OnAction** parameter from the custom ribbon control that was created.

Usefully, the Custom UI Editor assists you in doing this. If you look at the toolbar displayed, the icon on the far right has a label of "Generate Callbacks," which you can see if you hover your mouse over the icon. Click this and you will see skeleton code for all three custom buttons within the XML. Open the VBA Editor window in your Excel spreadsheet and insert a module by clicking Insert | Module. Make sure that you insert it in the workbook that has the custom ribbon; otherwise, it will not work.

Copy the skeleton code from the Custom UI Editor window by selecting all of it and pressing CTRL-C. Select the module on the VBA Editor window and press CTRL-V to paste it into your code. Your screen should now look like Figure 21-4.

If you go back to the Excel spreadsheet window, select your custom ribbon group, and click one of the buttons, you will now find that no error message now appears. Nothing actually happens, but just copying in the skeleton code has provided code for the **OnAction** parameter and has suppressed the error message.

You now need to add some code in to the callback code to make the buttons do something. You could make the code for the first button as follows:

```
'Callback for customButton1 onAction
Sub conBoldSub(control As IRibbonControl)
ActiveCell.Font.Bold = True
End Sub
```

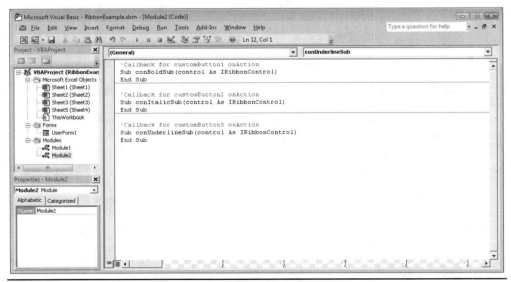

Figure 21-4   *VBA Editor window showing skeleton callback code*

This simply sets the active cell bold attribute. Pretty simple stuff, but by using your imagination you could go a lot further on this.

The preceding example only provides code that will take a specific action when the ribbon button is clicked.

You can also include code that will pass back a return value for the purposes of the title of the group, which then allows us to alter the title of the ribbon group programmatically. To do this, you need to exit your sample Excel file and then load it into the Custom UI Editor. The element for group should be altered to read

```
<group id="customGroup" getLabel="MyLabel">
This originally read:
<group id="customGroup" label="Contoso Tools">
```

Instead of specifying a static label for the group, you are now going to alter this dynamically using the subroutine MyLabel. In the module for this spreadsheet, insert the following code:

```
Sub MyLabel(control As IRibbonControl, ReturnValue As Variant)
ReturnValue = "My new title"
End Sub
```

The code is similar to the **OnAction** code that was created, but there is now an additional parameter called **ReturnValue**. This passes back a string called "My new title", which is used as the title for the ribbon group. If you now click Contoso, you will find that the custom group title has changed to the new text. The restriction on using this code is that it is only called when the Excel file is loaded in. This gives opportunities for the title to be changed according to a certain parameter such as the day of the week, but once it has changed, it cannot be called again without loading the file again.

Images

You can use all the images available in the add-in Office2007IconsGallery on the MSDN web site to customize your ribbon buttons. The best way to access this add-in is to go to http://msdn.microsoft.com and then search for Office2007IconsGallery. This will take you straight to the page to download this Excel add-in.

For example, if you want to use a smiley face, you use the parameter imageMso="HappyFace" instead of imageMso="Bold".

How Can You Use VBA Code with the Ribbon

From a VBA programming angle, the big question is how can you use VBA code dynamically with the ribbon. The answer to this, unfortunately, is that your opportunities are fairly limited.

Using VBA, you can find out if a particular ribbon control is enabled, is visible, or has been clicked. You can get the control's label, screentip or supertip (screentip and supertip are essentially the same thing), and you can display the control's image. You can also execute a particular control.

As you have already seen, you can add code to a control and you can change the title of a ribbon group, but this can only take place when the Excel file is loaded in.

Excel 2007 has over 1,700 ribbon controls, and each has a name. You use this name to identify the control in the collection when you are working with it.

A simple example of code to access a ribbon control is as follows:

```
MsgBox Application.CommandBars.GetEnabledMso("FontSizeDecrease")
```

This should return **True** in that the FontSizeDecrease control is enabled. Note that these names are case sensitive and if you put in "fontsizedecrease," this will produce an error.

The next question is, how do you get the name of a particular control with so many available? To do this, you need to place your cursor on the menu bar of the Excel spreadsheet and right-click. Take the option Customize Quick Action Toolbar or press C. You will see a form displayed as shown in Figure 21-5.

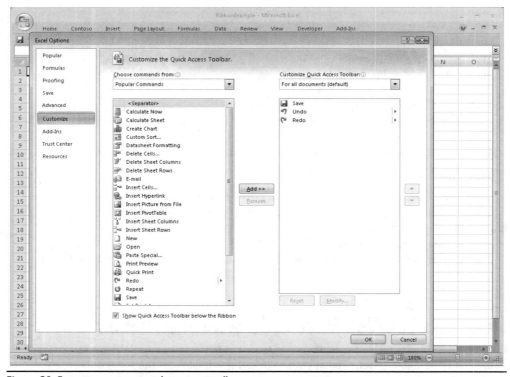

Figure 21-5   *Customize Quick Action Toolbar screen*

By selecting the drop-down Choose Commands From in the top left-hand corner of the form, you can select control lists in any of the menu tabs or any of the other groups available. You can even see the custom tab called Conteso that you created earlier.

If you select one of these options, you will then see all the controls and groups associated with it. If you hover your cursor over any one of the controls, you will see the name of it shown in brackets at the end of the tooltip string.

One important rule is that the list shows both groups and controls within those groups. The controls have icons; the groups do not. If you try to use this code on a group name, you will get an error. For example, GroupFont is a group (there is no icon next to it), so the statement

```
MsgBox Application.CommandBars.GetEnabledMso("GroupFont")
```

will give an error. However, if you substitute "FontSizeDecrease" for "Font," the code will run correctly.

As already stated, you can see the custom ribbon group that you created earlier called Conteso. If you hover your cursor on your custom controls, you will see that they all have names, but the sad thing is that they all have the same name (CustomControl) and you cannot access them by using this code.

You can use the following methods in conjunction with the existing controls within Excel:

▶ **ExecuteMso**   Runs the control as if the user had clicked it.

▶ **GetEnabledMso**   Returns True or False according to whether the control is enabled.

▶ **GetImageMso**   Returns the control image into a variable defined as IPictureDisplay. You also need to define width and height.

▶ **GetLabelMso**   Returns the label for that control, which is often the same as the name.

▶ **GetPressedMso**   Applies to check box and toggle buttons and returns True if the control has been pressed.

▶ **GetScreentipMso**   Returns the string for the screentip for that control. This is often the same as the name and the label.

▶ **GetSupertipMso**   Returns the super screentip for the control and is usually more descriptive.

▶ **ReleaseFocus**   Releases the focus on the command bar object.

▶ **GetVisibleMso**   Returns True or False for a given ID of an Mso (Microsoft Office control).

You can also use the parameters defined in the callback code to access user actions, such as if the user checked a check box or entered some text into an edit box. You will see examples of this further on in this chapter.

The ExecuteMso method is probably the most useful. The GetImageMso is complicated to use but it can be used to display control images on to your spreadsheet:

```
Sub DisplayMsoImage()
    Dim MyMsoImage As OLEObject
    Set MyMsoImage = _
 ActiveSheet.OLEObjects.Add(ClassType:="Forms.Image.1", Left:=100,
    Top:=100)
    MyMsoImage.Object.Picture = _
        Application.CommandBars.GetImageMso("Copy", 32, 32)

End Sub
```

This will place the image for the Copy control on the current sheet at position 100, 100.
    To clear this image from the sheet, use the following code:

```
ActiveSheet.OLEObjects(1).Delete
```

More on the Ribbon

Using the custom UI Editor, try adding the following code to the sample spreadsheet that you constructed earlier. This should be added in after </group> and before </tabs>:

```
</tab>
    <tab idMso="TabHome">
        <group id="Group1" label="My Control">
        <checkBox id="Checkbox1"
        label="Checkbox sample"
        onAction="MyCheckbox"
        />

</tab>
```

Your example file in the Custom UI Editor should now look like this:

```
<customUI xmlns="http://schemas.microsoft.com/office/2006/01/customui">
    <ribbon>
        <tabs>
            <tab id="customTab" label="Contoso" insertAfterMso="TabHome">
                <group idMso="GroupClipboard" />
                <group idMso="GroupFont" />
                <group id="customGroup" getLabel="MyLabel">
                    <button id="customButton1" label="ConBold" size="large"
                        onAction="conBoldSub" imageMso="HappyFace" />
```

```
                <button id="customButton2" label="ConItalic" size="large"
                    onAction="conItalicSub" imageMso="Italic" />
                <button id="customButton3" label="ConUnderline"
                    size="large" onAction="conUnderlineSub"
                    imageMso="Underline" />
            </group>
            <group idMso="GroupEnterDataAlignment" />
            <group idMso="GroupEnterDataNumber" />
            <group idMso="GroupQuickFormatting" />

        </tab>
        <tab idMso="TabHome">
            <group id="Group1" label="My Control">
                <checkBox id="Checkbox1" label="Checkbox sample"
                    onAction="MyCheckbox" />

            </group>
        </tab>

    </tabs>
  </ribbon>
</customUI>
```

Note that you can have only one **Custom UI** root within the XML file. If you try to create a second root for this, you will get errors and the ribbon XML will not work.

The purpose of this extra XML is to create a sample check box in a custom ribbon control on the Home tab of the user interface. It uses four callbacks, but these have not yet been defined. If you open the Home tab, you will get error messages that the procedure **MyCheckbox** does not exist.

You have now defined a check box with a callback called **MyCheckbox**. Load your file into Excel and click Home on the menu bar. Your screen will now look like Figure 21-6, with your new ribbon control My Control at the end of the ribbon containing a check box.

You can use the Generate Callbacks icon to help generate the code for the callback. This helps you with the parameters passed across. For example, with a check box there is a parameter called "pressed."

Copy the callback for Checkbox1 and paste it into the module that you created earlier in the VBA Editor. Save the file and close it down. When you now load the file, there are no error messages, as the callback is now defined.

You can now enter code for when the user ticks the check box or unticks it:

```
Sub MyCheckbox(control As IRibbonControl, pressed As Boolean)
MsgBox pressed
End Sub
```

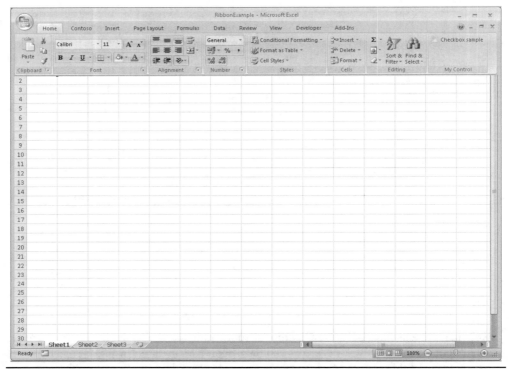

Figure 21-6   *Excel screen showing ribbon control*

When the user activates the check box, you will get a message box displaying "True," which becomes "False" when the box is deactivated. You can insert appropriate code here to deal with the check box being checked or unchecked by the user.

You can also use your ribbon control to capture user input by including an edit box in your ribbon control. To do this add in the following XML below your check box XML code:

```
<editBox id="Editbox1"
label="Editbox sample"
onChange="MyChange"/>
```

Note that in the case of the edit box, there is no **onAction** event. Instead, there is an **onChange** event. This different event can be confusing to the first-time user, but one of the ways of checking is to click the Generate Callbacks button. If you enter **onAction** instead of **onChange**, you will get an error message.

Your overall XML should now look like this:

```xml
<customUI xmlns="http://schemas.microsoft.com/office/2006/01/customui"
    onLoad="Startup">
    <ribbon>
        <tabs>
            <tab id="customTab" label="Contoso" insertAfterMso="TabHome">
                <group idMso="GroupClipboard" />
                <group idMso="GroupFont" />
                <group id="customGroup" getLabel="MyLabel">
                    <button id="customButton1" label="ConBold" size="large"
                        onAction="conBoldSub" imageMso="HappyFace" />
                    <button id="customButton2" label="ConItalic" size="large"
                        onAction="conItalicSub" imageMso="Italic" />
                    <button id="customButton3" label="ConUnderline"
                        size="large" onAction="conUnderlineSub"
                        imageMso="Underline" />
                </group>
                <group idMso="GroupEnterDataAlignment" />
                <group idMso="GroupEnterDataNumber" />
                <group idMso="GroupQuickFormatting" />

            </tab>
            <tab idMso="TabHome">
            <group id="customGroup1" label="My Control">
            <checkBox id="Checkbox1" label="Checkbox sample"
                onAction="MyCheckbox" />
            <editBox id="Editbox1" label="Editbox sample"
                onChange="MyChange" />


            </group>
        </tab>



        </tabs>
    </ribbon>
</customUI>
```

Save your file in the Custom UI Editor (making sure that it is not already open in Excel), and then load it into Excel. If you now click the Home menu item, you will see that your custom ribbon control My Control now has a text entry box as well as your original check box. If you type something into the text box and press ENTER, you will get an error message because the callback to MyChange has not yet been defined.

Again to create the callback, click the callback icon in the Custom UI Editor and copy and paste the code for Editbox1 **onChange**. This is a very useful feature because it gives you the correct passing parameters within the **callback** subroutine. The checkbox control had a parameter called **pressed** that was a Boolean (True or False), whereas the text box has a **text** parameter to to hold the value that the user typed in.

Your callback code should now look like

```
Sub MyChange(control As IRibbonControl, text As String)
MsgBox text
End Sub
```

This simply provides a message box to show what has been typed in. Go back to the spreadsheet and click Home on the menu bar. Enter some text into your new text box on the My Control ribbon control and press ENTER. Your text will then be displayed in a message box on screen.

Suppose you want to include something more complicated in your ribbon control such as a combo box (a drop-down control). This can also be accomplished in a fairly straightforward manner.

In the Custom UI Editor, add in the following XML below your edit box XML:

```
<comboBox
id="MyCombo"label="My Combo"
onChange ="OnChange"
getItemCount ="GetItemCount"
getItemLabel ="GetItemLabel"
/>
```

Your overall XML should now look like this:

```
<customUI xmlns="http://schemas.microsoft.com/office/2006/01/customui"
    <ribbon>
        <tabs>
            <tab id="customTab" label="Contoso" insertAfterMso="TabHome">
            <group idMso="GroupClipboard" />
            <group idMso="GroupFont" />
            <group id="customGroup" getLabel="MyLabel">
                <button id="customButton1" label="ConBold" size="large"
                    onAction="conBoldSub" imageMso="HappyFace" />
                <button id="customButton2" label="ConItalic" size="large"
                    onAction="conItalicSub" imageMso="Italic" />
                <button id="customButton3" label="ConUnderline" size="large"
                    onAction="conUnderlineSub" imageMso="Underline" />
            </group>
            <group idMso="GroupEnterDataAlignment" />
            <group idMso="GroupEnterDataNumber" />
            <group idMso="GroupQuickFormatting" />

            </tab>
            <tab idMso="TabHome">
            <group id="customGroup1" label="My Control">
            <checkBox id="Checkbox1" label="Checkbox sample"
                onAction="MyCheckbox" />
```

```
            <editBox id="Editbox1" label="Editbox sample"
                onChange="MyChange" />
            <comboBox id="MyCombo" label="My Combo"
                onChange ="OnChange" getItemCount ="GetItemCount"
                getItemLabel ="GetItemLabel" />
            </group>
            </tab>
        </tabs>
    </ribbon>
</customUI>
```

As with the edit box there is an **onChange** event, but there are also a **getItemCount** event and a **getItemLabel** event to define the combo box.

As before, save the file in the Custom UI Editor and then open it up in Excel. If you click Home in the menu bar and look at your custom ribbon control, this now has a drop-down, but it is not populated.

In the Custom UI Editor use the Create Callbacks icon to copy across the three callbacks for **OnChange**, **GetItemCount**, and **GetItemLabel**. Paste these into your VBA module. You need to also define an array to hold the values for the drop-down. Do this by putting the following statement in the declarations area of the module:

```
Dim ComboArray(3)
```

This will set up an array with four elements beginning at index 0.

You then need to add in the following code for your callbacks:

```
Sub GetItemCount(control As IRibbonControl, ByRef returnedVal)
returnedVal = 4
End Sub


Sub GetItemLabel(control As IRibbonControl, index As Integer, ByRef
returnedVal)
ComboArray(0)  = "Option1"
ComboArray(1)  = "Option2"
ComboArray(2)  = "Option3"
ComboArray(3)  = "Option4"

returnedVal = ComboArray(index)

End Sub


Sub OnChange(control As IRibbonControl, text As String)
MsgBox text

End Sub
```

Looking at these in turn, **GetItemCount** returns the number of items in the combo box list, which is 4.

GetItemLabel is more complicated. This populates the four-element array that you set up with option labels and then returns the array referenced by the index parameter (which is based on the number of items declared in **GetItemCount**).

Finally, **OnChange** displays the selected text when the user chooses an item from the combo box list.

Once you have put all this code in to your module, you must then save the file and close it. The reason for this is that **GetItemCount** and **GetItemLabel** are only called when the file is loaded into Excel. This means that you can only declare your combo list at this point and it cannot be changed dynamically during the operation of the spreadsheet. This is something of a drawback.

When you load your file, click Home in the menu bar and click the combo box in your custom control. You will see your four options listed (see Figure 21-7). Click one of those options and the text will appear in a message box on the spreadsheet screen.

In conjunction with the button control these examples provide simple ways for your ribbon control to interact with the user, and for you to provide code to deal with that interaction.

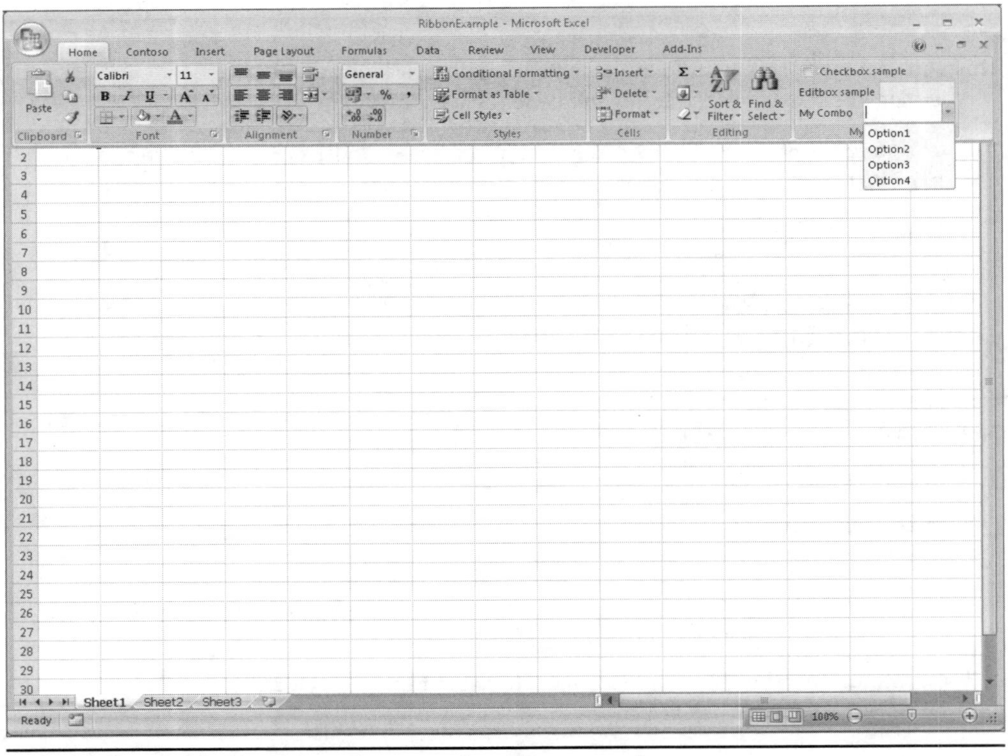

Figure 21-7   *Excel ribbon showing custom drop-down control*

Pivot Tables

I f you have used Excel's more advanced features, particularly for handling and analyzing large quantities of data, then you will have come across *pivot tables*. This feature is extremely powerful and allows you to use data in a spreadsheet that looks like a data table almost as if it were in a database. It is very useful for showing summaries of your data within a "cube" format and giving the user the means to summarize the data using different parameters and different conditions. You can effectively build in functionality similar to what you would find within an Access query if the data was held in an Access table.

A pivot table can be easily created in Excel, but you will also see that VBA provides a huge number of commands to control the pivot tables programmatically.

Creating a Simple Pivot Table from the Front End of Excel

Just in case you have never seen or used a pivot table before, here is how to create a simple pivot table so that you can understand the basic principles before moving on to the VBA side of things.

You first need to create some data in columnar format on a worksheet as shown in Figure 22-1. It is very important that you use column headings, as these are used within the pivot table to define groupings.

Next, click Insert on the menu bar and click the Pivot Table icon in the Tables group of the ribbon (far left of ribbon). A dialog will allow you to select a range of data to use in your pivot table. You select all the data shown in Figure 22-1 (A1.D11). Leave the other settings as they are and click OK.

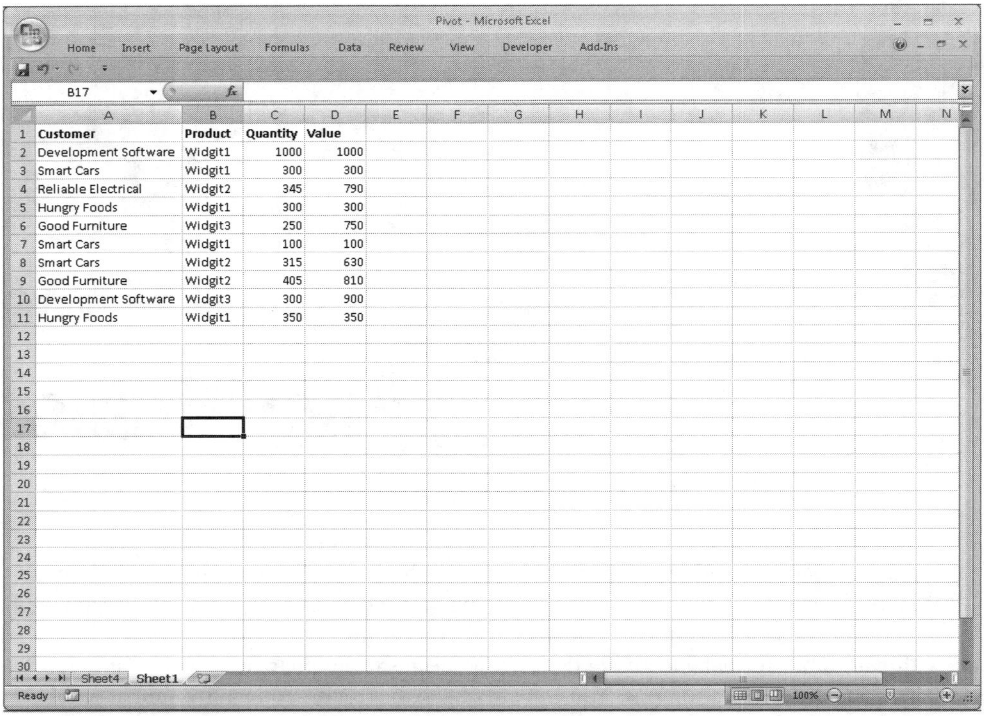

Figure 22-1   *Data in columnar format on a worksheet*

The Pivot Table window will appear, and your screen will look like Figure 22-2.

Note that you can also use an external data source for your pivot table, such as an ODBC connection to an external database. You can also put the pivot table into a new worksheet or keep it within the existing worksheet, and you can specify where it will appear within that worksheet. For the purposes of this exercise, accept the default settings and click OK. A new sheet will appear in your workbook, and your screen will look like Figure 22-3.

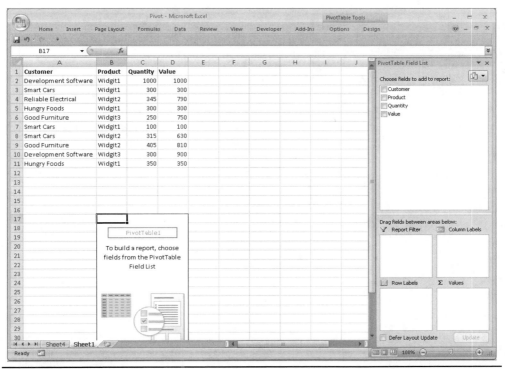

Figure 22-2   *Excel Pivot Table in the same worksheet example*

You now need to build the pivot table. Since it is a sales report, you want the customer name and product down the left-hand side of the pivot table. To do this, click Customer in the Pivot Table Field List and click the check box to the left of it. You will see your pivot table beginning to appear on the worksheet.

Click the check box for Product in the Pivot Table Field List and a subheading for the product will appear in your pivot table.

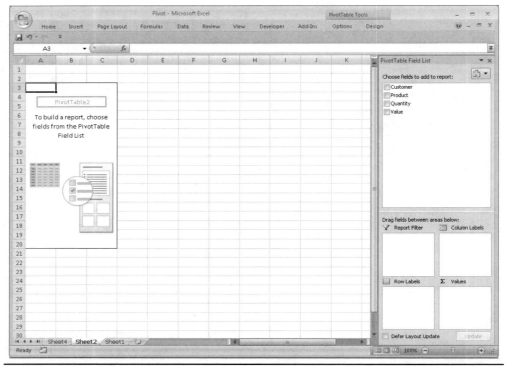

Figure 22-3 *Example of pivot table in a new worksheet*

You now need to show the actual quantities and values for the customers and products. Place your cursor on Quantity in the Pivot Table Field List, hold down the left mouse button, and drag it into the Sum of Values window (bottom right) in the Pivot Table Design window. Do the same thing for Value, and you will now see that you have a complete pivot table based on your data as shown in Figure 22-4.

The pivot table shows a summary of your data by customer and product in an easily readable format. If your data consisted of several thousand rows, there are obvious benefits to being able to present the data in a summarized format like this.

More advanced features for the pivot table are available to allow the user to extend and collapse headings and use filters. For presentation of data in Excel, this creates a very user-friendly way to do this and is extremely popular with users.

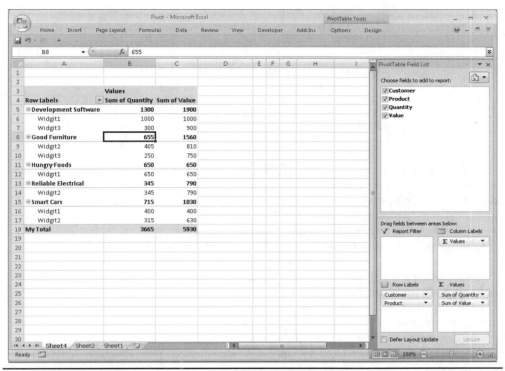

Figure 22-4   *A completed pivot table*

Creating a Pivot Table Using VBA

We have seen how to create a simple pivot table using the front end of Excel, but this can also be done using VBA code. The following code sample will create the identical pivot table:

```
Sub CreatePivot()
    Sheets.Add
    ActiveWorkbook.PivotCaches.Create(SourceType:=xlDatabase, _
        SourceData:="Sheet1!R1C1:R11C4", _
        Version:=xlPivotTableVersion12).CreatePivotTable _
        TableDestination:="Sheet4!R3C1", TableName:="PivotTable5", _
        DefaultVersion:=xlPivotTableVersion12
    Sheets("Sheet4").Select
    Cells(3, 1).Select
    With ActiveSheet.PivotTables("PivotTable5").PivotFields("Customer")
        .Orientation = xlRowField
        .Position = 1
    End With
```

```
   With ActiveSheet.PivotTables("PivotTable5").PivotFields("Product")
       .Orientation = xlRowField
       .Position = 2
   End With
   ActiveSheet.PivotTables("PivotTable5").AddDataField _
       ActiveSheet.PivotTables("PivotTable5").PivotFields("Quantity"), _
       "Sum of Quantity", xlSum ActiveSheet.PivotTables("PivotTable5") _
       .AddDataField ActiveSheet.PivotTables("PivotTable5") _
       .PivotFields("Value"), "Sum of Value", xlSum
End Sub
```

In order for this code to work successfully, notice that certain names are used for the worksheet name and the pivot table and these must not be already in use. The pivot table is added to Sheet4, which must not already be defined as a worksheet in the current workbook, since it is being created by this code. Similarly, PivotTable5 is the name reference given to the pivot table being created. Again, this must not already exist.

A further point is that the address references are in R1C1 format. You cannot use an address such as A1..D11 as a parameter, since this will produce an error.

The preceding code first creates a new worksheet and then defines a pivot cache. The *pivot cache* refers to the location of the data table that drives the pivot table, the location of the actual pivot table, the version of the pivot table being used, and the name of the pivot table for reference purposes. This effectively defines a blank pivot table without the row and column definitions.

The sheet where the pivot table will appear is then selected (Sheet4) and an offset to cell A3 is included so that the pivot table does not sit right at the top of the worksheet.

Next the two row fields are added (Customer and Product). Because the code has already created the pivot cache that directs where the data source is, all the columns within the data source are already included as index references within the pivot fields collection. In order to include the customer and product columns in the pivot table, all that is necessary is to set the Orientation property to **xlRowField** and the Order property to **1** or **2**, depending on the column order.

Finally, the two value columns are created. This is done by using the **AddDataField** method, passing the parameters for the Quantity and Value fields based on the source table, and including the optional parameters of **Caption** and **Function**. The **Function** parameter in each case is set to **xlSum**, although it could also be set to something like **xlCount**.

Using VBA with a Pivot Table

Because of the rich structure of the pivot table object model, there is a great deal that can be done in terms of changing the pivot table programmatically using VBA.

For example, if you wanted to turn the Quantity column in your pivot table into a count of items column, you would use the following code. The code assumes that you have a pivot table called PivotTable5.

```
With ActiveSheet.PivotTables("PivotTable5").PivotFields("Sum of Quantity")
      .Caption = "Count of Quantity"
      .Function = xlCount
   End With
```

To change it back to a sum of total, you would use the following code:

```
With ActiveSheet.PivotTables("PivotTable5").PivotFields("Count of Quantity")
      .Caption = "Sum of Quantity"
      .Function = xlSum
   End With
```

Notice that when you change the **Caption** property from "Sum of Quantity" to "Count of Quantity" in the first example, the name of the index in the **PivotFields** collection also changes. This means that when you use the same code a second time around to change the function back to **xlSum** from **xlCount**, you have to reference the pivot field in the **PivotFields** collection as "Count of Quantity" instead of "Sum of Quantity." If you do not follow this methodology, then you will get the error "Unable to get PivotTables property of the Worksheet class" when you run the code a second time.

You could also add in an additional "Count of Quantity" field:

```
ActiveSheet.PivotTables("PivotTable5").AddDataField ActiveSheet.PivotTables( _
      "PivotTable3").PivotFields("Quantity"), "Count of Quantity", xlCount
```

You can also change the visible appearance of the pivot table. If, for example, you wanted to show the product as the primary column with the customer as the secondary column, you would use the following code:

```
With ActiveSheet.PivotTables("PivotTable5").PivotFields("Product")
            .Position = 1
End With
```

There is no need to change the position for the field Customer, as this is changed automatically by VBA.

Your pivot table will now look like Figure 22-5.

To change the order of the pivot table back to its original status, you would use

```
With ActiveSheet.PivotTables("PivotTable5").PivotFields("Customer")
            .Position = 1
End With
```

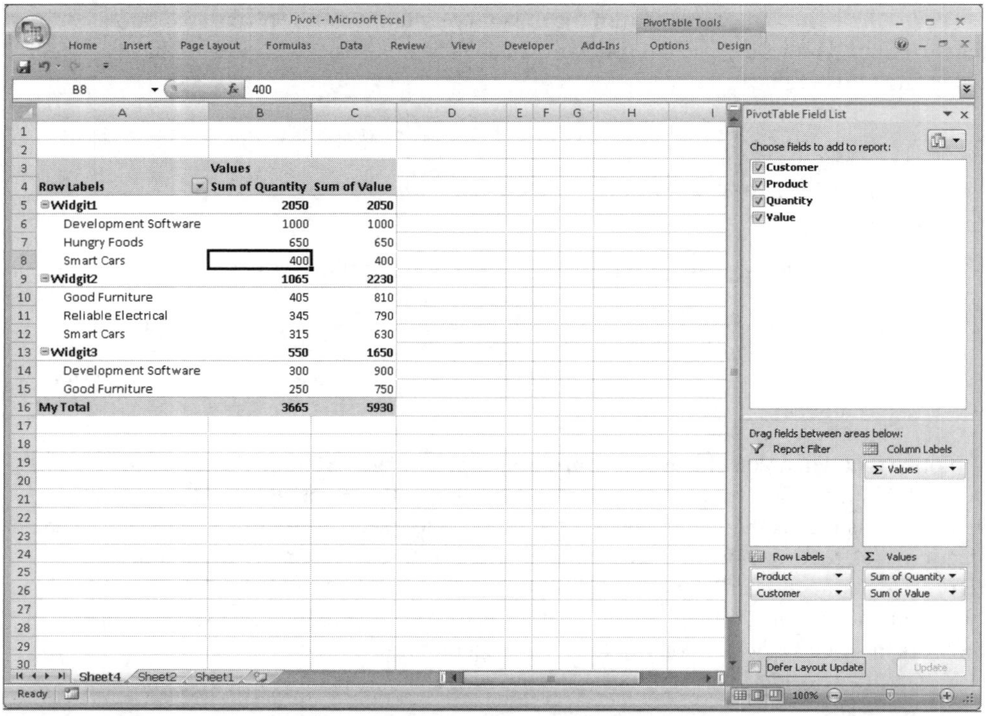

Figure 22-5 *Example of pivot table with column positions changed*

This is effectively the same as the user doing a drag and drop with the field names within the Pivot Table Field List window. It certainly opens up some interesting possibilities. If you wanted to offer your users a number of different complex views on the pivot table, you would write the VBA to do each of these and connect to buttons on the spreadsheet. The user would then just click the buttons without having to know how to manipulate the pivot table via the Pivot Table Field List window.

Other interesting views can easily be provided by using VBA. The following code will turn the Customer field into column labels, keeping the product field as a row label:

```
With ActiveSheet.PivotTables("PivotTable5").PivotFields("Customer")
            .Orientation = xlColumnField
End With
```

By pressing F2 to see the Object Browser and looking at the **PivotFields** collection, you will see that there are a whole load of properties you can use to programmatically change the appearance of your pivot table.

Advanced VBA for Pivot Tables

VBA code can also be used to introduce filters into your pivot tables and to hide or make items visible. For example, suppose that you had a user who wanted a separate view of the pivot table without Hungry Foods included. This is simple to code using the **PivotItems** collection:

```
With ActiveSheet.PivotTables("PivotTable5").PivotFields("Customer")
        .PivotItems("Hungry Foods").Visible = False
End With
```

The code selects the collection item indexed by "Hungry Foods" in the **PivotItems** collection and sets the **Visible** property to **False**. Setting the property back to **True** makes the item visible again.

You can also use VBA to create filters. If you only wanted to see customers beginning with the letter *R* in your pivot table, you could use the following code:

```
ActiveSheet.PivotTables("PivotTable5").PivotFields("Customer").PivotFilters. _
        Add Type:=xlCaptionEquals, Value1:="R*"
```

This adds a new item to the **PivotFilters** collection for the pivot field "Customer" using a wildcard. Notice that the standard wildcards * (string) and ? (single character) are available as criteria.

You are quite likely to get a request for a filter based on one of your value columns, such as all customers where the "'Sum of Quantity" column is greater than 500. The code to do this is as follows:

```
ActiveSheet.PivotTables("PivotTable5").PivotFields("Customer").PivotFilters. _
        Add Type:=xlValueIsGreaterThan, DataField:=ActiveSheet.PivotTables( _
        "PivotTable5").PivotFields("Sum of Quantity"), Value1:=500
```

Notice that the filter is added to the **PivotFilters** collection on the pivot field "Customer," not on the pivot field "Quantity." Filters will work correctly only if they are added to a row heading field. They will have absolutely no effect when added to a column heading, although the code will run without an error, and you will spend a lot of time scratching your head trying to understand why the filter has no effect on the pivot table.

Also you will notice that Value1 (500) is specified as a number. This could easily be changed to a variable or cell reference so that the filter can be updated dynamically when the user updates the pivot data. If Value1 referred to a figure input by the user, then this code could easily be added to the user input routine, making the pivot table change according to what figure the user had input.

To clear the filters for a particular column, the code is very straightforward:

```
ActiveSheet.PivotTables("PivotTable5").PivotFields("Customer").ClearAllFilters
```

VBA also allows you to access parameters that are not available via the user interface. An example of this is if you want to change the name "Grand Total" in your pivot table.

This appears at the bottom of the table, although it can be switched off through the user interface. However, you are stuck with the words "Grand Total," and you will not find an option to give this a new title. This is one of these silly things that users often want to change but cannot find a way to do so from the user interface.

The VBA code to change this is very simple:

```
ActiveSheet.PivotTables("PivotTable5").GrandTotalName = "My Total"
```

What about another thorny problem with pivot tables? What happens if your underlying data table changes in size in the worksheet? This could be an imported text file, and the number of rows could shrink or grow, in which case your pivot table would not pick up the correct information. This is certainly a common error that I have seen in pivot tables used in professional applications.

You will also notice that on the pivot table there is no option to change the source data range via the user interface. Strangely enough, in Excel 2003 it was quite easy for the user (with a bit of knowledge) to increase or shrink the source data range. However, in Excel 2007 it is difficult to do this.

If you insert rows into the source data table, then this will automatically feed into the pivot table, provided that you right-click a numerical cell and click Refresh. However, if your feed is from a text file import, you will not be able to do this, as Excel will be unaware of any extra or reduced rows within your import table.

Using VBA, you can easily find out how many rows have been imported. You can then adjust the source data for the pivot cache and refresh it using the following code:

```
ActiveWorkbook.PivotCaches(1).SourceData = "Sheet1!R1C1:R12C4"
ActiveWorkbook.PivotCaches(1).Refresh
```

This code assumes that the pivot table that you are working with is index 1. The code is actually very simple but gets around a huge problem.

Points to Bear in Mind on Pivot Tables

Excel 2007 pivot tables are not backwardly compatible to previous versions. If you use some of the VBA examples in this chapter, even if you save the file as XLS format, you may find that your code will produce errors in a previous version of Excel.

You can now develop far larger pivot tables with more rows, columns, fields, and pivot table items available to you.

You can also change the style of the pivot table by clicking Design in the menu bar and selecting a pivot table style. This can be done programmatically by

```
ActiveSheet.PivotTables("PivotTable6").TableStyle2 = "PivotStyleLight14"
```

You can also introduce conditional formatting into your pivot table, although this is done via selected cells and not as part of the pivot table. This introduces the problem that if the layout of the pivot table changes (grows or shrinks), you may get some unexpected results.

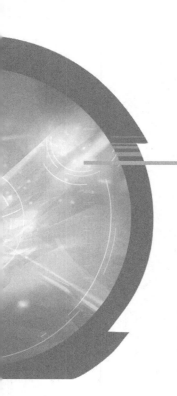

PART

IV

VBA in Action

You have learned the mechanics and techniques of VBA coding in the previous sections. It is now time for some practical experience that will enable you to put everything you have learned to work. This section contains a rich variety of practical examples for how to use Excel VBA. These examples will give you a good idea of how code can be used in Excel to make life easier and provide advanced functionality.

Many of these examples will allow you to achieve actions quickly that are not easy or may be impossible from the standard Excel user interface. Some of them could certainly be described as "hacks."

I have always felt that the best way to learn programming is to look at an example in action and see how it works and what it does. It may not necessarily do exactly what you require, but you can get a very good idea of the basics and feel confident enough to modify it to your own needs or branch out and write your own application.

The last chapter, Chapter 41, shows you how to pull all these examples into an Excel add-in and turn them into a professional and practical application.

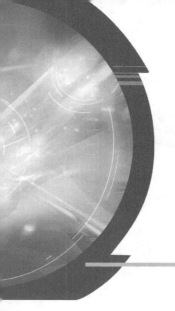

CHAPTER
23

Converting Labels to Numbers and Numbers to Labels

The example presented in this chapter allows the user to make a selection, which can go across several worksheets, and then make a conversion of labels into numbers or numbers into labels where necessary. If you often paste data in from other applications, you will frequently find that the data is pasted in as the wrong data type. Excel does not have a block command to get around this. You can use a formula to do it, but it means a great deal of copying and pasting to get the results you want. The process I will show here allows you to do it in one easy action.

If data is imported or pasted in from another application, it often ends up as labels rather than numbers. This means that it does not follow the normal numeric formatting and is usually left-aligned in a cell. If Excel thinks it is a label, even formatting numerically will not work. If there is a also a mixture of numeric and text characters within a cell, it's impossible to do anything with the formulas based on that cell because the cell will always be recognized as a string of characters rather than a number.

In writing the code, there are certain safeguards to bear in mind. The conversion must take place only if there is a numeric value within the string that is capable of being converted into a number. Also, if the cell holds a formula, conversion must not take place, because the formula will be lost, with disastrous results to the spreadsheet.

NOTE

Whenever you write an application or a macro, always try to think ahead about what the dangers might be to the user. Converting a formula is extremely dangerous, and you may end up with a number of unhappy users.

Here is the sample code:

```
Sub label_to_number()

Dim addr As String

For Each window In Windows
    For Each Worksheet In window.SelectedSheets

        For Each cell In Application.Selection

            addr = Worksheet.Name & "!" & cell.Address

            If IsNumeric(Range(addr).Value) = True And Range(addr).Text _
                <> "" And Range(addr).HasFormula = False Then

                Range(addr) = Val(Range(addr))

            End If

        Next cell

    Next worksheet
Next window
Application.Selection.NumberFormat = "0"
End Sub
```

Notice how the loops are nested and indented—there are several different levels that the macro works through.

The first thing to do is to define a variable to hold each cell address within the selected range; this is called **addr**. The subsequent code will then get the selected range.

The main problem with the macro is that the user may make a selection across a number of worksheets and want your macro to work across that selection. If you do not take this into consideration, you might find that your macro works only on the first selected worksheet, ignoring the rest of the selection. The user will think the macro has gone through the entire selection of worksheets because there is nothing to indicate that it has not. The user, discovering this later on, won't understand what has happened.

Therefore, you not only want the selection from the current worksheet, but you may also want to give the user the flexibility to be able to select multiple sheets by clicking the sheet tabs. The user may also wish to go across more than one workbook.

This gives some idea of the complexities involved when designing a macro. It is straightforward enough to deal with what is going on for a single worksheet, but what happens if multiple worksheets or workbook selections are made?

The selection object on the application object will give the actual cell addresses of cells that have been selected, but it will not tell you the name of the sheet it has occurred on or if there are multiple sheets involved. To do this, you first cycle through the **Windows** object using the syntax For Each..Next. Each worksheet creates a window that is part of the **Windows** collection. This is convenient because it does not matter how many sheets or workbooks are loaded. Do not confuse this with Windows itself—this collection is unique to windows within Excel. This will give you the name of each worksheet within Excel, regardless of the workbook it is in. You can then cycle through the worksheets, which are actually selected by using the **SelectedSheets** collection.

Within each selected worksheet, look at the **Selection** object. This is defined as the selection the user made by dragging the cursor over a group of cells so that a highlighted block appears. When this code is run, the **Selection** object will have the address of that selection.

There are a number of cells in the **Selection** object, so cycle through the selected cells using the syntax For Each..Next again. The cell address gives you the coordinates of that cell but does not tell us what worksheet it is sitting on. This is the reason for the first cycle through the **Windows** object to get the names of all the worksheets involved.

The cell address is then concatenated to the worksheet name using the ! character and stored in the variable **addr**. At this point, you need to check the cell for certain attributes, so you use an If statement. Use the **Range** method on the variable **addr** to do this.

The code checks that there is a numeric value in the cell, that the cell is not empty, and that it is not a formula. It uses the **IsNumeric** function and the **HasFormula** property. There is also a simple expression to check if the cell is empty. If all conditions are satisfied, it sets the cell value to the numeric value using the **Val** function.

The **End If** statement ends the If condition, and the remaining **Next** statements cycle through the collections until all the selections are completed. In this way, all selected sheets are worked through and all selected cells within those sheets are cycled through, as shown in Figure 23-1.

The final step in the code is to ensure that the format of the selection is changed to numeric. If the cells had been originally formatted to text, then they would still show as text in spite of the fact that the code entered numeric values.

Some label data has been placed in cells, and a formula has been put in at cell A1. To turn a number into a label, insert the single quote (') character first, and it will left-align as a label. Then make a selection by dragging the cursor across the range of data.

Run the macro, and anything that is a proper numeric will be changed to a number in the cell. Blank cells and formulas will remain the same.

With some ingenuity, it is not difficult to make this code go further. Strings that are partly numeric could have any nonnumeric characters stripped out from them and then converted to be numeric. The same code can also be used in reverse to convert cell contents back to labels:

```
Sub contents_to_label()
Dim addr As String
For Each window In Windows
    For Each Worksheet In window.SelectedSheets
```

```
        For Each cell In Application.Selection

            addr = Worksheet.Name & "!" & cell.Address

            If Range(addr).Value <> 0 Then Range(addr) = "'" & _
                CStr(Range(addr))

        Next cell
     Next worksheet

Next window
End Sub
```

This code is identical to the conversion of labels to numerics except for the actual conversion statement for the cell, which checks that there is a value there and uses the **CStr** function to change it to a string. It concatenates the single quote (') character in front so that it will be read as a label in the cell.

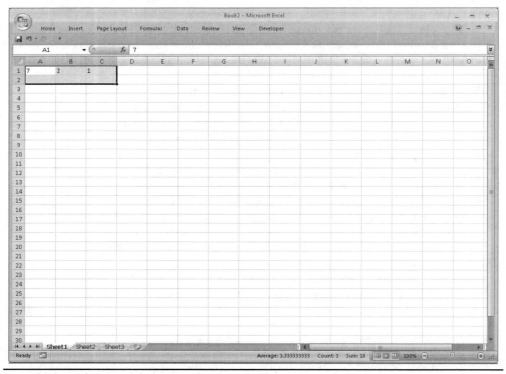

Figure 23-1   *Changing labels to numbers in a worksheet*

Transposing a Range of Cells

I t often happens that when you put a spreadsheet together, you suddenly find that you really need the row headings across the top and the column headings down the side in order to make the data readable. You can achieve this using copy and paste, but it takes several steps and there is always a danger of losing some data. The routine in this chapter shows how you can do this in one easy movement over a selected range.

This example presupposes that the worksheet Sheet1 will be used as a temporary store for data and will normally be blank. You could also use the next spreadsheet or create a new one.

Insert the following code into a module:

```
Sub transpose()
sel = Application.Selection.Address
For Each Window In Windows
    Set mysheets = Window.SelectedSheets
    For Each Worksheet In Window.SelectedSheets

    tempbook = ActiveWorkbook.Name

    Worksheet.Select

    Worksheet.Range(Application.Selection.Address).Copy

    Workbooks(tempbook).Activate
```

```
      temp = Application.ActiveCell.Address
      ActiveWorkbook.Sheets.Add
      ActiveSheet.Range("a1").PasteSpecial transpose:=True
      Worksheet.Range(sel).Clear
      copysheet = ActiveSheet.Name
      ActiveSheet.Range(Application.Selection.Address).Copy
      Worksheet.Range(temp).PasteSpecial

      Application.DisplayAlerts = False
      ActiveWorkbook.Sheets(copysheet).Delete
      Application.DisplayAlerts = True


   Next Worksheet
Next Window
mysheets.Select
End Sub
```

As in other examples, the code cycles through the windows within the **Windows** collection to find the selected sheets. A variable called **mysheets** holds the selected sheets. The code then cycles through each worksheet within the selected sheets collection.

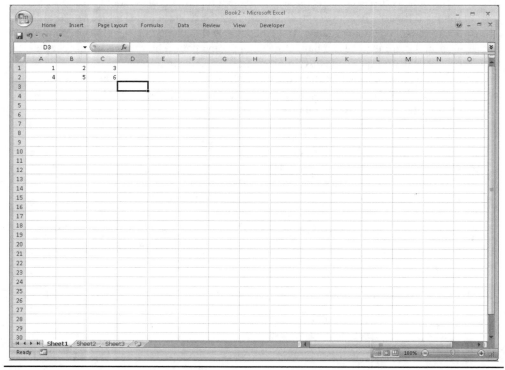

Figure 24-1   *A block of data ready to be transposed*

The name of the active workbook is stored in a variable called **tempbook**, and the selection address is stored in a variable called **sel**. The current worksheet being cycled through is selected. Because you cannot now copy and paste where the ranges overlap, the code inserts a dummy worksheet to paste and transpose the data onto, like a scratchpad.

The original range is cleared using the **sel** variable (as we do not want this to show the data in its nontransposed format), and then data is copied from the dummy worksheet and pasted back into the worksheet where the data is being transposed.

The dummy worksheet is then deleted, as there is no further use for it in this loop. Note that a **DisplayAlerts** statement turns off the alert messages because when a sheet is deleted, a warning message pops up to warn that data may be lost. We do not want to see this in our application, so this is a simple way of preventing it from appearing. Do not forget to switch it back on in your code; otherwise, no alert messages will ever appear and the consequences could be disastrous.

Finally, the sheets that were originally selected are reselected again using the variable **mysheets**. This ensures that the workbook ends up back in the state that the user started off with before running the code.

Enter a block of data, as shown in Figure 24-1 on the preceding page. Select this data by dragging the cursor over it, and then run the transpose code. The results are shown in Figure 24-2.

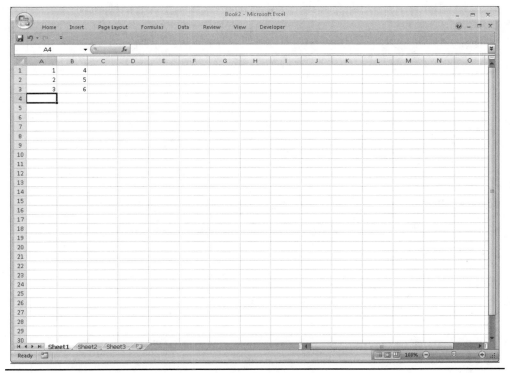

Figure 24-2   *The same block of data transposed*

25

Adding Formula Details into Comments

W hen you have a complex spreadsheet, you often need to check formulas to make sure that the results are correct, and this may involve looking through a number of cells where they are chained together. The only way in Excel to view a formula is to click the cell that contains it. This can be time-consuming and frustrating.

An easier way is to copy the formula into the comment for that cell. That way, you only need to sweep the cursor across that cell, and the formula will pop up in a comments box. You can see it instantly and without having to transfer your cell cursor position to that cell.

The only problem is that there could be many formulas in the spreadsheet—what happens if any are changed? Trying to check them manually would be a nightmare.

The following code adds any formulas into the comments box for a user selection. If there is a comment already there, it preserves the comment, and if there is already a formula/comment there, it updates the comment. The pipe (|) symbol (SHIFT-\) is used to separate existing comments from the formula.

```
Sub note()

For Each window In Windows
    For Each Worksheet In window.SelectedSheets

        For Each cell In Application.Selection

            addr = Worksheet.Name & "!" & cell.Address
```

```
temp = ""

On Error Resume Next

temp = Range(addr).Comment.Text

If InStr(temp, "|") Then

    temp = Mid(temp, InStr(temp, "|") + 1)

End If

Range(addr).ClearComments

If Range(addr).HasFormula = True Then

    Range(addr).AddComment (cell.Formula & "|" & temp)

Else

    If temp <> "" Then Range(addr).AddComment temp

End If
        Next cell

    Next worksheet

Next window
End Sub
```

The code cycles through each window in the **Windows** collection and through each worksheet in the selected sheets to find out which worksheets have been selected. Each cell in the user selection on that sheet is then worked through. The variable **addr** holds the worksheet name and the cell address, concatenated with the ! character.

A variable called **temp** is used to build the **note** string, which is set to **Null** initially. It is then loaded with the text of any existing comment using the **comment.text** property. If there is no comment, then an error can occur, which is why this is preceded by **On Error Resume Next**.

A search is then made within the **temp** string using the **Instr** function to see if there is a | symbol. If found, it means that the routine has already been run for that cell and that it already contains a formula. If you already use the | symbol for something else in comments, you may wish to alter the preceding code to use a different symbol, such as a backslash (\).

If there is already a formula in the comment, you need to remove it. Do this by setting the **temp** string to all characters after the | symbol so that the current formula for that cell can be added in.

The next step is to clear the comments from that cell, since you have the comments in the **temp** string.

The code then checks whether the cell has a formula by checking the **HasFormula** property. If it does, it adds in a new comment by concatenating the formula, then the | symbol to denote the end of the formula, and then the original comment if it was there. Bear in mind that if there was no comment previously, **temp** was initially set to **Null** for each loop, so no comment would show. If there was no formula, then the old comment is added back using

```
If temp <> "" Then Range(addr).AddComment temp
```

If it is a null string (because there was no previous comment), then no comment is actually set because of the **If** statement at the start of this line.

Make a selection on a spreadsheet by dragging the cursor over a range of cells and then run the code. The result should look like Figure 25-1.

Try changing the formula and rerunning the code. The formula part of the comment will change, but the original comment will stay the same.

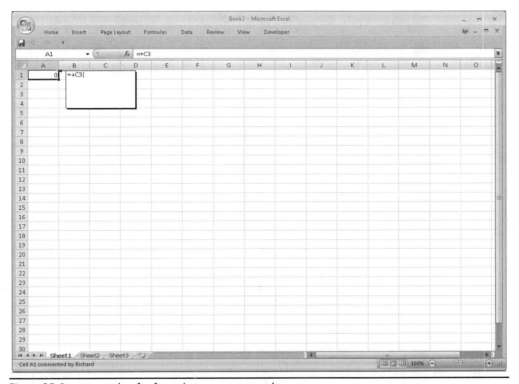

Figure 25-1   *Example of a formula in a comments box*

Calculating a Range

I f you have a complex spreadsheet, it often takes time to calculate, particularly if you have complex formulas and a number of worksheets. Of course, you can set calculation to manual by clicking the Office Start button, clicking Excel Options, and selecting Advanced, but this will calculate the entire workbook and can take more time than necessary when you only want to calculate one sheet or a range of cells. Microsoft has built a **range.calculate** method into the Excel object model, but strangely enough, it is not available from the spreadsheet menu. To use it, you need the following code in a module:

```
Sub range_calculate()

For Each window In Windows

    For Each Worksheet In window.SelectedSheets

        For Each cell In Application.Selection

            addr = Worksheet.Name & "!" & cell.Address

            Range(addr).Calculate

        Next cell

    Next worksheet

Next window

End Sub
```

The user selects a range by dragging the cursor across it. The user can select multiple sheets by holding down the CTRL key and clicking the sheet tab at the bottom of the Excel window. The selection needs to include cells that have a formula in them.

The code cycles through each window in the **Windows** object and through each worksheet in the **window.selectedsheets** object to find the sheets the user has selected.

Each cell within the selection is then gone through. The variable **addr** holds the selected worksheet name and is concatenated with the cell address using the ! character.

The cell is then calculated. Basically, only the cells within the selected range and on the selected sheets are calculated, which saves a large amount of time.

Try putting some data onto a spreadsheet, including formulas. Set the calculation to manual by clicking Formulas in the menu bar and then clicking the Calculation Options icon in the Calculation control of the ribbon (far right-hand side). Change the data and then select the range. Leave some cells with formulas outside the range. Run the code and check the results. The formulas within the range will recalculate; the ones outside will not.

Reversing a Label

If you import data into a spreadsheet from another application or another file, it is frequently not in the format you would like to see it in. For example, a list of names from another file might be in the format *last name, first name* (e.g., "Shepherd Richard"), and you may want them in the format *first name, last name* (e.g., "Richard Shepherd") in your spreadsheet. There might be thousands of names being imported into your spreadsheet, so how should you deal with it? Should you change each one manually? I have seen some people do this. No, it is much better to write some code to do this and, now that you are aware of the capabilities of Excel VBA, it is fairly straightforward:

```
Sub reverse_label()

For Each window In Windows
    For Each Worksheet In window.SelectedSheets

        For Each cell In Application.Selection

            addr = Worksheet.Name & "!" & cell.Address

                If Len(Range(addr).Text) > 0 Then

                    temp = Range(addr).Value

                    x = InStr(temp, " ")

                    If x=0 Then

                        temp = Mid(temp, x + 1) & " " & Left(temp, x - 1)
```

```
                    Range(addr).Value = temp

             End If

        End If

Next cell
    Next worksheet

Next window

End Sub
```

The user selects a range by dragging the cursor across it. Multiple sheets may also be used. The code cycles through each window in the **Windows** object and through each worksheet in the **window.selectedsheets** object to find the sheets that the user selected. Each cell within the selection is then gone through. The variable **addr** holds the selected worksheet name and is concatenated with the cell address using the ! character. The text in the cell is tested to ensure that there is something in there; the code does not do anything if there is no text.

Next, a variable called **temp** is loaded with the cell value. Using the **Instr** function, a search is made for a space character. The code assumes that there is only one space character between the first name and last name, although you could easily substitute another character for the space, if required. This address is loaded into variable **x**.

If **x** has a nonzero value—that is, if it is a true value—then the space has been found. The variable **temp** is loaded with the part of **temp** after the space, followed by the space itself, and then the part of **temp** before the space. Look at this example:

```
temp = "Richard Shepherd"
x = InStr(temp, " ")
```

The variable **x** will have the value of 8 because the space is the eighth character in the string.

```
temp = Mid(temp, x + 1) & " " & Left(temp, x - 1)
```

Here, **Mid(temp, $x + 1$)** is the same as writing **Mid(temp, 9)**, in this case. Both mean take all characters from the position of character 9 to the end, since I have not specified how many characters to take. This gives the result "Shepherd." **Left(temp, $x - 1$)** is the same as writing **Left(temp, 7)**, in this case. This gives the result "Richard" (seven characters from the left).

The two parts are concatenated together with a space in the middle, and the result is "Shepherd Richard." The string **temp** is then returned to the cell.

Try entering a list of names into a range on a spreadsheet. Leave a space in the middle of some and not in others. Select the range by dragging the cursor over it. Run this code, and you will see that where there is a space, the name has been reversed.

This code can be used for a number of situations and can be easily modified to deal with commas (,) or slashes (/) instead of space characters. For example, if the names were listed "Shepherd, Richard", you would need to search for the comma character.

If there is a middle initial, you will need to modify the code to look for the second space within the search string (assuming that the string is something like "Richard J Shepherd").

28

Who Created the Workbook?

T he Excel standard functions provide a wealth of information that can be placed into the spreadsheet, but one of the things not included is details of who actually created the workbook and the date and time it was created. Of course, you can click the Excel Start button, click Prepare, and then click Properties to find this out, but it would be far simpler to have a standard formula that picks this information up and shows it directly on the spreadsheet.

As you saw in Chapter 3, you can write your own functions, so it is easy enough to write a function that tells the user who created the workbook:

```
Function WHO()

temp = "Created by "

Dim Workbook As Workbook

Set Workbook = Application.ActiveWorkbook

For Each property In Workbook.BuiltinDocumentProperties

    On Error Resume Next

    If property.Name = "Author" Then temp = temp & property.Value
```

```
      If property.Name = "Creation date" Then temp = temp & " on " &
         property.Value

Next property

WHO = temp

End Function
```

Remember, this is a function, not a subroutine, so it works slightly differently from previous examples you have seen so far. No parameters are being passed because you are only picking up data from properties held within Excel and passing them back to the formula on the spreadsheet.

The first thing to do is set up a variable called **temp** holding the string "Created by". This will be the first part of the return string for inclusion in the spreadsheet; the rest will be supplied by the properties.

A variable called **Workbook** is defined as a **Workbook** type. The variable **Workbook** is then set to the active workbook, which currently has the focus and is where the formula will be entered. This is necessary because if there were several workbooks loaded, the formula would be useless if it took the details of the first workbook it came to rather than the one in which the formula is actually being entered.

The code then cycles through each property within the **BuiltInDocumentProperties** collection. This collection is common to all Office applications, so the **BuiltInDocumentProperties** collection contains an enormous number of parameters, many of which are not applicable to an Excel application. The main properties are the same as if you clicked the Office button, selected Prepare from the left-hand menu, and then selected Properties. You will see properties such as **Title**, **Subject**, and **Author**, which can all be used within the code sample shown earlier. An **On Error Resume Next** statement is necessary here because some of the properties cannot be displayed and would cause an error.

If the property name is **Author**, then you concatenate the value onto the **temp** string, so it will read "Created by Richard Shepherd." Note that when **temp** was created, the last character was a space so that the username would concatenate the next property properly. If the next property name is **creation date**, then you concatenate the word " on " being careful to include a leading and trailing space, and then concatenate the property value. This will automatically default to a long date as defined in Windows in the Control Panel's Regional and Language Options dialog. You can easily use the properties in a different order and concatenation to show date created and then author name. However, by using the **Format** function, you can make this appear differently. See earlier details on the **Format** function in Chapter 5.

The variable **WHO** is then loaded with the value of **temp** and passed back to the spreadsheet. You do not need to run the code to try this—just enter a formula (**=WHO()**) as you normally would on the spreadsheet. If you click the Formula Paste icon on the Formula toolbar, this formula will appear in the User Defined Formula section, and you can use it as you would any other formula. If you enter any parameters, you will get the standard Excel errors.

Once you have entered the code into a module, type **=WHO()** into a cell. Note that you must still use the parentheses even though there are no parameters to pass over. The result should look like Figure 28-1.

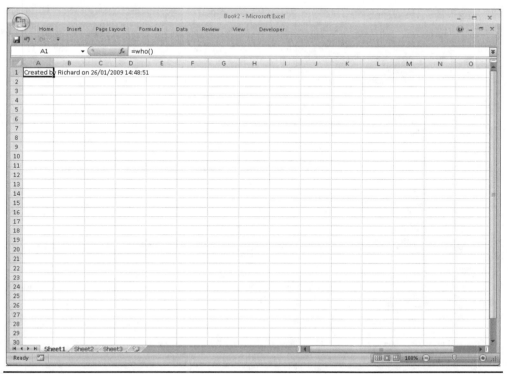

Figure 28-1   *Example of using the WHO function*

Evaluating a Cell

S ometimes in a spreadsheet a cell will contain both numeric characters and letter characters. For example, a cell that contains RJS123 will hold the characters as text. You may wish to separate out the numeric part of this text so that the cell only contains 123, but it is not easy to do this. The function **Value** will convert a label holding numeric data into a real number, but this will not work if there are alpha characters involved as well.

You can write your own function to do this, however. For example, if the cell has the label ART3478BC, you may wish to extract the number, which is 3478. You could use a **Mid** function to do this, but that assumes that the structure of the letters will always be the same. If you do not always have three letters followed by four numbers followed by two letters, then you will have to keep changing your criteria. The following code provides a reliable means to extract numbers from labels:

```
Function EVAL(cell_ref As Object)
    Application.Volatile
    t = ""
    For Each cell In cell_ref
        temp = cell.Value

        For n = 1 To Len(temp)

            If IsNumeric(Mid(temp, n, 1)) Then

                t = t & Mid(temp, n, 1)

            End If
```

```
        Next n
   Next cell
   EVAL = Val(t)

End Function
```

This is a function as opposed to a subroutine, and it behaves differently than a subroutine. A range is passed into it in the form of an object called **cell_ref**.

Application.volatile ensures that the function must be recalculated when any cells on the worksheet are recalculated. The user can then select a cell or range of cells by dragging the cursor in much the same way as you would with the **SUM** function. If only one cell is selected, it is very apparent where the numeric has come from; for example, ABC1234 will be shown as 1234. However, this can have odd results if multiple cells are used because all the numerics will be concatenated together.

A variable called **t** is set to empty, which builds up the numeric string for return back to the cell. Each cell within the **cell_ref** object is then cycled through. A variable called **temp** is loaded with the cell value.

The code then uses a For..Next loop to work through the string of the cell value one character at a time. It tests each character to see if it is numeric using the **IsNumeric** function. If it is numeric, the code concatenates it onto the variable **t**.

When all cells in the selected range are completed, the code takes the value of **t** using the **Val** function and returns it using the variable **EVAL**. To try this out, do not run the code, just enter a formula (for example, **=EVAL(A1)**) as you normally would in the spreadsheet itself.

If you click the Formula Paste icon on the Formula toolbar, this formula will be under the User Defined Formula section, and you can use it as you would for any other formula. If you put in no parameters, you will get the standard Excel errors.

Once you have entered the code into a module, type **ABC1234RS** into cell A1 and type **=EVAL(A1)** into another cell. The cell with the formula will give the result 1234 as a number. Your formula should look like Figure 29-1.

You may want to use this function if you have imported or pasted data in from another source such as a database. If there is a reference code imported that consists of letters and numbers, you may wish to separate out the numbers.

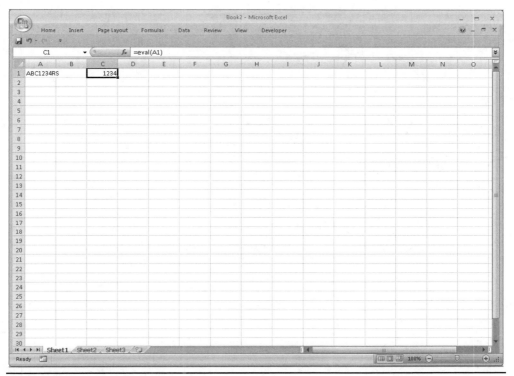

Figure 29-1   *Example of EVAL function*

Sorting Worksheets into Alphabetical Order

As workbooks are developed, the number of worksheets rises, and they often end up in a haphazard order. Of course you can drag sheets about using the sheet tabs, but this can be a complex process when there are many sheets. This chapter deals with code that can quickly and efficiently sort your worksheets by name on the tabs at the bottom. If they have alpha names, they will be sorted alphabetically, and if they have numeric names, they will be sorted numerically. Numeric names are sorted before alpha names.

Insert the following code into a module:

```
Sub sortsheet()
For i = 1 To Sheets.Count

    For j = 1 To Sheets.Count - 1

        If UCase$(Sheets(j).Name) > UCase$(Sheets(j + 1).Name) Then

            Sheets(j).Move after:=Sheets(j + 1)

        End If
    Next j
Next i
End Sub
```

This code is only designed to work on the current workbook—that is, the one that has the focus. Only one workbook can be active and have the focus.

The code cycles through the **Sheets** collection by using the **Count** property and a For..Next loop based on that count. It then has a nested loop that cycles through the same sheets less the final one. This is because the code looks at the current sheet and the next sheet in index order. On the final sheet, there is no next sheet, so this would cause an error in the code. The code tests to see if the name of the current sheet in the For..Next loop is greater than the next sheet.

First, the function **Ucase** is used to convert names into uppercase text because differences between upper- and lowercase could give incorrect results. If the name is greater than the next sheet, then the **Move** method is used to place it after the next sheet (if you are sorting in ascending order, it should be after the next sheet) by setting the **after** parameter to the next indexed sheet. Worksheets within a workbook cannot have the same name, so the code does not have to deal with this problem. In this way a "bubble sort" takes place, and the sheets are sorted into order.

Rename your worksheets by right-clicking the sheet tab at the bottom and selecting Rename. Use random names and ensure that the order of sheet names is mixed up. Run the code, and the sheets will be transferred into the correct order, together with their contents.

Replacing Characters in a String

The code in this chapter creates a worksheet function that replaces all instances of a specified character in a string with another specified character. For example, if you had a cell in your spreadsheet containing the text "***Replacement String***," you could use the Replace formula to replace the * character with the ! character so that the string will read "!!!Replacement String!!!"

This is quite useful for data imported or pasted in from another application. Imported data sometimes includes extraneous characters that need to be removed altogether or changed to another character.

Because this is a public function, it can also be used inside your own VBA code. Insert the following code into a module:

```
Function REP(target As String, r As String, s As String)
temp = ""
For n = 1 To Len(target)

    If Mid(target, n, 1) = r Then

      temp = temp & s

    Else
```

```
        temp = temp & Mid(target, n, 1)
    End If
REP = temp
Next n
End Function
```

This is a function, and it behaves differently than a subroutine in that it is called from the spreadsheet itself by entering a formula, which returns a result to the spreadsheet cell it is in. Three parameters are passed to it:

Name	Type	Description
target	String	String to be searched or a cell reference to it
r	String	Character to be searched for
s	String	Character to replace searched character

A variable **temp** is set to null. This will be used to build the new string. A For..Next loop is then used to move through **target** one character at a time. The **Mid** function breaks out each character from the string and tests it to see if it equals the search character. Note that it has to be an exact match because the match is case sensitive.

If there is a match, the character represented by **s** is concatenated onto the end of **temp**. If there is no match, the original character is concatenated onto **temp**. Finally, the variable **REP**, which represents the function, is given the string value of **temp**, and this places it back into the cell.

You do not need to run the code to try this—just enter a formula as you normally would within a cell of the spreadsheet:

```
=REP(A1,"*","!")
```

If you click the Formula Paste icon on the Formula toolbar, this formula will be under the User Defined Formula section, and you can use it as you would any other formula. If you do not put in the proper parameters, you will get the standard Excel errors. Your worksheet should look like Figure 31-1.

TIP

A handy way to remove a particular character from a string is to set the search string as normal and then set the replacement string as an empty string:

```
=REP(A1,"*","")
```

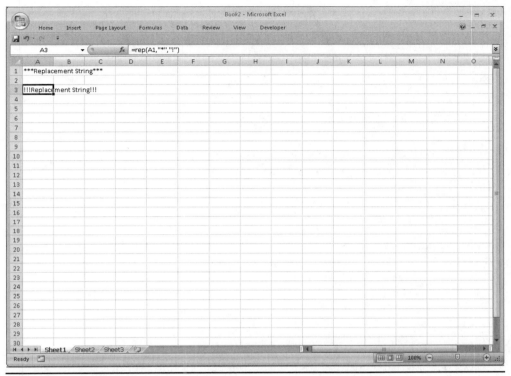

Figure 31-1   *Example of replacement function*

Timed Events

When you write an application, you often might want a procedure to be executed at a regular time interval. For example, you might want to emulate the autosave add-in in Excel and call a save routine or recalculate the workbook every five minutes. If the workbook is large and full of complex formulas, you should use manual calculation to ensure that every five minutes every calculation is up-to-date.

If you have used Visual Basic for Windows, then you are aware that there is a timer control available. All you have to do is to set the timer interval and then put your code on the timer event. Unfortunately, there is nothing like this in VBA, and it is a complicated procedure to make a timed event happen. You can do it, however, by using the **OnTime** method. The code in this method provides a time in the future and a subroutine to call when the current time equals the time you have set. Try entering the following code into a module:

```
Private Sub time_set
Dim w As Workbook
Application.OnTime Now + TimeValue("00:05:00"), "time_set"
For Each w In Application.Workbooks
    MsgBox w.Name
Next w
End Sub
```

This procedure needs to be called only once. You can call it from the **Workbook_Open** event when your workbook is first loaded.

In the preceding code, first a variable **w** is dimensioned as a workbook. Next, the **OnTime** statement states that in five minutes (the current time defined by **Now**, plus a time value of five minutes) the same routine of **time_set** is to be called again. The code then cycles through and saves each loaded workbook (using a For..Each loop). Five minutes later, the routine is called again. It then sets itself up to be called in another five minutes and saves all the workbooks again.

You have so far used only two of the parameters in **OnTime**: **EarliestTime** and **Procedure**. You can also specify the **LatestTime**, which is the latest time the procedure should run. Once the current time has passed the latest time you specify, the **OnTime** procedure will no longer be called. The **Schedule** parameter can be set to True or False. This switches the **OnTime** function on or off. If **Schedule** is set to False, it will not run.

You can also specify the latest time at which you want the timed event to stop:

```
Application.OnTime Now + TimeValue("00:05:00"), _
"time_set", TimeValue("22:00:00")
```

In this example, the procedure **time_set** is called every five minutes until 10:00 P.M. To stop the automated procedure, you set the **Schedule** parameter to False:

```
Application.OnTime Now + TimeValue("00:05:00"), "time_set", , False
```

If you are thinking of writing VBA macros for the shareware industry, this is a great way to introduce "nag" message boxes to get the user to register the product! You can also nag the user to do something every *x* minutes.

Auto-Totaling a Matrix of Numbers

A problem most spreadsheet users run across at some point is auto-totaling a matrix of numbers. That is, you have a large range of values that make up a matrix of numbers, and you need totals across the bottom of each column and down the right-hand side of each row, with a grand total in the bottom right-hand corner. It can be time-consuming to set this up, and you can sometimes end up with mistakes, especially if you get a different total across the bottom from the total down the right-hand side.

The following piece of code works on a user-selected range and generates all the totals for you, even working across several selected sheets (note it needs the function **convert_asc**, which is detailed next):

```
Sub matrix_total()

If Application.Selection.Count = 1 Then MsgBox "Select a range": Exit Sub

Dim rr As Range
Dim coord(4) As String
temp = Application.Selection.Address & "$"
Set rr = ActiveWindow.RangeSelection
coord(0) = rr.Column
coord(2) = rr.Column + rr.Columns.Count - 1
coord(1) = rr.Row
coord(3) = rr.Row + rr.Rows.Count - 1
```

```
For Each window In Windows
    For Each Worksheet In window.SelectedSheets
        con = 1

        For n = coord(0) To coord(2)
            formulastr = convert_asc(VAL(coord(0)) + con - 1) & _
                coord(1) & ".." & convert_asc(VAL(coord(0)) + _
                con - 1) & coord(3)

            Worksheet.Cells(VAL(coord(3)) + 1, n).Formula = _
                "=sum(" & formulastr & ")"
            con = con + 1
        Next n

        con = 1
        For n = coord(1) To coord(3) + 1
            formulastr = convert_asc(VAL(coord(0))) & (coord(1) + _
                con - 1) & ".."  & convert_asc(VAL(coord(2))) & _
                (coord(1) + con - 1)

            Worksheet.Cells(n, VAL(coord(2)) + 1).Formula = _
                "=sum(" & formulastr & ")"
            con = con + 1
        Next n




    Next Worksheet
Next window
End Sub
```

This code is somewhat complicated because the program has to first figure out the top-left and bottom-right coordinates of the selected range. If there is only one cell in the selected range, it will cause problems with the coordinate selection routine. Also, the result would be pointless, so the procedure is exited if the cell count is only 1.

If the cell count is more than 1, an array is set up to hold the coordinates found for the selected range. A variable called **temp** holds the actual address of the selected range. This is always held in absolute format using $ characters, for example, $B$4:$D$6. An extra $ sign is added for searching purposes.

A variable called **rr**, which has been dimensioned as a range, is then set to hold the selected range. From this, the coordinates of the four corners of the range can be worked out using the column and row properties.

The macro then cycles through the **Windows** collection and through each worksheet to pick up the selected sheets. Within the selected sheet, a For..Next loop then works through the selected columns from the array (elements 0 and 2). Element (0) holds the start column number, and element (2) holds the end column number. The variable **con** keeps track of the column number offset and is incremented for each loop.

At this point, the formula has to be devised for each column so that it sums it up. A variable called **formulastr** holds the coordinate portion. For example, this could be D4..D10. This uses a function called **convert_asc**, which performs the reverse of the conversion done earlier and converts the number back into column letters. The code for **convert_asc** is as follows:

```
Private Function convert_asc(target As Integer) As String
high = Int(target / 26)
low = target Mod 26
temp = ""
If high > 0 Then temp = Chr(high + 64)
temp = temp & Chr(low + 64)
convert_asc = temp
End Function
```

A number representing the column number is passed across as an integer. This is split into the high part of the number—that is, the part representing the first letter in a two-column number. If it is only a one-column number, this is set to 0.

The low part uses the **Mod** function to get the remainder, which represents the second column. The high part has 64 added, and the **Chr** function converts the numeric value back to a letter. The significance of the number 64 is that A (uppercase) is ASCII code 65. You already have a system whereby 1 represents column A. If you add 64 to 1, you get 65, which is the ASCII code for *A*. Once the algorithm moves on to double-letter columns such as AA, it gets more complicated, however. The high and low variables split the number (such as 27 for column AA) into its two-letter parts by dividing the number by 26 for the high part (first letter of the column) and then using the modulus for the low part (second letter of the column). The low part has 64 added, and the **Chr** function converts the numeric value back to a letter. The letter is then concatenated with the high letter (if it has a value), so the resulting value of the concatenation returns the column reference in letters.

Moving back to the main procedure, you are trying to achieve a formula string for each column within the selected range. If the user selects the range D4..F6, you have to provide **SUM** formulas for columns D to F, and they must read **SUM(D4..D6)**, **SUM(E4..E6)**, and **SUM(F4..F6)**.

The first part of the formula will be the column letter, which is provided by the start point from the array; the offset, **con**, is then added and 1 is subtracted. This is converted into letters. The next part of the formula is the top row number, which is provided by element 1 of the array. Two dots (..) are now concatenated to separate the start and finish parts of the address. The same column reference is used as before for the next part of the address, and the bottom row reference is provided by element 3 of the array. This now gives the address of a single column within the selected range, for example, D3..D7.

The **SUM** formula now needs to go into the worksheet directly under the selected range and in the same column the formula refers to. For example, the formula **SUM(D4..D6)** has to go into the cell D7. The cell is referred to using the final row from the third element and adding 1 to it (to get to the row below the bottom of the matrix) and using **n** for the column because the For..Next loop works through column numbers. The word **=sum** and parentheses are concatenated to the variable **formulastr**, and a valid formula for totaling a column in the selected range is placed on the row below it. This is repeated using the For..Next loop for all the columns within the selected range.

The variable **con**, representing the column offset, is incremented. The result is that all columns now have totals. Next, you move on to the rows using another For..Next loop based on elements 1 and 3 of the array (top row and bottom row of user selection). Note that 1 has been added to the final value—this is to get a grand total in the bottom right-hand corner of the selection, which is done in the same way as before: the copy of the array that was held in **coord** is used this time for the column letters, since they were not changed to numeric in this array. The cells going down the right-hand side of the matrix are then filled with a **SUM** formula adding across the rows, and the totals filled in column by column from before are summed up to get the grand total.

This now gives totaling formulas along the bottom and right-hand side of the user selection with a grand total in the bottom right-hand corner. An example of matrix totaling is shown in Figure 33-1.

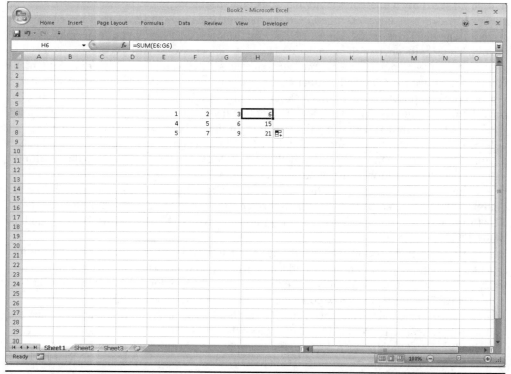

Figure 33-1   *Results of matrix additions*

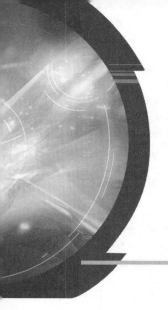

Absolute and Relative Formulas

A
s you know, formulas can be entered using absolute or relative addressing for cell references. For example, the address A1 in a formula is relative; that is, if you copy the formula to a new location, the cell address will change relative to where you copy it. If you use an absolute address such as $A$1, however, it will always reference cell A1, no matter where it is copied to on the spreadsheet.

It is easy enough to change one cell formula to be absolute, but what if you have a whole range of formulas that needs to be changed? You end up having to change every formula in each cell manually, and mistakes can creep into your spreadsheet.

You can write code to automatically convert formulas to use absolute references in one procedure based on a user selection, and what is more, you can offer users options about how they want absolute and relative formulas to appear in the spreadsheet. For example, you can offer the choice of the column and row both being absolute ($A$1), the column relative and the row absolute (A$1), the column absolute and the row relative ($A1), or the column and row both relative (A1). There are four options involved:

Absolute and Relative States	Format
Relative Row, Relative Column	A1
Relative Row, Absolute Column	A$1
Absolute Row, Relative Column	$A1
Absolute Row, Absolute Column	$A$1

To offer the user a choice on this, you need to insert a UserForm. You will also need to define a global variable called **canc** (short for Cancel) to check whether the user clicks the Cancel button on the form. You need to put the following code in the declarations part of your module:

```
Global canc As Integer
```

See the example of the form in Figure 34-1.

A set of radio buttons based within a frame control makes it easy for the user to see what is happening. Two command buttons (OK and Cancel) have also been added. You can set one of the radio buttons on by default by setting its **Value** property to True, so you do not have to worry about the user selecting a button.

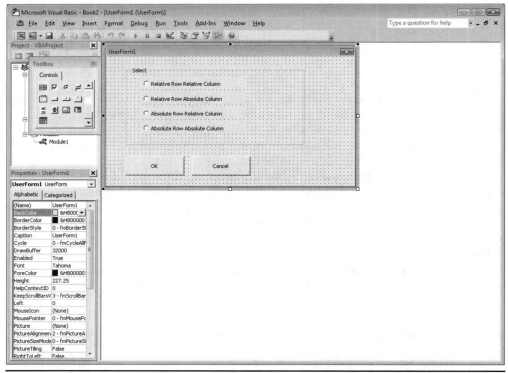

Figure 34-1 *Setting up the UserForm to provide the GUI interface*

Drag the controls onto the form from the toolbox. You need two command buttons, a frame, and four radio buttons. You can change the captions on the radio buttons and the form by changing the **Caption** property on each control. If you have any difficulty doing this, see Chapter 9 on form construction.

The two command buttons are for the **OK** and **Cancel** functions. It is assumed in this example that the OK button is the first button (CommandButton1) and the Cancel button is the second button (CommandButton2).

The command buttons need code behind them, or they will do nothing. Double-click the command button, which will take you into the code window showing the **Click** event for that button. Enter the following code:

```
Private Sub CommandButton1_Click()
     UserForm1.Hide
     canc = 0

End Sub
Private Sub CommandButton2_Click()
     UserForm1.Hide
     canc = 1


End Sub
```

In each case, the UserForm is hidden using the **Hide** method, which makes it invisible to the user and passes execution back to the code that called the form.

The variable **canc**, which you defined as a global variable, is set to 0 if the user clicked OK and 1 if the user clicked Cancel. This is so you can tell from the code what action the user took and then act accordingly.

The main code for the Absolute and Relative procedure must be inserted into a module as follows:

```
Sub conv_formula()
UserForm1.Show
If canc = 1 Then Exit Sub
If UserForm1.OptionButton1.Value = True Then act = xlRelative
If UserForm1.OptionButton2.Value = True Then act = xlRelRowAbsColumn
If UserForm1.OptionButton4.Value = True Then act = xlAbsolute
If UserForm1.OptionButton3.Value = True Then act = xlAbsRowRelColumn
For Each window In Windows
    For Each Worksheet In window.SelectedSheets
```

```
        For Each cell In Application.Selection

            addr = Worksheet.Name & "!" & cell.Address

            If Range(addr).HasFormula = True Then Range(addr).Formula = _
            Application.ConvertFormula(Formula:=Range(addr).Formula, _
            fromreferencestyle:=xlA1, toreferencestyle:=xlA1, toabsolute:=act)

        Next cell

    Next worksheet
    Next window
End Sub
```

You also need to define the variable **canc** as a global variable:

```
Global canc as Integer
```

The first thing the code does is show the UserForm you created in the form designer and display it using the **Show** method. This then hands execution over to the form, which waits until one of the two buttons (OK or Cancel) is clicked.

The user selects a radio button for an option and clicks OK, which hides the form. The main code starts executing again. The variable **canc** is checked to see if the user clicked the Cancel button. If the value of **canc** is 1, the Cancel button was selected and a simple **Exit Sub** is all that is required to ensure that nothing takes place. However, if the user clicked OK on the form, then **canc** will be 0 and the user has chosen to execute the macro.

The next four rows check which action the user took on the radio buttons. Note that only one radio button can have a True value because as soon as another one is clicked, it takes the value True and gives all the others the value False.

Depending on which radio button has the True value, a variable called **act** is loaded with a constant value. The constants used here are already defined in VBA and work with the **ConvertFormula** method.

The code then cycles through all the windows in the **Windows** collection, through each worksheet within the selected sheets of that window, and then through each cell within the selection.

A variable called **addr** is loaded with the worksheet name and the cell address. The code then checks that the cell in question has a formula (because there is no point trying to convert something that is not a formula). The formula is then converted using the **ConvertFormula** method and the constant provided by the radio buttons.

Run the code by clicking the Run symbol in the VBE window (with the cursor on the **conv_formula** code), and the UserForm will appear as shown in Figure 34-2.

Make your selection from the radio buttons and click OK; check the formulas selected. The $ will have been added or removed all the way through the selected range as appropriate.

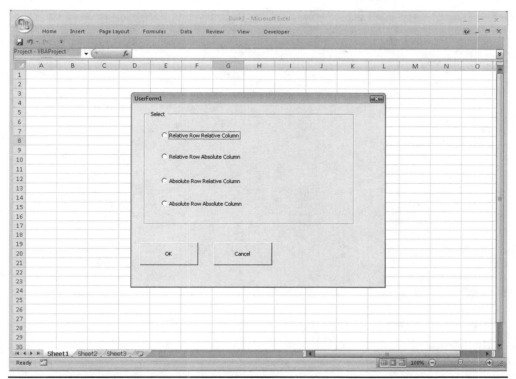

Figure 34-2   *The GUI interface displayed*

Coloring Alternate Rows and Columns of the Spreadsheet

Sometimes when you have many rows of data on your spreadsheet, it is difficult to read across them, particularly when you print them out or they are very long. A solution is to color alternate rows—you may remember the old "music line" paper that spreadsheets used to be printed on for just this reason.

When writing this routine, you can restrict the shading to one particular color and make life easy for yourself. However, when writing professional code, it's important to give users as much choice as possible, and this means giving users a screen to select the color of their choice for shading.

This may sound complicated, but there are easy ways to use an API call to display the standard color selection dialog and to then use the choice made within your code. Suddenly, the shading process becomes easy! You don't even need to design a UserForm to allow the user to select the color because it has all been done for you.

You do need a blank UserForm to hold the code for the API call to call the color selection dialog.

First you will need to insert the declaration for the API call and also a variable type declaration into the declaration section of the module for the user form. This area is at the very top of the module. The code for the declarations is as follows:

```
Private Type COLORSTRUC
  lStructSize As Long
  hwnd As Long
  hInstance As Long
  rgbResult As Long
  lpCustColors As String
  Flags As Long
  lCustData As Long
  lpfnHook As Long
  lpTemplateName As String
End Type

Private Const CC_SOLIDCOLOR = &H80

Private Declare Function ChooseColor _
    Lib "comdlg32.dll" Alias "ChooseColorA" _
    (pChoosecolor As COLORSTRUC) As Long
```

This will set up a variable type for COLORSTRUC to be used by the API call, and the declaration for the function ChooseColor. It will also create a constant called CC_SOLIDCOLOR.

Insert the following code into the module:

```
Sub shade()
Dim x As Long, CSel As COLORSTRUC, CustColor(16) As Long

  CSel.lStructSize = Len(CSel)
  CSel.Flags = CC_SOLIDCOLOR
  CSel.lpCustColors = String$(16 * 4, 0)
  x = ChooseColor(CSel)
For Each window In Windows

    For Each Worksheet In window.SelectedSheets

        addr = Worksheet.Name & "!" & Selection.Address

        For counter = 1 To Application.Selection.Rows.Count

            If counter Mod 2 = 1 Then

                Range(addr).Rows(counter).Interior.Color = _CSel.rgbResult

            End If
```

```
        Next counter
    Next worksheet

Next window

End Sub
```

Because you are dealing only with rows within the selection and not cells, the routine is less complicated than the previous examples. It cycles through each window in the **Windows** collection and then through each worksheet within the **SelectedSheets** object. A variable called **addr** is loaded with the worksheet name and the selection address. A For..Next loop works through all the rows within the selection by using the **rows.count** property. Each row number is tested to see if it is odd or even by using the **Mod** function. If there is a remainder of 1, then the row is odd numbered and needs coloring. The row is set to the color selected in the ChooseColor API call.

Make a selection of a range on the spreadsheet and then run the code. The result should look similar to Figure 35-1, which is based on selecting the range A1..D13.

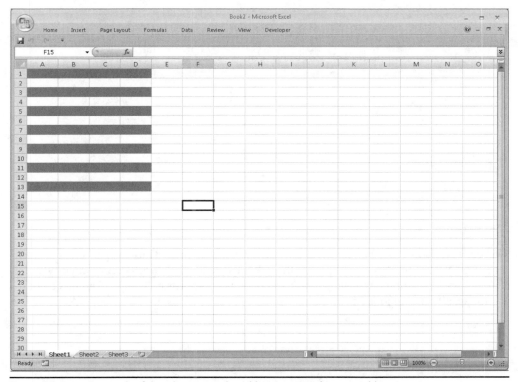

Figure 35-1   *The result of the alternate colored lines macro (horizontal lines)*

With some small modification, you can also make the code color in alternate columns:

```
Sub shade1()
Dim x As Long, CSel As COLORSTRUC, CustColor(16) As Long

  CSel.lStructSize = Len(CSel)
  CSel.Flags = CC_SOLIDCOLOR
  CSel.lpCustColors = String$(16 * 4, 0)
  x = ChooseColor(CSel)



For Each window In Windows

    For Each Worksheet In window.SelectedSheets

        addr = Worksheet.Name & "!" & Selection.Address

        For counter = 1 To Application.Selection.Columns.Count

            If counter Mod 2 = 1 Then

              Range(addr).Columns(counter).Interior.Color = _
                 CSel.rgbResult

            End If

        Next counter

    Next worksheet

Next window

End Sub
```

This code works pretty much the same way as the previous code. The only part that changes is the For..Next loop; it is now checking the columns using the **column.count** property and changing the color of the row, which now refers to the **Columns** collection. Run this code, and the results should look like Figure 35-2. This is based on a selected range of A1..C17.

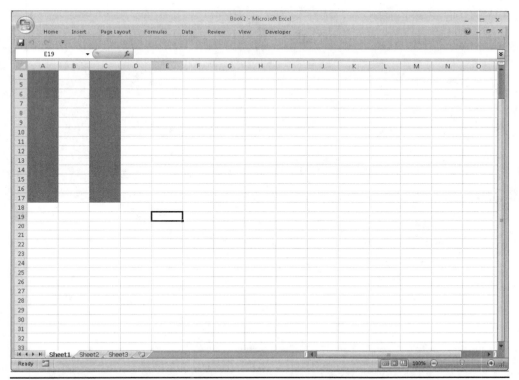

Figure 35-2   *The result of the alternate colored columns macro (vertical columns)*

Coloring Cells Containing Formulas

O n complex spreadsheets, it is not always easy to see which cells have actual numbers and which cells are formulas. You can use different displays to fix this by switching to a view showing cell formulas within the spreadsheet, but it does display with wider columns, and you cannot see the original result, only the formula.

The code example in this chapter shows you how to color cells with a formula based on a user selection of cells in the spreadsheet and a user-chosen color. The user chooses the color by using a color selector dialog driven by an API call.

First you will need to insert the declaration for the API call and also a variable type declaration into the declaration section of the module for the user form. This area is at the very top of the module. The code for the declarations is as follows:

```
Private Type COLORSTRUC
   lStructSize As Long
   hwnd As Long
   hInstance As Long
   rgbResult As Long
   lpCustColors As String
   Flags As Long
   lCustData As Long
   lpfnHook As Long
   lpTemplateName As String
End Type
```

```
Private Const CC_SOLIDCOLOR = &H80

Private Declare Function ChooseColor _
    Lib "comdlg32.dll" Alias "ChooseColorA" _
    (pChoosecolor As COLORSTRUC) As Long
```

This will set up a variable type for COLORSTRUC to be used by the API call, and the declaration for the function ChooseColor. It will also create a constant called CC_SOLIDCOLOR.

Insert the following code into the module:

```
Sub col_cell()
Dim x As Long, CSel As COLORSTRUC, CustColor(16) As Long

  CSel.lStructSize = Len(CSel)
  CSel.Flags = CC_SOLIDCOLOR
  CSel.lpCustColors = String$(16 * 4, 0)
  x = ChooseColor(CSel)
For Each window In Windows
    For Each Worksheet In window.SelectedSheets

        For Each cell In Application.Selection

            addr = Worksheet.Name & "!" & cell.Address

            If Range(addr).HasFormula Then Range(addr).Interior.Color = _
                CSel.rgbResult

        Next cell

    Next worksheet
Next window
End Sub
```

Once the user selects a color from the dialog, the code cycles through the windows in the **Windows** collection and through the worksheets within the selected sheet's collection for each worksheet. Each cell within the selection is then gone through. The variable **addr** holds the name of the worksheet concatenated with the cell address using the ! character. The code then tests to see if that cell has a formula. If it does, it sets the color to the user's selection from the **CommonDialog** form using the **Interior.Color** property.

Make a selection of cells that have a combination of formulas and numbers, and then run the code. You should have results similar to Figure 36-1.

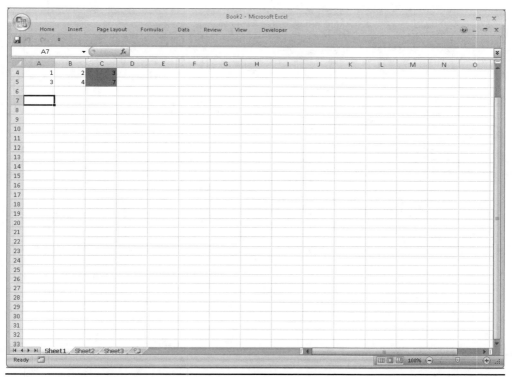

Figure 36-1   *Example of coloring cells containing formulas*

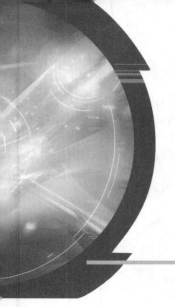

Summing Cells by Reference to a Master Cell

As you saw in early chapters of this book, you can create your own functions to use as formulas within the spreadsheet, just as if Microsoft had written them instead of you. This chapter shows how to create a more complicated function. When users are summing a row or column of cells, they sometimes want to include only particular values in the sum. These values are typically based on some attribute of the cell such as a font property or a background color.

Occasionally, people ask me, "Can I just add up the numbers in italics or in bold?" I have to tell them that there is no built-in way to do this in Excel. However, with the flexibility of VBA, you can write your own formula to do this. The syntax on your spreadsheet is as follows:

SUMCELLSBYREF (*range*, *reference*, *attribute*)

The *attribute* contains the font attribute, as defined next, that you wish to sum by. You can, for example, use the attribute of Bold to sum all cells that are in Bold font. This is fully explained in the table that follows.

▶ The *range* is a range of cells defined in the same way as the standard **SUM** function. Select this by entering the formula and then dragging the cursor over your range of cells.

► The *reference* is a single cell reference set to the attributes you wish to sum, such as those in italic. You need to format this cell to your reference attribute such as bold or italic.

► The *attribute* is a string containing one of the following:

Attribute	Description
Color	Sums all cells with the same font color as in the reference cell.
Italic	Sums all cells set to the same italic font setting as the reference cell.
Bold	Sums all cells set to the same bold font setting as the reference cell.
Size	Sums all cells set to the same font size as the reference cell.
Underline	Sums all cells set to the same underline setting as the reference cell.
Subscript	Sums all cells set to the same subscript setting as the reference cell.
Superscript	Sums all cells set to the same superscript setting as the reference cell.

The code to do all of this is shown here. Place the following into a module:

```
Public Function SUMCELLSBYREF(cells_to_sum As Object, r As Object, p _
As String)
Application.Volatile
total = 0
For Each cell In cells_to_sum

    If p = "bold" And cell.Font.Bold = r.Font.Bold Then

        total = total + cell.Value

    End If

    If p = "color" And cell.Font.Color = r.Font.Color Then

        total = total + cell.Value

    End If

    If p = "italic" And cell.Font.Italic = r.Font.Italic Then

        total = total + cell.Value

    End If

    If p = "name" And cell.Font.Name = r.Font.Name Then

        total = total + cell.Value

    End If
```

```
    If p = "size" And cell.Font.Size = r.Font.Size Then

        total = total + cell.Value

    End If

    If p = "underline" And cell.Font.Underline = r.Font.Underline Then

        total = total + cell.Value

    End If

    If p = "subscript" And cell.Font.Subscript = r.Font.Subscript Then

        total = total + cell.Value

    End If

    If p = "superscript" And cell.Font.Superscript = r.Font.Superscript _
        Then

        total = total + cell.Value

    End If
Next cell
SUMCELLSBYREF = total
End Function
```

This function has to be declared as a **Public** function for it to be available within the spreadsheet. As per the syntax, three parameters are passed over:

Name	Type	Description
cells_to_sum	Object	Range address of cells to sum
r	Object	Address of reference cell, which is formatted to the attribute to be summed by, such as bold
p	String	Attribute type; for example, the string "color2" or the string "font size"

The statement **Application.Volatile** allows a range of cells to be selected dynamically from within the formula. It works in the same way as the **SUM** function in that you can drag the cursor over the range while within the formula. A variable called **total**, which will hold the overall value of the sum, is set to 0. Using a For Each..Next loop, each cell within the **cells_to_sum** object is cycled through.

There are condition statements set up for each of the values that can be held by **p**, the attribute statement. For example, if **p** states "**bold**", the code tests the condition that the cell bold attribute equals the reference cell bold attribute. This could be true or false, depending on what you are trying to achieve in your summation. If the attributes agree, the variable

total is increased by the cell value. The **total** variable contains a running total as the cells are processed.

When all the cells have been examined, the variable **SUMCELLSBYREF** is given the value of **total**, and this is the returned value to the spreadsheet.

To try this out, you do not need to run the code—just enter a formula as you normally would within Excel:

```
=SUMCELLSBYREF(A1..A4,C1,"bold")
```

You will find that if you click the Formula Paste icon on the Formula toolbar, the formula will appear under the User Defined Formula section, and you can use it as you would any other formula. If you miss any parameters, you will get the standard Excel errors.

Try entering some data and then put the formula in. Bear in mind that if you have Recalc set to manual, it will not recalculate the result automatically. A sample result is shown in Figure 37-1.

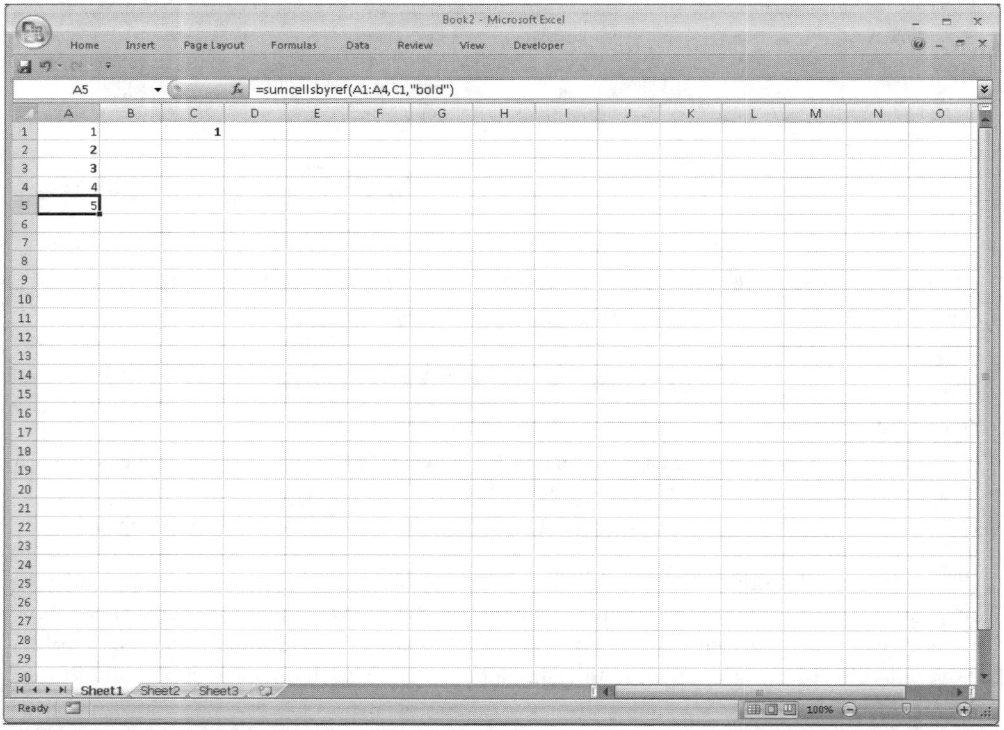

Figure 37-1 *Example of SUMCELLSBYREF in action*

Globally Changing a Range of Values

W hen you have a large amount of data on a spreadsheet, you may wish to change a range of numbers by a set value or a percentage. For example, you may want every value in a range to increase by two, or, if the spreadsheet shows sales figure projections for the coming year, you may want to see the impact of a 10 percent change on all numbers across a range. You can use scenarios in Excel to place individual values into cells, but you cannot apply a global factor across a range of cells.

The code in this chapter gives the user the ability to apply a global factor such as adding ten to every cell or decreasing all numbers by 5 percent. To make it work, a UserForm must be built to allow the user to input a factor. Insert a new UserForm by selecting Insert | UserForm from the VBE menu.

The dialog needs a label control to hold the description of the input, a text box to capture the user input, and two command buttons for OK and Cancel. The title of the form can be changed by clicking the form itself and then changing the caption property in the properties window. Drag the controls from the toolbox onto the form. The UserForm shown in Figure 38-1 is intended as a guide. So long as you have a text box for input, other controls are flexible.

The OK and Cancel buttons need code attached to them or they will do nothing. If you have not already done so in a previous example, you also need to set up a global variable called **canc** in the declarations section of your module to hold a value that says whether the user clicks OK or Cancel.

The whole idea of the UserForm is to capture a parameter string that can be applied to a range of cells. If you want to increase all the numbers by three, enter **+3**.

```
Global canc As Integer
```

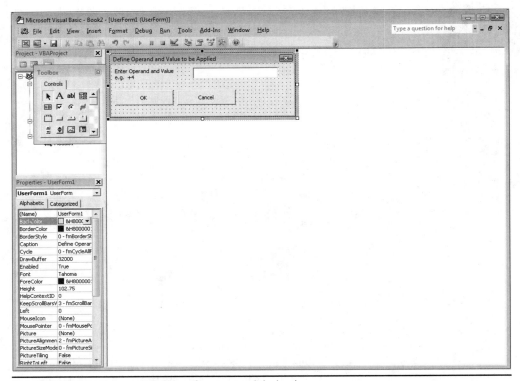

Figure 38-1 *Defining a UserForm for setting global values*

Add the following code in the **Click** events for the OK and Cancel buttons. Do not put this in your module. Instead, double-click the OK button and you will go into the code for the **Click** event.

```
Private Sub CommandButton1_Click()

'This button is for OK
  UserForm2.Hide
  canc = 0
End Sub

Private Sub CommandButton2_Click()
'This button is for Cancel
  UserForm2.Hide
  canc = 1
End Sub
```

Each of these routines hides the UserForm with the **Hide** method. This means that execution is transferred back to the original code that displayed the form. However, if the user clicks OK, **canc** is set to 0 (false); otherwise, it is set to 1 (True). Because **canc** is a global variable, you can access it from anywhere. You then insert the following code into a module:

```
Sub change_val()
UserForm2.Show
If canc = 1 Then Exit Sub
op = UserForm2.TextBox1.Text
Dim addr As String
For Each window In Windows
    For Each Worksheet In window.SelectedSheets

        For Each cell In Application.Selection

            addr = Worksheet.Name & "!" & cell.Address

            On Error Resume Next

            If Range(addr).Value <> "" _
                And IsNumeric(Range(addr).Value) _
                And Range(addr).HasFormula = False Then

                Range(addr).Value = "=" & Val(Range(addr).Value) & op

                Range(addr).Copy

                Range(addr).PasteSpecial xlPasteValues

            End If

        Next cell
        Next worksheet

Next window
End Sub
```

You also need to define the variable **canc** as a global variable in your module:

```
Global canc as integer
```

The first thing that this code does is to display the UserForm that you inserted, which allows users to input information into the text box and click OK or Cancel, depending on their action.

After the form is hidden by one of the click events, the code tests the variable **canc** to see if the Cancel button was clicked. If the value of **canc** is 1 (meaning the Cancel button was pressed), then a simple **Exit Sub** is all that is required.

If OK was clicked, the input entered into the text box is captured in the variable **op**. Validation code could be inserted at this point if the user did not input anything, but it makes no difference to subsequent code because all values will remain the same.

A variable called **addr** is set up as a string. The code then loops through each window in the **Windows** collection and goes through each worksheet in the selected worksheets collection. The variable **addr** is loaded with the current worksheet, and the current cell address concatenated with the ! character. The value of the cell defined by **addr** is then tested to check that it is not empty, that it has a numeric value, and that it is not a formula. If you apply an operand and a value to the cell, there must already be a value that is not a formula for it to work on, since the formula value will be automatically updated because of the change to the numeric cells.

If all conditions are met, the cell value is filled with a string containing the = sign concatenated with the existing cell value concatenated with the variable **op**, which holds the details of how the cell has to change—for example, "*90%".

This puts the whole thing in as a formula. To tidy it up, a copy and paste operation is then performed on that cell, copying the cell to the clipboard using the **Copy** method. The **PasteSpecial** method then pastes the value back into the cell so that only the new number appears.

Place a range of data into a spreadsheet (include some formulas inside it as well) and select it by dragging the cursor across it. Run the code and enter ***90%** in the text box on the UserForm. Click OK, and all the cells will hold 90 percent of their previous value. Formula cells will be unchanged, but they will show an actual value of 90 percent based on the other cells.

To put the numbers back to their previous values, simply do the reverse. Enter **/90%**, and they will be back to their starting position.

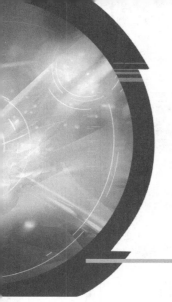

Displaying Hidden Sheets Without a Password

T his example shows the real power of the VBA language. If you hide a worksheet and protect it with a password, you are not supposed to be allowed to view it. There are password-cracking programs on the market, but later versions of Excel have encrypted the passwords so that they cannot be easily cracked. Knowing this, you might assume that your worksheet is safe.

In the Excel object model, however, Microsoft left a "back door" that you can exploit. You cannot view the passwords, but you can go through the **Worksheets** collection and find the hidden ones. Once you have the name of the worksheet, you can simply copy its contents onto a visible worksheet and view everything there.

Before you do anything, you will need to create a hidden worksheet within your current workbook. This is a very different procedure from the one that you were used to in earlier versions of Excel.

Click the Home item in the menu and then click Format in the Cells control of the ribbon (over to the right-hand side of the ribbon). You will see a pop-up menu from which you select Hide & Unhide on the Visibility tab.

A further pop-up will appear with the option to hide the current sheet.

For this code, you will need to insert a new UserForm to provide an interface to the user. You do this using Insert | UserForm from the VBE menu. Your UserForm needs to look like Figure 39-1.

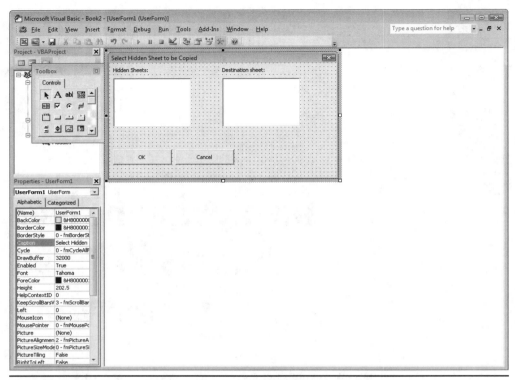

Figure 39-1   *Designing a UserForm for viewing hidden sheets*

This form has two list boxes, one to show all the hidden sheets and one to show the possible destination sheets (which are visible). The user clicks a hidden sheet to select it and then clicks a sheet in the visible list to select the destination.

You need to include two label controls to hold the headings for the list boxes so that the user can see what each one represents. You also need two command buttons for OK and Cancel actions. The caption on the form can be changed by clicking the form and altering the **Caption** property in the Properties window.

This example UserForm is different from previous ones in that the form has to be populated with information before it is displayed. If you do not do this, the user will only see two empty list boxes, which will not be very useful.

To write the code to do this, double-click the form to enter the code window for the UserForm. The first piece of code needs to go in the UserForm activate event, which is called whenever the form is first displayed. On the module, select UserForm in the top-left drop-down menu and select Activate in the top-right drop-down menu. Insert the following code:

```
Private Sub UserForm_Activate()
ListBox1.Clear
ListBox2.Clear
```

```
For Each Worksheet In ActiveWorkbook.Worksheets
    If Worksheet.Visible = False Then

        ListBox1.AddItem Worksheet.Name

    End If
Next
For Each Worksheet In ActiveWorkbook.Worksheets
    If Worksheet.Visible = True Then

        ListBox2.AddItem Worksheet.Name

    End If
Next
End Sub
```

The first thing the code does is ensure that both list boxes are completely empty by using the **Clear** method.

The code then cycles through each worksheet within the **ActiveWorkbook Worksheets** collection. Notice that you are only using the active workbook here and not all workbooks that may be loaded. If you used all workbooks, they could be difficult to show in the list boxes, and it could lead to addressing problems. Although you could show all of them by concatenating on the workbook name or adding another list box, it would get quite confusing.

The code checks whether the worksheet is hidden by checking the **Visible** property. If it is set to false, it uses the **AddItem** method of the list box to add the worksheet name to the first list box.

It then goes through the worksheets again, checking to see if the sheet is visible. If it is, it uses the **AddItem** method to add the worksheet name to the second list box. When the code opens the UserForm, the user sees two list boxes, one with all the hidden sheets in it and the other with all the visible sheets.

You also need some code attached to the OK and Cancel buttons. For this you will insert a global variable in the declarations part of a module called **canc**:

```
Global canc as Integer
```

You can then add the following code into the UserForm module under the two command button click events:

```
Private Sub CommandButton1_Click()
'code for OK button

UserForm1.Hide

canc = 0

End Sub
```

```
Private Sub CommandButton2_Click()
'code for Cancel button

UserForm1.Hide

canc = 1

End Sub
```

With this code, both command buttons hide the form and transfer execution back to the code that originally displayed the form. However, in the case of the OK button, the global variable **canc** is set to 0, and it is set to 1 if the Cancel button is clicked.

Having set the user interface up, you need to add some code into a module:

```
Sub hidden_sheets()
UserForm1.Show
If canc = 1 Then Exit Sub
s1 = UserForm1.ListBox1.Text
s2 = UserForm1.ListBox2.Text
If s1 = "" Or s2 = "" Then Exit Sub
Range(s1 & "!a1. xfd1048576").Copy
Range(s2 & "!a1").PasteSpecial
Range(s2 & "!a1").Select
End Sub
```

To show the user form and make the code run, you click your cursor anywhere on the hidden_sheets code and click the Run symbol in the VBE toolbar. To make this easier to use, you could define a button on a spreadsheet and harness this to your code. You could also define a menu item (see Chapter 11) to allow the user to call this procedure.

The code is fairly straightforward for what it does. The first line shows your UserForm using the **Show** method. This allows the user to see all the names of the hidden sheets and make a selection of where they would like them copied.

When the form is hidden and execution is transferred back to the **hidden_sheets** routine, the **canc** variable is checked. If the user clicked Cancel, the procedure is exited and nothing happens. If the user clicked OK, the **hidden_sheets** procedure is executed.

Two variables, **s1** and **s2**, are loaded with the text selected from each list box. If no selection was made in one or the other of the list boxes, the procedure is exited and nothing happens.

The entire hidden sheet is copied onto the clipboard using the **Copy** method. The name of the sheet is concatenated with **a1. xfd1048576** using the ! character. Notice that we make use of all the new available rows and columns in Excel 2007 (this does have the disadvantage that it will fail if used in an earlier version of Excel).

This ensures that every cell is picked up. It is then pasted to the chosen destination using the **PasteSpecial** method. In the example code, the cell A1 is the destination. Cell A1 is then selected on the destination sheet, which makes it the current worksheet and moves the focus to it.

To test out the sample, set up a sheet in a workbook and put some data onto it. Click the Home item in the menu and then click Format in the Cells control of the ribbon (over to the right-hand side of the ribbon). You will see a pop-up menu from which you select Hide & Unhide on the Visibility tab.

Now protect the entire workbook with a password. Click the Review item in the menu bar and then click the Protect Workbook icon in the Changes control of the ribbon (right-hand side of ribbon). Click Protect Structure and Windows in the pop-up that appears and check both the structure and windows boxes. Set a password.

If you try to make your hidden sheet appear, it is impossible. Try clicking Home in the menu bar and then click Format in the Cells control of the ribbon. Click the Hide & Unhide option in the pop-up and you will see that the Unhide Sheet option is now disabled.

Without the password, you cannot see the sheet; but run the code and you will see a screen similar to Figure 39-2.

In your new user form, select the hidden sheet and then select a destination sheet. Click OK, and the contents of the hidden sheet will appear on your destination sheet. Remember, this procedure does not check whether the destination sheet is blank. Any data on it will be completely overwritten and lost.

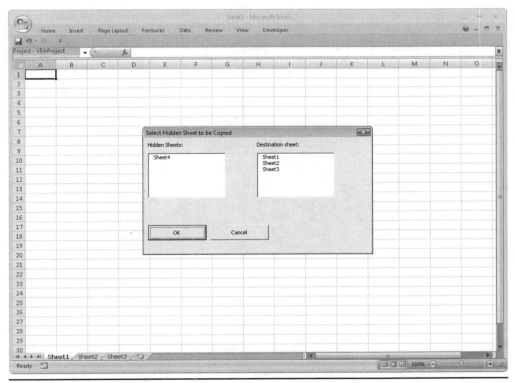

Figure 39-2   *The hidden sheets UserForm in action*

Searching Multiple Sheets and Workbooks

Excel already has a built-in search facility that you access by pressing CTRL-F while on a worksheet, but this method will only search the current worksheet. You can select a group of worksheets and search across those, but you do have to make the selection first, and you cannot search across all workbooks. Using the standard search facility can be cumbersome, but you can write code to produce your own search facility that will work across several spreadsheets or workbooks without having to first select them.

Because of the flexibility of the Excel object model, all the search features are already there. All you need to do is to make them work across worksheets and workbooks.

The first thing that you need is a UserForm for the user interface. Because you want to build in the same functionality as the existing search facility, the UserForm should be fairly close to the existing search form, as shown in Figure 40-1.

There are four command buttons, one each for Find Next, Close, Replace, and Replace All. There is a text box for both the find text and the replacement text along with labels to describe what they each mean.

There are two combo boxes for selection of the type of search and two labels to give the description. Finally, there are two check boxes for matching the case and finding entire cells.

The controls are dragged from the toolbox onto the form. If you are uncertain about which control is which in the toolbox, use the tooltip text on each control in the toolbox to tell you.

The form caption can be changed by clicking the caption bar to highlight the form itself and then editing the caption property in the properties window. You need to set up a global

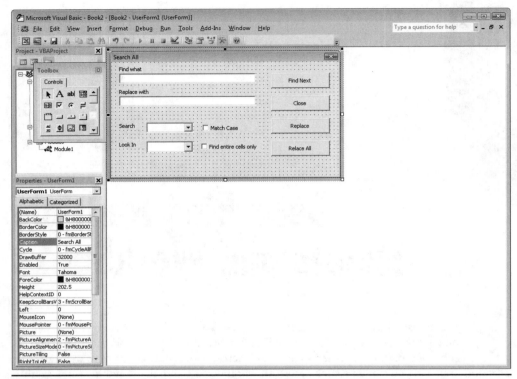

Figure 40-1   *Designing the UserForm for the Search facility*

variable **canc** in a module to hold users' actions based on which command button they click. This is placed in the declarations section of a module.

```
Global canc As Integer
```

Because there are four command buttons, **canc** will now have to hold a greater range of values than you have seen in previous examples.

You now need to add the following code to the UserForm module for it to operate. Double-click any control on the form to be taken into the code window for the form. The code is as follows:

```
Private Sub CommandButton1_Click()
'code for Find Next button
FindDialog.Hide
canc = 0

End Sub
```

```
Private Sub CommandButton2_Click()
'code for Close button
FindDialog.Hide
canc = 1
End Sub

Private Sub CommandButton3_Click()
'code for Replace button
FindDialog.Hide
canc = 2
End Sub

Private Sub CommandButton3_MouseMove(ByVal Button As Integer, _
ByVal Shift As Integer, ByVal X As Single, ByVal Y As Single)
ComboBox2.Visible = False
Label3.Visible = False
End Sub

Private Sub CommandButton4_Click()
'code for Replace All button
FindDialog.Hide
canc = 4
End Sub

Private Sub CommandButton4_MouseMove(ByVal Button As Integer, _
ByVal  Shift As Integer, ByVal X As Single, ByVal Y As Single)
ComboBox2.Visible = False
Label3.Visible = False
End Sub


Private Sub TextBox2_MouseMove(ByVal Button As Integer, ByVal Shift _
   As  Integer, ByVal X As Single, ByVal Y As Single)
ComboBox2.Visible = False
Label3.Visible = False
End Sub


Private Sub UserForm_Activate()

ComboBox1.Clear

ComboBox1.AddItem "ByRows"
ComboBox1.AddItem "ByColumns"
```

```
ComboBox2.Clear

ComboBox2.AddItem "Formulas"
ComboBox2.AddItem "Values"
ComboBox2.AddItem "Comments"
End Sub


Private Sub UserForm_MouseMove(ByVal Button As Integer, ByVal Shift _
  As Integer, ByVal X As Single, ByVal Y As Single)
ComboBox2.Visible = True
Label3.Visible = True
End Sub

Private Sub UserForm_Terminate()
canc = 1
End Sub
```

This is a more complicated UserForm than previous examples in this book because there are a lot of events being used. Each procedure will be dealt with in turn.

Command Button1 represents the Find Next button. When this is clicked, the UserForm (FindDialog) is hidden and execution is transferred back to the procedure that displayed the form. The global variable **canc** is set to 0.

Command Button2 represents the Close button. When this is clicked, the UserForm (FindDialog) is hidden and execution is transferred back to the procedure that displayed the form. The global variable **canc** is set to 1.

Command Button3 represents the Replace button. When this is clicked, the UserForm (FindDialog) is hidden and execution is transferred back to the procedure that displayed the form. The global variable **canc** is set to 2.

Command Button4 represents the Replace All button. When this is clicked, the UserForm (FindDialog) is hidden and execution is transferred back to the procedure that displayed the form. The global variable **canc** is set to 3.

For **Command Button3**, the **Mouse Move** event on that button is also utilized because when the Replace option is used, the **LookIn** parameters (shown on Figure 40-1) are not required, as defined by **ComboBox2** and **Label3**. This code sets the visible properties of **ComboBox2** and **Label3** to False so that they cannot be seen on the form at that point. The same thing happens for the **Mouse Move** event on **Command Button4**, which represents Replace All.

Also, if the user enters text in TextBox2, the **Mouse Move** event makes **ComboBox2** and **Label3** disappear from the form. These are the **ComboBox** and **Label** that define the **LookIn** parameters, and they are not required for a Replace.

When the UserForm is activated, the combo boxes need to have values in their lists for the user to select. This is done in the **UserForm_Activate** event, and the **AddItem** method adds the items into the combo box lists. The boxes are cleared first using the **Clear** method.

Where the mouse **Move** events were used on command buttons and text boxes to make certain controls vanish, the mouse **Move** event on the form makes them visible again by setting the **Visible** property to True.

Finally, if the form is closed, the **UserForm_Terminate** event is called; this sets **canc** to 1, which means the Close button was clicked and no further action is to be taken.

You next need to insert the following code into the same module where you inserted the other global variable.

```
Sub findsheet()
flag = 0
sflag = 1
temp = ""
Dim a As Range, s As Worksheet, w As Workbook

FindDialog.TextBox1.Text = ActiveCell.Value
 Set a = ActiveCell

For Each w In Workbooks
     Set a = w.Sheets(1).Range("xfd1048576")

    For n = 1 To w.Worksheets.Count

loopa:

        If sflag = 1 Then FindDialog.Show

        sflag = 0

        If canc = 1 Then FindDialog.Hide: canc = 0: Exit Sub

        On Error Resume Next

        sstr = FindDialog.TextBox1.Text 'Search string

        rep = FindDialog.TextBox2.Text 'Replacement string
            If canc = 2 Then 'single replacement
            a.Replace sstr, rep
            sflag = 1
            GoTo loopa 'go back to form after replacement
            End If

        On Error Resume Next
'set up li variable for 'look in'
        If FindDialog.ComboBox2.Text = "Formulas" Then li = -4123
```

```
        If FindDialog.ComboBox2.Text = "Values" Then li = -4163

        If FindDialog.ComboBox2.Text = "Coments" Then li = -4144
'set up so variable for search order
        If FindDialog.ComboBox1.Text = "ByRows" Then so = 1

        If FindDialog.ComboBox1.Text = "ByColumns" Then so = 2

        mc = FindDialog.CheckBox1.Value 'Match Case flag

        la = FindDialog.CheckBox2.Value 'Look At flag

        If la = True Then lat = 1 Else lat = 2 'set Look At T flag _
            (lat)
        If canc = 4 Then


                    p = w.Sheets(n).Range("a1", " xfd1048576"). _
Replace(sstr, rep, lat, so,  mc) 'search string, replace string, _
look at, search order, match case

        End If
        If a.Address = "" Then Set a = Sheets(n).Range("xfd1048576")

        Set a = w.Sheets(n).Range("a1", " xfd1048576"). _
Find(sstr, a, li, lat, so, ,mc) 'search string, replace string, _
look at, search order, match case

        If a.Address = "" Then sflag = 0 Else sflag = 1

        If InStr(temp, w.Name & Sheets(n).Name & a.Address) Or _
        a.Address = ""  Then sflag = 0: GoTo bypass 'search is
'complete - break out of loop

        w.Activate

        Sheets(n).Activate

        a.Activate

        temp = temp & " " & w.Name & Sheets(n).Name & a.Address

        GoTo loopa
bypass:
```

```
        temp = ""

    Next n
Next w
MsgBox "No further occurrences of " & sstr, vbInformation
Exit Sub

End Sub
```

The first thing this code does is set up variables for flags, temporary strings, and range, workbook, and worksheet.

The text box on the UserForm for "Find what" is set to the active cell value. This is the cell that currently has the cursor on it, so when the UserForm is displayed, it will have the value of that cell in the "Find what" text box by default. The variable **a**, which was dimensioned as a range, is set to the active cell.

The code cycles through all the workbooks loaded using a For Each..Next loop. The variable **a** is set to the very last cell in the first indexed worksheet within the workbook.

The code then uses a For..Next loop to cycle through the worksheets within the workbook. A label is included at this point called **loopa** for reference purposes so that your code can loop back to it under certain circumstances.

If the variable **sflag** is 1, the UserForm for searching is displayed. The user can then enter their selection of what they wish to find and whether they want to replace it. Depending on which action the user takes, the global variable **canc** will be set to one of four values.

The variable **sflag** is set to zero. This variable determines whether the UserForm is shown. This depends on certain conditions, and initially, you do not want it shown again until the search text is found in the first instance, so **sflag** is set to 0.

If **canc** is set to 1, it means the user clicked the Close button, so the UserForm is then hidden, **canc** is set to 0, and the subroutine is exited with no further action.

Next, two variables are set up to hold the values of "Find what" and "Replace with" on the UserForm. The variable **sstr** holds the value of "Find what," and the variable **rep** holds the value of "Replace with."

If the user clicked the Replace button on the form, **canc** will be set to 2. This means that the user has already found an instance of the search string and wishes to replace it with the replacement string. This is done using the **Replace** method based on the range held in variable **a**. The variable **sflag** is set to 1, which means display the UserForm again, and the code loops to the label **loopa**, which shows the UserForm again.

If the user has not clicked the Replace or the Close button on the form, then other options are likely to involve searching the worksheet. At this point, the other search options from the UserForm are brought into play, using the values of combo boxes and check boxes:

▶ Based on the value of ComboBox2 text, which holds the choice of where to look in, the value of a variable **li** is set. This is set to values used within the Find and Replace methods.

▶ Based on the value of ComboBox1 text, which holds the choice of whether the search is made by rows or columns, a variable called **so** is set.

▶ The value of CheckBox1, which dictates whether case should be matched in the search, is placed in a variable called **mc**.

▶ The value of CheckBox2, which dictates whether whole cells only should be found, is placed in a variable called **la**. If the value of **la** is true, then a variable called **lat** is set to 1; otherwise, it is set to 2.

▶ If the user has clicked the Replace All button, **canc** will have the value of 4 and everything matching the search pattern within the worksheet will be replaced using the variables holding information taken from the UserForm.

▶ If the **Range** object held in variable **a** has no address, it is set to the very last cell on the spreadsheet.

▶ The **Range** object **a** is set to the next available find of the search string on the worksheet using the variables holding information taken from the UserForm. The **Find** method works by moving on from the last find on that worksheet, so there is no need to update the actual search range.

Eventually, no further occurrences of the search string will be found, and the range object address will be set to Null. When this happens, **sflag** is set to 0, which means no display of the UserForm; otherwise, it is set to 1 to display the UserForm.

You now use a variable called **temp** to keep track of all finds of the search string. The problem with the standard **Find** method is that it goes through one worksheet, finally produces a null address (meaning no further instances can be found), and then starts again at cell A1 on the same worksheet. To make it move on to the following worksheet and start searching there, some extra code is required so that the **Find** method can keep track of what it has found and move it onto a new sheet where required.

If the cell address in the form of workbook, worksheet, and cell is already in the string variable **temp**, which means that the **Find** method has gone back to cell A1 and started again, or the address of the **Range** object **A** is set to Null, then **sflag** is set to 0 (meaning do not display UserForm) and the execution moves to a label called **bypass**.

If a proper find was made, then the workbook, worksheet, and cell are all activated using the **Activate** method. This means that the cursor is moved to the next instance of the search text.

The name of the workbook, name of the worksheet, and cell address are all added into the variable **temp** so that checks can be made to see whether a search is complete on a worksheet. Execution then branches back to **loopa**, where the UserForm is displayed and the user can then search to the next instance.

The **bypass** label allows the code to clear the variable **temp** and to move on to the next available worksheet. It then moves through the worksheet until it comes to an instance of the search string, at which point the UserForm is displayed again to see whether the user wants to replace the instance.

Once all the worksheets and workbooks have been cycled through, a message box is displayed saying "No further instances of the search string."

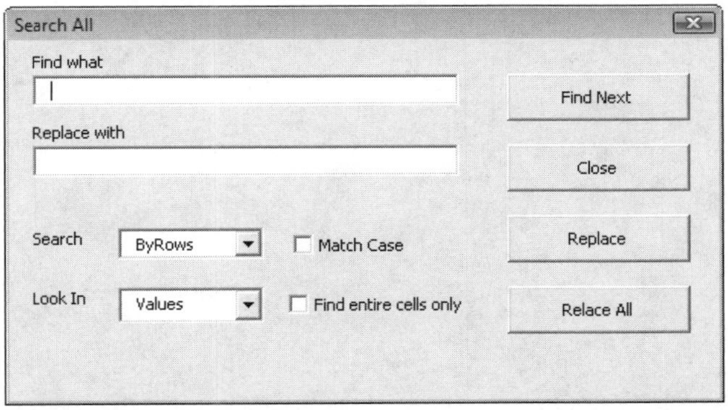

Figure 40-2 *Example of the Search All facility*

Try running the code. You run the subroutine **findsheet** to start the search procedure and display your form. Your screen should look like Figure 40-2.

The operation should work exactly the same as the normal **Find** method from the Excel spreadsheet menu does but with the additional feature of searching through all spreadsheets and workbooks.

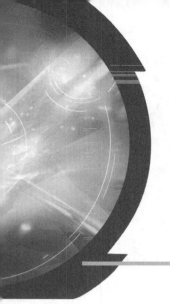

Brighten Up Your Comments

Y ou should be familiar with comments in an Excel spreadsheet—the yellow boxes assigned to a cell that pop up when you sweep your cursor across that cell. Comments are generally used for providing information about that cell. In Chapter 22, you learned how to include formulas in comments.

You can also write code to modify the appearance of comments boxes—for example, there is an enormous range of shapes you can use for your comments boxes. This is a very good example of being able to do something in VBA through the Excel object model that cannot be done through the normal Excel menu: all the code is there behind the scenes, but the user doesn't have access to it.

Effects can be quite stunning on a spreadsheet, particularly if you have never seen them before. The code to add effects assumes the user has already made a selection of cells where some cells contain comments. You first need to create a user interface form, as shown in Figure 41-1.

This form includes two list boxes to allow the user to choose a shape type and a gradient type. The shape type lets the user choose from predefined shapes such as a cube or a balloon. The gradient type lets the user choose the color gradation and whether it is from the center or the top corner.

There are two label controls to define the list boxes. In addition, the four command buttons to allow for user options are: OK to use the settings for comments, Cancel to do nothing, Select Color to choose the color that the user wants, and Default to return to the default settings for comments.

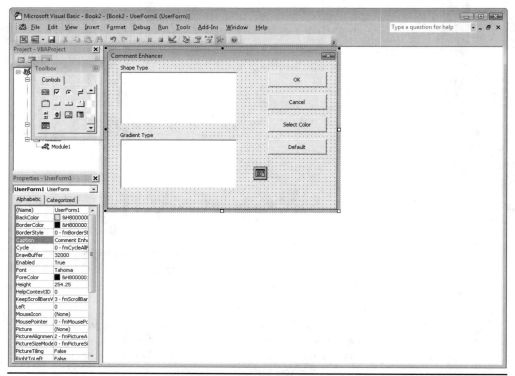

Figure 41-1 *Designing the UserForm for providing graphic comments*

To allow the user to select a color an API call is used to display the common dialog for color selection. To do this, you will need to add the following code into the definition part of a module:

```
Private Type COLORSTRUC
    lStructSize As Long
    hwnd As Long
    hInstance As Long
    rgbResult As Long
    lpCustColors As String
    Flags As Long
    lCustData As Long
    lpfnHook As Long
    lpTemplateName As String
End Type

Private Const CC_SOLIDCOLOR = &H80
```

```
Private Declare Function ChooseColor _
    Lib "comdlg32.dll" Alias "ChooseColorA" _
    (pChoosecolor As COLORSTRUC) As Long
```

This defines the API call to the 'ChooseColor' function in the library comdlg32.dll and defines a variable type to be used (COLORSTRUC) with this API call.

These controls are all dragged onto the form from the toolbox. If you have trouble identifying the controls in the toolbox, then use the tooltips on each control to identify them.

The form caption is changed by clicking the form title and editing the **caption** property in the properties window.

You then need to add the following code to the form so that all the controls work:

```
Private Sub CommandButton1_Click()
UserForm1.Hide
canc = 0
End Sub


Private Sub CommandButton2_Click()
UserForm1.Hide
canc = 1
End Sub


Private Sub CommandButton3_Click()
Dim x As Long, CSel As COLORSTRUC, CustColor(16) As Long

On Error GoTo errhandler2


  CSel.lStructSize = Len(CSel)

  CSel.Flags = CC_SOLIDCOLOR
  CSel.lpCustColors = String$(16 * 4, 0)
  x = ChooseColor(CSel)
  col = CSel.rgbResulterrhandler2:
Exit Sub
End Sub


Private Sub CommandButton4_Click()
UserForm1.Hide
canc = 2
End Sub
```

```
Private Sub UserForm_Initialize()
ListBox1.AddItem "msoShape32PointStar"
ListBox1.AddItem "msoShape24PointStar"
ListBox1.AddItem "msoShape16PointStar"
ListBox1.AddItem "msoShape8PointStar"
ListBox1.AddItem "msoshapeBalloon"
ListBox1.AddItem "msoShapeCube"
ListBox1.AddItem "msoshapeDiamond"
ListBox2.AddItem "msoGradientDiagonalDown"
ListBox2.AddItem "msoGradientDiagonalUp"
ListBox2.AddItem "msoGradientFromCenter"
ListBox2.AddItem "msoGradientFromCorner"
ListBox2.AddItem "msoGradientFromTitle"
ListBox2.AddItem "msoGradientHorizontal"
ListBox2.AddItem "msoGradientMixed"
ListBox2.AddItem "msoGradientVertical"


End Sub
```

You also need to set up a global variable called **canc** if you have not already done so from previous examples. This variable holds a record of the user's actions so that it can be transferred to other modules. You also need a global variable called **col** to hold the user's choice of color. You need to put this in the declarations section of a module:

```
Global canc As Integer
Global col as Long
```

Working through the code, the four command buttons' click events are similar, apart from the Color button (Button3). When the user clicks OK, Cancel, or Default, the UserForm is hidden and **canc** is set to a value to indicate which button the user clicked (OK is 0, Cancel is 1, and Default is 2).

The Color button (Button3) is different because you have to display a dialog to let the user choose a color.

The code sets the **CancelError** property to True, which means if the user clicks Cancel, an error is generated that the code can use to check for the Cancel action.

The **Flags** property is set to H1, and an error condition is entered. The purpose of setting the flag is to display the Color Option dialog properly. If an error is generated by the user clicking Cancel, then the execution jumps to **errhandler2** and exits the subroutine.

The **Action** property is set to 3, which displays the Color Selection common dialog and allows the user to select a color, which is then inserted into the global variable **col**.

When the UserForm loads, the list boxes must be populated. This is done on the **Form Initialize** event using the **AddItem** method of the **ListBox** object. This example adds the actual constant names to the list boxes, but it can be modified to use abbreviated names or more friendly names.

The constant names added into **ListBox1** represent a small selection from all the shapes available. If you use the Object Browser (F2 in the code window) and search on

msoAutoShapeType, you will find an extensive range of shapes that can be used. Unfortunately, it is not possible to enumerate constant names using a For..Each loop, so they need to be placed in the list box line by line. This is because they are constants, not objects, and thus not part of a collection.

You then need to write the procedure for displaying the UserForm and reacting to the user's selections. Place the following code within a module:

```
Sub comment_enhance()
Dim param As Long, grad As Long
UserForm1.Show
If canc = 1 Then Exit Sub
Select Case UserForm1.ListBox1.Text
Case "msoShape32PointStar"

    param = msoShape32pointStar
Case "msoShape24PointStar"

    param = msoShape24pointStar
Case "msoShape16PointStar"

    param = msoShape16pointStar
Case "msoShape8PointStar"

    param = msoShape8pointStar
Case "msoshapeBalloon"

    param = msoShapeBalloon
Case "msoShapeCube"

     param = msoShapeCube
Case "msoshapeDiamond"

     param = msoShapeDiamond

End Select

Select Case UserForm1.ListBox2.Text
Case "msoGradientDiagonalDown"

   grad = msoGradientDiagonalDown
Case "msoGradientDiagonalUp"

   grad = msoGradientDiagonalUp
Case "msoGradientFromCenter"
```

```
        grad = msoGradientFromCenter
Case "msoGradientFromCorner"

        grad = msoGradientFromCorner
Case "msoGradientFromTitle"

        grad = msoGradientFromTitle
Case "msoGradientHorizontal"

        grad = msoGradientHorizontal
Case "msoGradientMixed"

        grad = msoGradientMixed
Case "msoGradientVertical"

        grad = msoGradientVertical
End Select

If canc = 2 Then
For Each window In Windows

    For Each Worksheet In window.SelectedSheets

        For Each cell In Application.Selection

            addr = Worksheet.Name & "!" & cell.Address

            On Error Resume Next

            temp = ""

            temp = Range(addr).Comment.Text

            Range(addr).Comment.Delete

            If temp <> "" Then

                Range(addr).AddComment (temp)

            End If

        Next cell
    Next worksheet

Next window
```

```
Exit Sub
End If

For Each window In Windows

    For Each Worksheet In window.SelectedSheets

        For Each cell In Application.Selection

            addr = Worksheet.Name & "!" & cell.Address

            On Error Resume Next

            Range(addr).Comment.Shape.Fill.OneColorGradient grad, 1, 1

            Range(addr).Comment.Shape.Fill.BackColor.RGB = col
            Range(addr).Comment.Shape.AutoShapeType = param

        Next cell
    Next worksheet

Next window
End Sub
```

Initially, two variables are set up, one called **param**, which holds the user's choice of shape, and one called **grad**, which holds the user's choice of color gradation. The UserForm is then displayed and the user makes a choice of shape, color, and color gradation.

The code then tests the variable **canc** to see if it has a value of 1, indicating the user clicked Cancel on the form. If it does, a simple **Exit Sub** is all that is required, and no further action is taken.

If the user clicks a button other than Cancel, then you need to find out what selection they made. Unfortunately, the list boxes only hold text strings of the names of constants and the user selections have to be converted into a real constant using the **Case** method, based first on **listbox1**. The variable **param** is set with the real constant value based on the text selected in the list box. The same thing is done for the second list box, setting the variable **grad** to the constant value selected.

Next, the code tests to see if **canc** has a value of 2. If it does, the user clicked the Default button, which returns all comments to their default shape and color. If Default has been selected, the code cycles through each window in the **Windows** collection and then through each worksheet within the selected sheet's object.

To actually reset the comments within the selected cells back to the default, you need to go through several steps because there is no specific command within the Excel object model to do this. You must make a copy of the text of the comment, delete the comment, and then recreate it using the copied text. The new comment takes the default shape and color.

The code works through every cell within the user selection and loads a variable **addr** with the selected sheet name and the cell address, concatenated with the ! character. The **On Error Resume Next** statement is used because there is no way in the Excel object model to test whether a cell has a comment attached to it.

NOTE

*You can find out if a cell has a formula by looking at the **HasFormula** property, but there is no **HasComment** property because looping through cells without comments would cause error messages to appear, which would halt the flow of the program.*

A variable called **temp** is set to Null, which is then loaded with the text from the comment for a particular cell. It is important when looping through cells like this to clear **temp** out by setting it to an empty string; otherwise, there is a danger of notes being replicated throughout the selected range.

The comment is deleted using the **Delete** method, and a test is performed to see if the variable **temp** has any text in it—that is, to see if there is a comment in that cell. If there is, the comment is added back in using the **AddComment** method with all the default settings, giving the user the impression that the comment has been reset.

Once all the cells have been cycled through for the default option, the procedure is exited and no further action is taken.

If the code is still running, it can only be because the user clicked OK, meaning that changes need to be made to the comments.

Again the code cycles through the windows in the **Windows** collection and the worksheets within the **windows.selectedsheets** object in order to find all the selected sheets.

It then cycles through each cell within the application selection and loads a variable **addr** with the worksheet name and the cell address, concatenated with the ! character.

On Error Resume Next is used again to cover cells without comments.

First, the gradient is set using the **Fill.OneColorGradient** method and setting it to the variable held in **grad**. If you are going to change the color of the comment, then it is important to set the gradient first of all.

Next, the color is set by setting the **BackColor.RGB** property to the global variable **col**. We use a global variable so that we can access its value from other modules.

Finally, the shape of the note is set by setting the **AutoShapeType** property to the variable **param**.

It is important to keep these last three instructions in this order, since you may get incorrect results if you do not.

Test It Out

Place some comments on a spreadsheet by right-clicking the cell and choosing Insert Comment from the pop-up menu. Make a selection of cells including your comments cells by dragging the cursor over them.

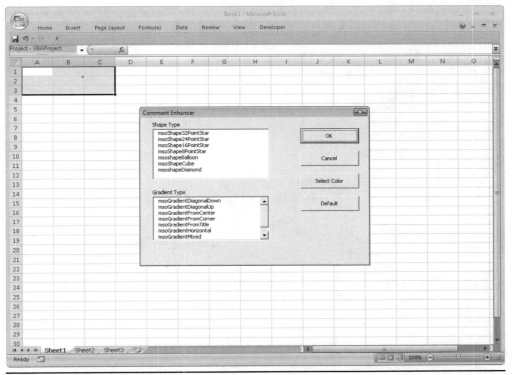

Figure 41-2   *The Comment Enhancer UserForm in action*

Run the code and your screen should look Figure 41-2.

Select a shape and a gradient type. Click the Color button and select a color from the dialog. Click OK and then look at your comments. They should now look similar to Figure 41-3, depending on your selections.

When using this procedure, the user does not have to select both a shape and a color and gradient. It can be either/or. However, if color is being changed, a gradient must be selected; otherwise, the color change will not take place.

Sometimes when altering shapes of comments, the shape does not resize perfectly to the amount of text shown, and some text is lost. This usually happens with circular shapes, such as stars. You can work around this by setting the **Height** and **Width** properties of the comment shape as follows:

```
Range(addr).Comment.Shape.Height = 100
Range(addr).Comment.Shape.Width = 100
```

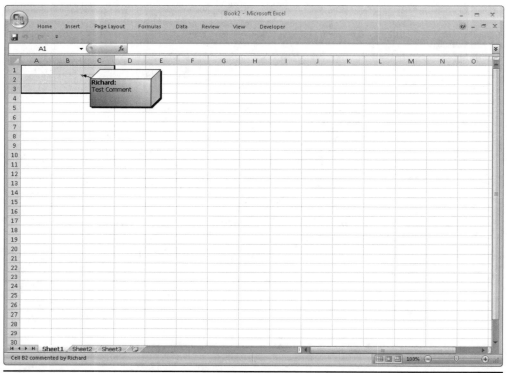

Figure 41-3   *An example of a comment enhanced to a cube graphic*

Importing a CSV File Containing Leading Zeros

A major problem with all versions of Excel is the way in which CSV (comma-separated value) files are imported into a spreadsheet. If you click the Excel Start button and select Open from the menu on the left-hand side of the window and then open a CSV file, Excel will import it in almost as if it was a worksheet, offering no options for how you wish to see your data.

Many applications are capable of outputting data in CSV format, and this is not restricted to Excel. Many users find Excel somewhat arrogant in the way it decides on the format without giving you the chance to specify your own choice.

If you happen to have a field in your CSV file that is all numeric characters but begins with a zero, Excel automatically removes the leading zero and converts the field into a number.

This can be extremely frustrating if you are dealing with telephone numbers that commence with a zero or account codes with a leading zero on them. Even placing quote marks around the field in question will not solve the problem. Excel will still interpret this as a number and will remove the leading zero.

If you search on the Internet, you will find that many people have come across this problem and the only way around it is to rename the file with a TXT suffix, open the file, and use the Import Wizard that then appears to specify that your field has to be text, not general, format. This dictates to Excel that the field is a text field, not a number, and the leading zero is kept.

This is not a simple process when all you really want to do is to import a simple CSV file. In a workplace environment it is not straightforward and needs careful explaining to any new member of staff in a work situation.

Happily, this is a process that can easily be automated using VBA, and the process can then be attached to a button in the worksheet or to a menu item, or you could even turn it into an Add-In (see Chapter 44).

First you need to create a dummy CSV file with some leading zero data in it. Rather than create this in Excel, it is best to create this in Notepad (which is a simple text editor) so that the file commences as totally independent of Excel.

To open Notepad, click the Windows Start button at the bottom left-hand corner of your screen, click All Programs, and then click Accessories. This will provide an expanded list of applications, which will include Notepad. Click Notepad to open it.

Type in the following text into the Notepad window:

```
FirstName,LastName,N1,N2,N3
Richard,Shepherd,01234,03456,1752
Alexander,Shepherd,0345,02384,345
```

Your Notepad window should now look like Figure 42-1. The sample data provides a combination of leading zero and non–leading zero data.

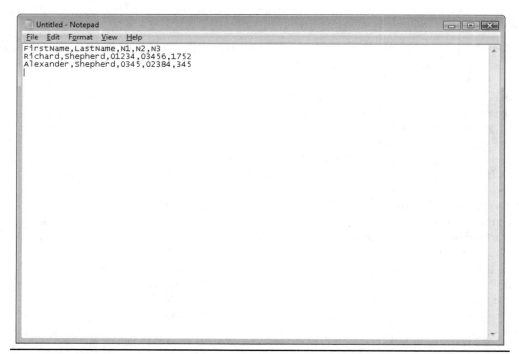

Figure 42-1   *A Notepad window with data entered into it*

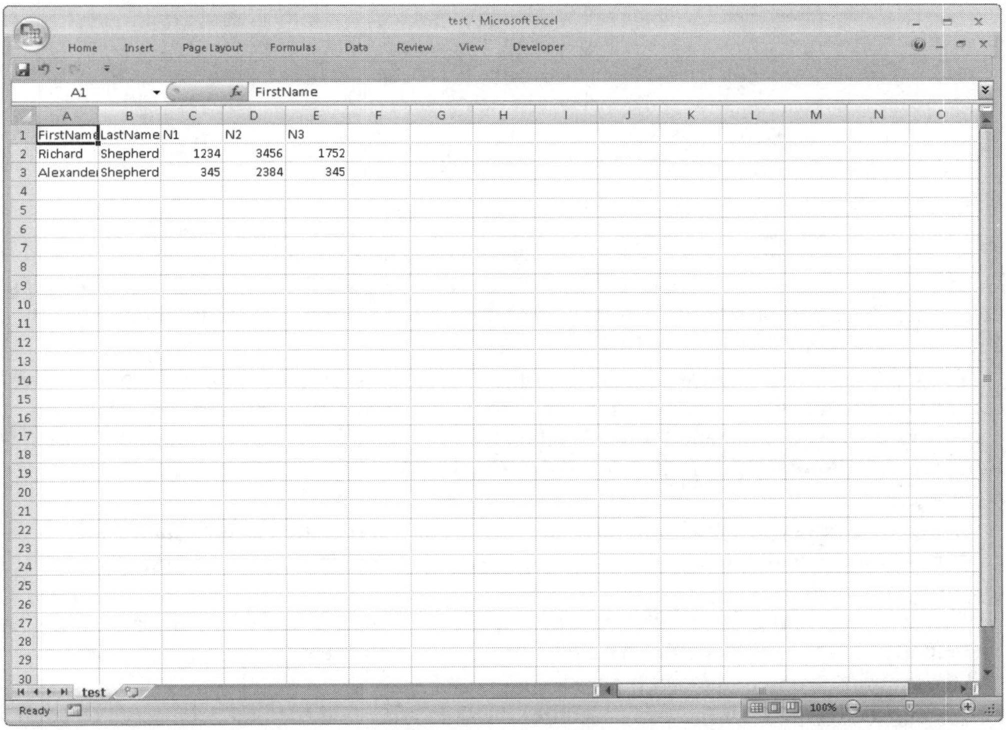

Figure 42-2   *A CSV file imported into Excel*

Click File | Save in the Notepad menu bar and you will be prompted for a location and a filename. Call the file LeadingZero.CSV. You must make sure that you include the CSV suffix so that the file is treated as a CSV file and not a text file.

In Excel, click the Excel Start button in the top left-hand corner of the screen and click Open in the menu on the left-hand side. Select Text Files as the file type and locate your CSV file. Click Open and the CSV file will be imported in. Your worksheet will now look like Figure 42-2.

As you can see, the problem is that the import process has removed the leading zeros in your file and turned the numeric fields into numbers, which was exactly what you did not want to happen.

Press ALT-F11 and insert a module using Insert | Module on the VBE menu. Enter the following code:

```
Sub ImportLeadingZeros()
On Error Resume Next
Kill "C:\temp\LeadingZero.txt"
On Error GoTo 0
Name "C:\temp\LeadingZero.csv" As _"C:\temp\LeadingZero.txt"
```

```
    Workbooks.OpenText Filename:="C:\temp\LeadingZero.txt", Origin _
        :=xlMSDOS, StartRow:=1, DataType:=xlDelimited, TextQualifier:= _
        xlDoubleQuote, ConsecutiveDelimiter:=False, Tab:=False, _
        Semicolon:=False, Comma:=True, Space:=False, Other:=False, _
        FieldInfo:=Array(Array(1, 1), Array(2, 1), Array(3, 2), _
        Array(4, 2), Array(5, 2)), TrailingMinusNumbers:=True
End Sub
```

The code assumes that the file LeadingZero.csv that you created earlier is located at C:\temp.

The first thing the code does is to delete the file LeadingZero.txt (if it already exists) using the Visual Basic command "Kill." If this is not done, then an error may come about when the code renames your CSV file to a TXT file.

The On Error Resume Next statement turns off all error messages, since if there is no file to Kill (delete), this will create an error. On Error Goto 0 turns the error messaging back on.

The Visual Basic command "Name" is then used to rename your CSV file to a TXT file. Finally a **Workbooks.OpenText** command opens the TXT file according to specific parameters.

Using the **DataType** and **Comma** parameters, the file is specified as delimited with comma delimiters and the Text Qualifier is specified as a double quotation mark, although this quotation mark is not used in our sample file.

The most interesting part is the **FieldInfo** parameter, which is formed by an array. The first element of the array specifies the field number. In our sample file we have five fields, and these simply go in numerical order (1–5).

The second element for the array specifies the field type. Fields 1 and 2 are set to General format and use the parameter of 1 (xlGeneralFormat). However, we want fields 3, 4, and 5 to be set to Text format so that our leading zeros are interpreted correctly, so their format is set to Text format and use a parameter of 2 (xlTextFormat).

Run the code and your worksheet screen will look like Figure 42-3. The green triangles showing in the top left-hand corners of some of the cells indicate that Excel has detected a number formatted as text and is warning the user of this. However, this is the situation that we wish to see, so there is no problem.

The leading zeros are maintained and formatted to text fields. Of course your CSV file has been renamed to a TXT suffix. You cannot rename it back within this code, because the file is now Open and is locked, but this is something to bear in mind.

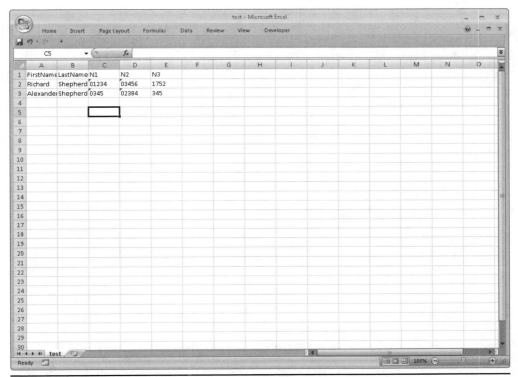

Figure 42-3   *A CSV file imported into Excel with leading zeros showing*

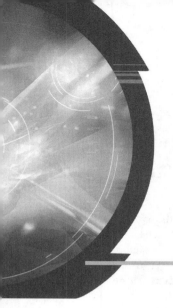

43

Working with Shapes

Y ou may already know that you can insert shapes into a spreadsheet. After all, objects such as graphs and comments are shapes. You may have already used the AutoShapes menu on the Drawing toolbar to insert a shape onto your worksheet and even experimented with the 3-D options, but what you probably don't know is that VBA gives you an enormous choice of shapes to use that you cannot get from the Excel menus.

Shapes can also be manipulated through VBA to give you a greater selection of shapes to use. The user interface in Excel is quite tricky to operate to get these effects, but in VBA it is more straightforward and you can more easily see what is going on. You can make your spreadsheet look more interesting by using unusual shapes as well as color and 3-D effects.

Try putting the following code into a module:

```
Sub test_shad()
Dim w As Worksheet
Set w = worksheets("sheet1")
Dim myshape As Shape
Set myshape = w.Shapes.AddShape(msoShapeBalloon, 90, 90, 90, 40)
myshape.TextFrame.Characters.Text = "Test Message"
myshape.TextFrame.Characters.Font.Bold = True
With myshape.ThreeD

    .Visible = True

    .Depth = 40

    .ExtrusionColor.RGB = RGB(255, 100, 255)
```

```
        .PresetLightingDirection = msoLightingTop

End With

myshape.BottomRightCell = ""

End Sub
```

Here, a variable **w** is dimensioned as a worksheet and then set to **sheet1** within the **Worksheets** collection. A variable called **Myshape** is dimensioned as a shape. This is set to a new shape added to the worksheet, represented by the variable **w**, using a **Set** statement. The shape being used is a balloon (speech bubble), and the parameters set the **Left**, **Top**, **Width**, and **Height** properties of the balloon. The text is set to "Test Message" using the **TextFrame** object, and the font is set to bold.

Using the **With** statement, the shape's 3-D settings are now made. The **Visible** property is set to True so that the 3-D part of the object can be seen. The depth of the 3-D effect is set to 40, and the extrusion color is set to the RGB value for purple. The extrusion is the 3-D effect behind the actual shape.

Lighting direction is set to come from the top; it can also be set to come from other angles by using the different constants available. You can see these constants by using the Object Browser (press F2 when in the VBE) and searching on **msoPresetLightingDirection**.

Finally, the bottom-right cell of the shape is set to an empty value. This may seem unnecessary, but it ensures that the shape will actually appear on the worksheet. If you leave it out and run the code, you will not see the shape until you scroll the worksheet down and then up again.

Try running the code from the module, and you should see the result in Figure 43-1.

Shapes can also be used to activate macros. Add the following code to a module that you have inserted yourself:

```
Sub text_message()
      MsgBox "My shape message"
End Sub
```

This displays a simple message box. Now add the following line to your **Shape** macro:

```
myshape.OnAction = "text_message"
```

This sets the **OnAction** property to call the subroutine that you just created called **text_message**. When you click the shape, it will run your code.

Delete the previous shape by clicking the extrusion of the shape and pressing DELETE; then rerun your macro. When you wipe the cursor across the new shape, it will have a hand icon. Click the shape, and the message box will appear.

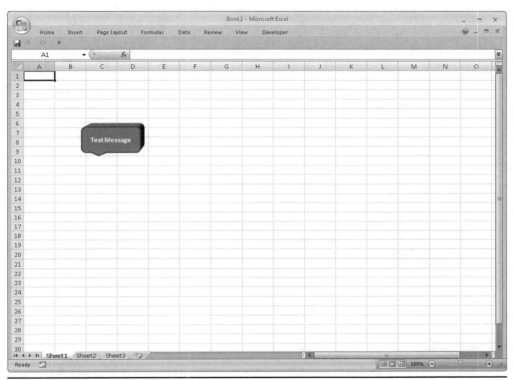

Figure 43-1   *Example of a VBA-defined shape in Excel*

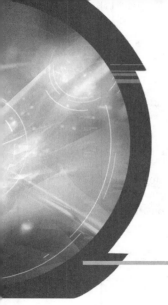

Turning Your VBA Code into an Add-In

Throughout this book, you have built samples as macros that have all been run from the code window or from a command button on the spreadsheet. This is fine if you are writing these just for your own use or for a power user. You know exactly how the code works and how to invoke it because you wrote it.

However, what if you want a wider audience for your macros? This could be in your workplace, or you could even be thinking about producing a commercial application. Other users will not want to mess about running odd bits of VBA code. They probably have no idea how the code modules work, and you probably don't want them viewing your code, because you don't want them to change something and cause a bug. Most likely, users will also want to use it in conjunction with their own spreadsheets.

The answer is to create an add-in. You are probably already familiar with third-party add-ins for Excel. If you click the Excel Start button in the top left-hand corner of your screen and then click the Excel Options button at the bottom of the window, you will see an Add-Ins option in the menu on the left-hand side. Click this and you will be able to see what Add-Ins are available and loaded and to manage your Add-Ins.

Fortunately, it is relatively easy to turn your code into an add-in file.

The first thing you need is a proper user interface to call all your procedures. The best way to do this is to add your own menu onto the Excel menu structure. This was explained in Chapter 11, although how it is built in to the menu structure is more restricted in Excel 2007.

You will be creating an add-in called Magic, as reflected in the menu and naming conventions in the code.

Assuming that you have entered in all the code from the previous examples and inserted the appropriate UserForms, you must now add the following code for the menu structure. If you have entered the code into different files, you can use Copy and Paste to collect all your code into one module to insert in a final file. If you have not done all the examples, then you can choose not to include the menu bar command for that particular example. The easiest way to do this is to **Rem** out the lines you do not need by putting the single quote (') character in front of the line. The line will turn green and will become a comment instead of actual code. For example, if you want to remove the Calculate Range option, you **Rem** out the following statements:

```
'.Controls.Add(Type:=msoControlButton).Caption = "Calculate Range"

    '.Controls("Calculate Range").OnAction = "range_calculate"
```

This removes the line that sets up the option on the menu and the line that provides the action.

```
Sub menu()

Dim newsubitem As Object

CommandBars("Worksheet menu bar") _
.Controls.Add(Type:=msoControlPopup).Caption = _
    "Magic"

Set newsubitem = CommandBars("worksheet menu bar") _
    .Controls("magic")

With newsubitem

    .Controls.Add(Type:=msoControlButton).Caption = _
        "Absolute Relative Formula"

    .Controls("Absolute Relative Formula").OnAction = _
        "conv_formula"

    .Controls.Add(Type:=msoControlButton).Caption = _
        "Calculate Range"

    .Controls("Calculate Range").OnAction = _
        "range_calculate"

    .Controls.Add(Type:=msoControlButton).Caption = _
        "Change Values"
```

```
.Controls("Change Values").OnAction = "change_val"

.Controls.Add(Type:=msoControlButton).Caption = _
    "Color Alternate Columns"

.Controls("Color Alternate Columns").OnAction = _
    "shade1"

.Controls.Add(Type:=msoControlButton).Caption = _
    "Color Alternate Rows"

.Controls("Color Alternate Rows").OnAction = _
    "shade"

.Controls.Add(Type:=msoControlButton).Caption = _
    "Color cells with Formula"

.Controls("Color Cells with Formula").OnAction = _
    "col_cell"

.Controls.Add(Type:=msoControlButton).Caption = _
    "Contents to Label"

.Controls("Contents to Label").OnAction = _
    "contents_to_label"

.Controls.Add(Type:=msoControlButton).Caption = _
    "Copy Hidden Sheets"

.Controls("Copy hidden Sheets").OnAction = _
    "hidden_sheets"

.Controls.Add(Type:=msoControlButton).Caption = _
    "Enter Formulae as Notes"

.Controls("Enter Formulae as Notes").OnAction = _
    "note"

.Controls.Add(Type:=msoControlButton).Caption = _
    "Label to Number"

.Controls("Label to Number").OnAction = _
    "label_to_number"
```

```
     .Controls.Add(Type:=msoControlButton).Caption = _
          "Matrix Total"

     .Controls("Matrix Total").OnAction = _
          "matrix_total"

     .Controls.Add(Type:=msoControlButton).Caption = _
          "Reverse Label"

     .Controls("Reverse Label").OnAction = _
          "reverse_label"

     .Controls.Add(Type:=msoControlButton).Caption = _
          "Search"

     .Controls("Search").OnAction = "findsheet"

     .Controls.Add(Type:=msoControlButton).Caption = _
          "Sort Sheets"

     .Controls("Sort Sheets").OnAction = "sortsheet"

     .Controls.Add(Type:=msoControlButton).Caption = _
          "Transpose"

     .Controls("Transpose").OnAction = "transpose"

End With

End Sub
```

Initially, a variable called **newsubitem** is dimensioned as an object. A new menu item is then added to the Tools menu bar—but notice it is not added as a standard menu item but as a pop-up (**type=msoControlPopup**), which means it can have a submenu beneath it. This submenu will hold all the routines.

The variable **newsubitem** is set to this menu item. Using the **With** statement, the individual menu items are added to the submenu. Each one is added as a control button (**type=msoControlButton**), and the **OnAction** property is set to the name of the subroutine.

Enter the preceding code into a module and run it. There will be an option called Magic on the AddIns menu across the top of the worksheet. Select it, and you will see a submenu, as shown in Figure 44-1.

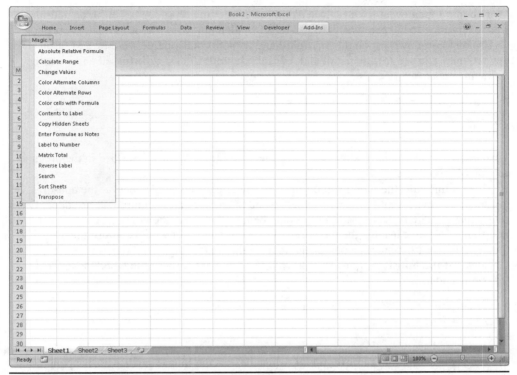

Figure 44-1   *Example of creation of a pop-up submenu*

Having created this menu, you also need code to remove it. Users of your add-in may not want to retain it on their copy of Excel, and they need a way to remove the menu. This is done by simply deleting the Magic menu using the **Delete** command:

```
Sub remove_menu()
  CommandBars("Worksheet menu bar"). _
Controls("magic").Delete
End Sub
```

From the user's angle, how will these routines be enacted? When the add-in is installed, the menu structure needs to appear. When the add-in is uninstalled, the menu needs to be removed. Fortunately, there are events built in to take care of this. On the Project tree in the VBE (VBA Editor window), open Microsoft Excel Objects and double-click **ThisWorkbook**. This is the object for the workbook for your add-in. This will default to the

Workbook_Open event if you select Workbook in the first drop-down, but for an add-in, you want everything to happen when the add-in is installed, not when the workbook is opened.

Use the drop-down list on the top right-hand corner of the module window and scroll upward until you see **AddinInstall** and **AddinUninstall**. Click **AddinInstall** and enter the following code:

```
Private Sub Workbook_AddinInstall()
  Call menu
End Sub
```

This assumes that you have already created the subroutine "Menu" described in the previous section of this chapter.

This routine calls the **menu** subroutine that you already coded. Whenever the add-in is installed, the **menu** subroutine will be called and the new menu structure will be added. One safety feature here is that the add-in can only be installed once; the only other option is to uninstall it. This means that the menu can only appear once—it would confuse the users if they ended up with more than one menu item for the same thing.

Click **AddinUninstall** in the drop-down in the top-right corner of the module and add the following code:

```
Private Sub Workbook_AddinUninstall()
  Call remove_menu
End Sub
```

This calls the subroutine **remove_menu**, which deletes the Magic menu. This happens when the user uninstalls your add-in so that no trace is left of it.

You almost have a complete add-in. The next step is to name it so that when users install it they can easily identify it. To do this, select Tools | VBAProject Properties on the VBE menu, and you will see a form called VBAProject Project Properties. Enter the project name—this sets the name of the add-in and the filename, so choose sensibly. You can also choose a description.

You may want to prevent your users from viewing your code and changing it. You can do this by clicking the Protection tab on the VBA Project Properties window, as shown in Figure 44-2. Check the Lock Project for Viewing box and enter and reenter your password. Click OK. Do not under any circumstances forget your password! If you do, there is no way to view your code and, unless you have a backup copy without a password on it, all your hard work will be lost.

All that remains to be done is to turn your project into an add-in file. Select the Worksheet screen, click the Excel Start button in the top left-hand corner of your screen, and select Save As from the menu. Select Other Formats from the menu that appears and the Save As

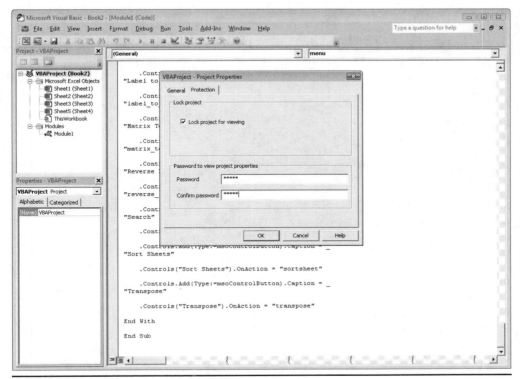

Figure 44-2   *Setting a password to protect your add-in*

window will open. On the Save As Type drop-down, there is an option to save as Microsoft Excel Add-In, as shown in Figure 44-3. Do not select Excel97-2003 Add-In unless you specifically want to create an add-in for a previous version of Excel. Use the default path of <username>\AppData\Roaming\Microsoft\Addins so that Excel will automatically pick up the location and you will not have to browse for the file.

Select the Addin filter and click OK. Your file will now be saved with an xlam extension.

Exit Excel and reopen it to test your add-in. Click on the Excel Start button in the top left-hand corner of the worksheet screen and then click the Excel Options button at the bottom of the next window. Click Add-Ins in the menu on the left-hand side of the window and you will see your new add-in listed under Interactive Application Add-Ins. To install it, click the Manage drop-down at the bottom of the screen and select Excel Add-Ins (this should be the default). Click Go.

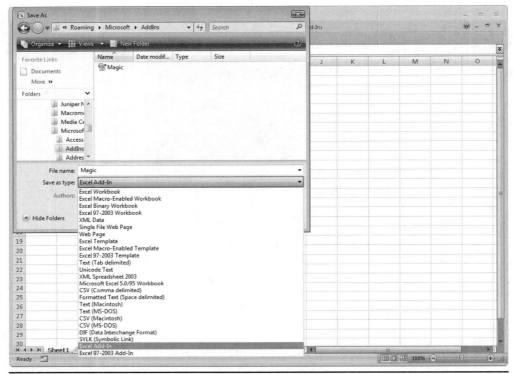

Figure 44-3 *Saving your file as an add-in*

You should see it automatically listed in the pop-up window, but if you don't, use the Browse button to locate the file. Figure 44-4 shows the Add-Ins window and the Browse button. Check the box next to the add-in that you have selected.

Click OK. Your add-in is now installed. On the Excel menu bar you will now have an item called Add-Ins. Click this and you will see a ribbon control called Menu Commands with your Magic menu in it. If you click this, you will see a pop-up menu containing all the menu commands that you entered in earlier, as shown in Figure 41-1. Select some cells and try out the options to make sure they all work.

Notice that when you select the Window menu from the spreadsheet menu, there is no indication of your add-in being there. This is because the workbook belonging to the add-in exists only virtually. It can be used by the VBA code, as you saw in the example for transposing a range of cells in Chapter 24, but it cannot appear onscreen.

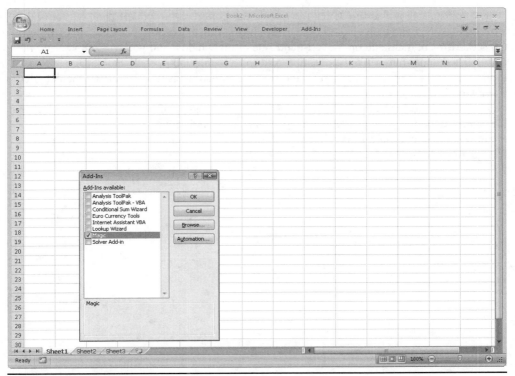

Figure 44-4   *Installing your add-in*

NOTE

Once you have created an add-in, you cannot turn it back into an Excel spreadsheet at a later date.

Press ALT-F11 and look at the VBA code screen. You will see an object in the Project tree called **Magic.xlam**, which represents your add-in. If you used password protection, you will be prompted for the password when you double-click it to open it.

You can still edit the VBA code and make changes, add other menu options, and insert new forms. However, now that it is an add-in, the only way to save your changes is by using File | Save Magic.xlam from the VBE menu. When you save your changes, make sure that you are saving the right code by clicking the cursor on the add-in within the Project tree. There are also modules for the current workbook, and you can easily save these instead of your add-in data. If in doubt, click the add-in in the Project tree and make sure that the File | Save option on the VBE menu has the name of your add-in.

Try uninstalling the add-in. Click the Excel Start button in the top left-hand corner of the worksheet screen and then click the Excel Options button at the bottom of the next window. Click Add-Ins in the menu on the left-hand side of the window and you will see your new add-in listed under Interactive Application Add-Ins. To uninstall it, click the Manage drop-down at the bottom of the screen and select Excel Add-Ins (this should be the default). Click Go.

Locate your add-in in the list. Uncheck the check box and click OK. You will now see that the Magic menu has disappeared from the Menu Commands control of Add-Ins. If your menu was the only customized menu available, then the Add-Ins item will also disappear from the menu bar.

ASCII Character Codes

This appendix is a listing of the 255 ASCII (American Standard Code for Information Interchange) character codes that Excel uses. They work in conjunction with the functions **Asc** and **Chr**. **Asc** will give the ASCII number of a character, and **Chr** will give the character based on an ASCII number.

All these characters can be used to produce text strings by using the **Chr** function (see Chapter 5). Here is an example that will produce the string "ABC":

```
MsgBox Chr(65) & Chr(66) & Chr(67)
```

You can also insert carriage return and line feed characters to make your text wrap at the correct point.

In the table, the _ symbol indicates that there is not a displayable character.

Beyond character 128 Excel uses an extended character set (which is not real ASCII), which partially depends on the locale of the user and the PC being used. For example, =CHAR(153) in a spreadsheet cell will give a TM (trademark) symbol. However, you may need to experiment with these beyond character 128.

ASCII Code	Character	ASCII Code	Character
1	_	8	_
2	_	9	Horizontal tab
3	_	10	Line feed
4	_	11	Vertical tab
5	_	12	Form feed
6	_	13	Carriage return
7	_	14	_

ASCII Code	Character	ASCII Code	Character
15	_	51	3
16	_	52	4
17	_	53	5
18	_	54	6
19	_	55	7
20	_	56	8
21	_	57	9
22	_	58	:
23	_	59	;
24	_	60	<
25	_	61	=
26	_	62	>
27	_	63	?
28	_	64	@
29	_	65	A
30	_	66	B
31	_	67	C
32	Space	68	D
33	!	69	E
34	"	70	F
35	#	71	G
36	$	72	H
37	%	73	I
38	&	74	J
39	'	75	K
40	(	76	L
41	)	77	M
42	*	78	N
43	+	79	O
44	,	80	P
45	-	81	Q
46	.	82	R
47	/	83	S
48	0	84	T
49	1	85	U
50	2	86	V

ASCII Code	Character	ASCII Code	Character
87	W	123	{
88	X	124	|
89	Y	125	}
90	Z	126	~
91	[	127	_
92	\	128	„
93	]	129	_
94	^	130	‚
95	_	131	F
96	`	132	„
97	a	133	…
98	b	134	†
99	c	135	‡
100	d	136	^
101	e	137	‰
102	f	138	Š
103	g	139	‹
104	h	140	Œ
105	i	141	_
106	j	142	Ž
107	k	143	_
108	l	144	_
109	m	145	‘
110	n	146	’
111	o	147	“
112	p	148	”
113	q	149	•
114	r	150	–
115	s	151	—
116	t	152	~
117	u	153	™
118	v	154	š
119	w	155	›
120	x	156	œ
121	y	157	_
122	z	158	ž

ASCII Code	Character	ASCII Code	Character
159	Ÿ	195	Ã
160		196	Ä
161	¡	197	Å
162	¢	198	Æ
163	£	199	Ç
164	¤	200	È
165	¥	201	É
166	¦	202	Ê
167	§	203	Ë
168	¨	204	Ì
169	©	205	Í
170	ª	206	Î
171	<<	207	Ï
172	¬	208	Ð
173	–	209	Ñ
174	®	210	Ò
175	¯	211	Ó
176	°	212	Ô
177	±	213	Õ
178	²	214	Ö
179	³	215	×
180	´	216	Ø
181	µ	217	Ù
182	¶	218	Ú
183	·	219	Û
184	¸	220	Ü
185	¹	221	Ý
186	º	222	Þ
187	>>	223	ß
188	¼	224	À
189	½	225	Á
190	¾	226	Â
191	¿	227	Ã
192	À	228	Ä
193	Á	229	Å
194	Â	230	Æ

ASCII Code	Character	ASCII Code	Character
231	Ç	244	Ô
232	È	245	Õ
233	É	246	Ö
234	Ê	247	÷
235	Ë	248	Ø
236	Ì	249	Ù
237	Í	250	Ú
238	Î	251	Û
239	Ï	252	Ü
240	Đ	253	Ý
241	Ñ	254	Þ
242	Ò	255	Ÿ
243	Ó		

Index

L

Label control, 104
labels
    charts, 184–185
    converting to numbers, 261–264
    reversing, 275–276
LBound statement, 24
Lcase function, 47–48
leading zeros data, 347–351
Left property, 99
Len function, 49
Let property, 207
Like operator, 79–80
list boxes, 105–107
ListBox control, 105–107
ListBox object, 340
local variables, 16
logic errors, 82
logical operators, 75–79
Long data type, 20, 21
Loop keyword, 24
loops, 39–43
    animations, 214–216
    described, 35
    Do Until, 41–42
    For Each, 41
    early exit of, 42–43
    For..Next, 22–23, 40–41
    indexes and, 40, 41, 43
    nested, 41, 43, 216, 262, 286
    While..Wend, 42

M

macro recorder, 185
macros
    calling code from, 28
    charts, 185
    comments, 149
    creating simple, 7–10
    described, 3–4, 147
    location of, 4
    naming, 147
    recording, 147–149
    running, 8–9, 27
    saving, 11–12

    subroutines available as, 32–33
    using subroutines with, 28
Magic menu, 357–366
main objects, 151–169
master cells, 313–315
MatchRequired property, 105
mathematical functions, 30–32
mathematical operators, 30, 71, 72–74
matrix, 293–296
matrix additions, 293–296
memory
    arrays and, 20, 23
    creating Workbook objects in, 145–146
    data types and, 20
    inadequate, 24
    Windows and, 24
menu bars, 3, 123–130, 358
menu commands, 124–128, 133, 364, 366
menu entries, 124–125
menu items, 124–127, 147, 360
Menu Items control, 124
message boxes, 66–69. *See also* dialogs
    conditional statements, 38
    constants, 67–69
    MsgBox function, 66
    MsgBox statement, 7–10
    overview, 66–67
    Select Case statement, 39
    using in debugging, 88–90
methods. *See also specific methods*
    calling, 138–142
    described, 134–135, 138
    examining in Object Browser, 143–144
    examples of, 134–135, 138
    object models, 134–142
    overview, 134–136
    ribbon, 241–242
Microsoft Access, 188–190
Microsoft Common Dialog control, 113–121
Microsoft Developer Network (MSDN), 194
Microsoft dialogs, 113–121
Microsoft Excel Objects, 6
Microsoft Office. *See* Office
Microsoft Outlook, 174–176
Microsoft Word, 171, 172–174
Mid command, 46–47
Minute function, 61

Stop Hackers in Their Tracks

**Hacking Exposed,
6th Edition**

**Hacking Exposed
Malware & Rootkits**

**Hacking Exposed Computer
Forensics, 2nd Edition**

**24 Deadly Sins of
Software Security**

**Hacking Exposed
Linux, 3rd Edition**

**Hacking Exposed
Windows, 3rd Edition**

**Hacking Exposed
Web 2.0**

**Hacking Exposed:
Web Applications, 2nd Edition**

**Gray Hat Hacking,
2nd Edition**

**Hacking Exposed
Wireless**

**Hacking Exposed
VoIP**

**IT Auditing: Using Controls to
Protect Information Assets**

Expert CompTIA® certification guides
FOR SUCCESS ON EXAM DAY AND BEYOND

Gregory White,
Wm. Arthur Conklin, et al.
A comprehensive CompTIA Security+™ exam guide and essential on-the-job reference.
978-0-07-160127-6

T.J. Samuelle
Concise coverage of only what you need to know to pass the CompTIA Security+™ exam.
978-0-07-160123-8

Tom Carpenter
The #1 classroom-proven CompTIA Convergence+™ training and exam prep tool.
978-0-07-159680-0

Ron Gilster and Helen Heneveld
A comprehensive CEA-CompTIA DHTI+™ exam guide and essential on-the-job reference.
978-0-07-154665-2

Practice exams, e-books, and more on CD-ROMs